W9-AHG-505

What Leaders Are Saying about Women's Bible Journals

"This Bible study has it all—great illustrations, accurate information, simple explanations, and relevant applications! Well done, Lenya Heitzig and Penny Rose. It is with joy that I heartily recommend this Women's Bible Journal."
—Anne Graham Lotz, Bible teacher and author of the best-selling *Just Give Me Jesus*

"I'm touched and blessed by your heart for His kingdom."
—Kay Arthur, Bible teacher and author of many best-selling Bible studies

"This Bible study will take you into a deeper relationship with Christ, bringing about transformation in your life."
—Ruth Bell Graham, speaker, poet, and author of *Footprints of a Pilgrim*

"Lenya's love for the Lord and knowledge of His Word uniquely equips her to help other women discover the pathway to God through these in-depth Bible studies."
—Kay Smith, wife of Chuck Smith (Calvary Chapel)

Ruth & Esther

Women's Bible Journal

pathway to
God's Plan

Lenya Heitzig | Penny Pierce Rose

TYNDALE HOUSE PUBLISHERS, INC. • WHEATON, IL

Visit Tyndale's exciting Web site at www.tyndale.com

Pathway to God's Plan: Ruth and Esther

Copyright © 2002 by Lenya Heitzig and Penny Pierce Rose. All rights reserved.

Cover photograph copyright © 2001 by Mark Lewis/Getty Images. All rights reserved.

Many illustrations used have been taken from the *Bible Illustrator for Windows*. Parsons Technology, 1997–1998. Illustrations copyright © 1998 by Christianity Today, Inc. All rights reserved. Portions copyright © 1984–1995 Faircom Corp.

Authors' photos copyright © 2001 by Frank Frost Photography. All rights reserved.

Designed by Kelly Bennema

Edited by Lynn Vanderzalm and Mary Horner Collins

Unless otherwise indicated, all Scripture quotations are taken from the New King James Version. Copyright © 1979, 1980, 1982 by Thomas Nelson, Inc. Used by permission. All rights reserved.

Scripture quotations marked NLT are taken from the *Holy Bible,* New Living Translation, copyright © 1996. Used by permission of Tyndale House Publishers, Inc., Wheaton, Illinois 60189. All rights reserved.

Scripture quotations marked NIV are taken from the *Holy Bible,* New International Version®. NIV®. Copyright © 1973, 1978, 1984 by International Bible Society. Used by permission of Zondervan Publishing House. All rights reserved.

Scripture quotations marked KJV are taken from the *Holy Bible,* King James Version.

Printed in the United States of America

07 06 05 04 03 02
8   7   6   5   4   3   2   1

Contents

Introduction

*C*ourageous pioneer women who accompanied their rough and rugged husbands on treacherous journeys across America's wild, wild West deserve the respect of those of us who live in relative ease. What made them tick? How could they leave the luxury of big city life to work their fingers to the bone building a little house on the prairie? Pioneers are driven to go where no one has gone before, motivated by a quest for knowledge, new territory, fame and fortune, or the thrill of adventure. Still others set out on expeditions for religious purposes.

We usually think explorers are men like Christopher Columbus or Lewis and Clark. However, history is full of women who possessed pioneer spirits too: Amelia Earhart flew solo across the Atlantic; Golda Meir made a pilgrimage from Milwaukee to Palestine and became Israel's first female prime minister; and Sally Ride climbed aboard the shuttle *Challenger*.

By the 1900s pioneers had conquered the known world. Yet the unquenchable urge to explore drew people toward new frontiers: the ocean depths and outer space. We've been to the moon and beyond, but still our search goes on. Perhaps humanity isn't really on a geographical journey but on a spiritual quest. Instead of searching for a new land, we're in pursuit of *the* Promised Land.

What about you? Are you a pioneer at heart? If you've dreamed of becoming a spiritual explorer, then the Women's Bible Journal will open the way to exciting discoveries in God's Word. Your journeys will lead you into experiences that will satisfy your pioneering spirit. Whether your expedition is in a small-group setting or alone in personal study, the Women's Bible Journal charts a clear path.

On this expedition you'll explore the Old Testament books of Ruth and Esther. These were two very different women living in very different worlds. But they had one thing in common: they followed the same God. As you dig into Israel's history and study these true stories, you'll be inspired. Ruth's pilgrimage to the Promised Land and her subsequent love story will thrill you with the romance of redemption. Esther will challenge you to become bold in your faith, taking advantage of the divine opportunities God places in your path. In both books the providential hand of God is clearly seen as He intervenes on behalf of His children.

Exploring God's Word can be as vast as a trip around the world, so we need a map to keep us on course. We've plotted the route by dividing each of the twelve lessons into five sections—one study for each weekday. Every day you will follow a pathway that leads you to a deeper understanding and application of God's Word. Allow us to familiarize you with the steps you'll take:

Preparation is where each day's journey begins. Start with the prayer designed to lead you into the lesson, then read the relevant promise from Scripture. The story at the beginning of each day's study will help you begin to think about how the theme of the day's study expresses itself in our contemporary lives. Most of the stories in this book are written from Lenya's point of view; the stories that reflect Penny's life are indicated with a parenthetical note.

Exploration is the next stop. Here you will ask, *What are the facts?* These are the who-what-when-where-how questions that will help you explore the passage verse by verse. Unless otherwise indicated, the definitions have been adapted from *Nelson's Illustrated Bible Dictionary*. Paranthetical abbreviations for sources used include *(Nelson's Index)* for *Nelson's Quick Reference Topical Bible Index; (Unger's)* for *New Unger's Bible Dictionary; (Vine's)* for *Vine's Complete Expository Dictionary of Old and New Testament Words; (Webster's)* for *Merriam-Webster's Collegiate Dictionary*. We have used the New King James Version in this study along with verses selected from the New Living Translation. Feel free to use other Bible translations as well.

Explanation sidebars will help you answer the question, *What does it mean?* Questions that have a related sidebar comment are marked with the symbol ❦, and the sidebar insight with the same number will help you understand what the passage means through contemporary illustrations, biblical principles, and key definitions. We have gleaned insights from various Bible scholars and have relied on the *PC Study Bible,* which contains many study resources (see bibliography).

Transformation exercises answer the question, *How should this change my life?* Here you will not only personally apply the lessons you have learned but also have the opportunity to reflect on what you've studied. The journal section of each lesson is an important place for you to open your heart and express your thoughts, goals, commitments, and prayers. It becomes a personal record of God's transforming work in your life. When you have completed all twelve lessons, you may want to take a few minutes to read through your journal responses, seeing how God has touched your heart and moved you to action during the weeks that you heard Him speak to you through Ruth and Esther. The story at the end of each day's study will again help you focus on the day's theme.

Contemplation ends the day with inspiring quotes and encouraging insights from Christians, past and present, who have learned much from their own journeys with God.

Before starting this study, read the How to Get the Most out of This Study section to find tips and checklists for individuals, groups, and group leaders.

Traveling to exotic places and experiencing new cultures may change your perspective, but exploring God's Word has the power to revolutionize your life. We pray that as you journey through Ruth and Esther, you will discover the wonder and assurance of God's providential care in your life.

In His love,
Lenya Heitzig and Penny Pierce Rose

How to Get the Most out of This Study

This book is ideal for discussion in a small-group setting as well as for individual study. The following suggestions will help you and your group get the most out of your study time.

PERSONAL CHECKLIST

___ **Be determined.** Examine your daily schedule, then set aside a consistent time for this study.

___ **Be prepared.** Gather the materials you'll need: the Bible, your Women's Bible Journal, and a pen.

___ **Be inspired.** Begin each day with prayer, asking the Holy Spirit to be your teacher and to illuminate your mind.

___ **Be complete.** Read the suggested Bible passage and finish the homework each day.

___ **Be persistent.** Answer each question as fully as possible. If you're unable to answer a question, move forward to the next question, or read the explanation, which may offer further insight.

___ **Be consistent.** Don't get discouraged. If you miss a day, use the weekend to catch up.

___ **Be honest.** When answering the transformation questions, allow the Lord to search your heart and transform your life. The journal questions will help you write out your thoughts, a form of reflection that has proved helpful to many fellow pilgrims. Take time to reflect honestly about your own feelings, experiences, sins, goals, and responses to God.

___ **Be blessed.** Enjoy your daily study time with God as He speaks to you through His Word.

SMALL-GROUP CHECKLIST

___ **Be prayerful.** Pray before you begin your time together.

___ **Be biblical.** Keep all answers in line with God's Word; avoid personal opinion.

___ **Be confidential.** Keep all sharing within your small group confidential.

___ **Be respectful.** Listen without interrupting. Keep comments on track and to the point so that all can share.

___ **Be discreet.** In some cases, you need not share more than absolutely necessary. Some things are between you and the Lord.

___ *Be kind.* Reply to the comments of others lovingly and courteously.

___ *Be mindful.* Remember your group members in prayer throughout the week.

SMALL-GROUP LEADER CHECKLIST

___ *Be prayerful.* Pray that the Holy Spirit will "guide you into truth" so that your leadership will guide others.

___ *Be faithful.* Prepare by reading the Bible passage and studying the lesson ahead of time, highlighting truths and applying them personally.

___ *Be prompt.* Begin and end the study on time.

___ *Be thorough.* For optimum benefit, allot one hour for small-group discussion. This should allow plenty of time to cover all of the questions and exercises for each lesson.

___ *Be selective.* If you have less than an hour, you should carefully choose the questions you will address and summarize the edited information for your group. In this way, you can focus on the more thought-provoking exploration questions. Be sure to grant enough time to address pertinent transformation exercises, as this is where you and the women will clearly see God at work in your lives.

___ *Be sensitive.* Some of the transformation exercises are very personal and may not be appropriate to discuss in a small group. If you sense that this is the case, feel free to move to another question.

___ *Be flexible.* If the questions in the Women's Bible Journal seem unclear, reword them for your group. Feel free to add your own questions to bring out the meaning of a verse.

___ *Be inclusive.* Encourage each member to participate in the discussion. You may have to draw some out or tone some down so that all have the opportunity to participate.

___ *Be honest.* Don't be afraid to admit that you don't have all the answers! When in doubt, encourage the women to take difficult questions to their church leadership for clarification.

___ *Be focused.* Keep the discussion on tempo and on target. Learn to pace your small group so that you complete a lesson on time. Though participants may get sidetracked, you should redirect the discussion to the passage at hand.

___ *Be patient.* Realize that not all people are at the same place spiritually or socially. Wait for the members of your group to answer the questions rather than jump in and answer them yourself.

Where Is God?

When our son Nathan was barely two, he'd squeeze his eyes shut and say, "I can't see, I can't see!" He thought that if he couldn't see me, then I couldn't see him either. Playing hide-and-seek was a breeze. I never had to run and hide; I'd simply whisper, "Close your eyes, Nathan, and count to ten," and I was hidden as far as he was concerned! There are times as an adult when I've made a similar mistaken assumption about my heavenly Father. If I don't "see" God, perhaps He can't see me or my inappropriate behavior. What about you? Have you ever thought that since God is invisible, maybe your actions were too?

The reality is that God in His providence sees everything, even before it happens. You can run, but you can never hide from His view. The word *providence* comes from two Latin words: *pro* meaning "before" and *video* translated "I see." Scripture says, "The eyes of the Lord run to and fro throughout the whole earth" (2 Chronicles 16:9). Have no doubt—though you may not see Him in your darkest night, He can always see you!

Throughout the book of Ruth we see God's providential care. It was a dark time for the nation of Israel, and tough circumstances had obscured the people's view of God. In the midst of foreign oppression and famine one family asked, "Where is God?" Instead of opening their spiritual eyes to see Him, they went their own way and ran to the land of Moab.

preparation

Father, thank You that there is nowhere I can escape from Your presence. When I walk through the valleys of this life, it's comforting to know You are right beside me. Help me to take Your hand as You guide me through. Amen.

PRESENCE
I can never escape from your spirit! I can never get away from your presence! If I ride the wings of the morning, if I dwell by the farthest oceans, even there your hand will guide me, and your strength will support me. Psalm 139:7, 9-10, NLT

explanation

SIN CYCLE
The book of Judges depicts Israel's tragic cycle of sin: *disobedience* to God's Word, *discipline* from the Lord, her cry of *despair*, followed by God's *deliverance*. If your life is spinning out of control, maybe you're stuck in the sin cycle too. Call on God and discover "deliverance is of the Lord" (Proverbs 21:31).

LESSON 1 - DAY 1

exploration

In today's lesson we meet the characters in the book of Ruth and gain an understanding of life during the time of the judges. We discover the choice one family made to seek greener pastures outside of the Promised Land and God's will.

Read Ruth 1; then focus on verses 1-2.

> **Now it came to pass, in the days when the judges ruled, that there was a famine in the land. And a certain man of Bethlehem, Judah, went to dwell in the country of Moab, he and his wife and his two sons. Ruth 1:1**

1. In what days did the story of Ruth take place? . . . .

   In the Days when the judges ruled :

2. Fill in the following chart to discover the spiritual condition of the nation of Israel during the time of the judges.

SCRIPTURE	SPIRITUAL CONDITION
Judg. 2:10	*didn't Know the Lord or what He had done*
Judg. 2:11-12	*did evil, forsook him, worshiped other gods*
Judg. 17:6	*Everyone did as they saw fit*

3. According to Ruth 1:1, what natural disaster was Israel experiencing?

FAMINE

4. Read Leviticus 26:18-20. How do these verses lead you to believe God was chastening His people?

Because God foretold what would happen if the people were disobedient. No crops = Famine

5. How did this man of Bethlehem respond to the famine?

Took his family and went to live in Moab

> *The name of the man was Elimelech, the name of his wife was Naomi, and the names of his two sons were Mahlon and Chilion—Ephrathites of Bethlehem, Judah. And they went to the country of Moab and remained there.* Ruth 1:2

6. What were the names of the man and his wife? Elimelech + Naomi

7. What were the names of their sons? How are they described?

Mahlon and Chilion - Ephrathites of Bethlehem

8. How long did they stay in Moab? for ever

transformation

9. Today we discovered the four stages of Israel's sin cycle. Think about your life. Are you at times caught in the same cycle?

5
TRADING PLACES
This family made a bad trade, exchanging the Promised Land for a land of pagans. They left Bethlehem (translated, "house of bread") for Moab, an enemy nation called "My washpot" (translated, "a pan of dirty water") in Psalm 60:8. The family turned away from glory and landed in the gutter.

6
PRODIGAL FAMILY
We know the Prodigal Son of the New Testament. He ran away, repented, and returned home (see Luke 15:11-32). Commentator J. Vernon McGee says of Naomi's family, "Here it's the story of a prodigal family." They ran to Moab when they should have stayed in the Promised Land; later they realized they needed to return home.

9
DIVINE DISCIPLINE
God disciplines His children for good reasons: to get their attention, correct their behavior, or express His love. "Don't ignore it when the Lord disciplines you. . . . For the Lord disciplines those he loves, and he punishes those he accepts as his children" (Hebrews 12:5-6, NLT).

10
KING
Elimelech's name meant "God is king" but he didn't let God rule his life. He led his family astray instead of submitting to God's sovereignty. "The Lord is king forever" (Psalm 10:16, NLT).

11
CONTROL
The word *Lord* denotes ownership with absolute control. It refers to owners of slaves or kings as the lords of their subjects (adapted, *Unger's*). Revelation 1:5 identifies Jesus as the King of kings and the Lord of lords. Therefore He holds complete control over all of humanity, including you and me.

Journal about a time when you have gone through these phases.

Disobedience (Example: I didn't trust God to provide financially so I went into debt.)

I didn't trust God to provide for us so we went and pawned Scott's viola.

Discipline (Example: I was turned over to collection agencies.)

We didn't get very much money for it

Despair (Example: "God, if You rescue me, I'll never do it again.")

It didn't make us feel any better about the circumstances

Deliverance (Example: A godly adviser showed me how to pay off my debt.)

The people in church blessed us beyond measure. Then we realized we were acting in the flesh.

10. In the days of the judges there was no king in Israel, and "everyone did what was right in his own eyes" (Judges 17:6). Check the boxes that indicate how you have sometimes made yourself the ruler, the queen of your world.

✓ I make the decisions.
✓ I don't listen to advice.
✓ I trust my intuition.
___ I boss others around.
✓ I want things my way.

___ My time is my own.
✓ I don't admit failure.
___ I'm smarter than that.
✓ My way's the best way.

11. Take time to think about the areas you want to control in your life. Then offer these up to God.

Journal the following verses into a personal prayer, submitting your "domain" to the lordship of Jesus Christ, the King of kings and Lord of lords. "At the name of Jesus every knee will bow, in heaven and on earth and under the earth, and every tongue will confess that Jesus Christ is Lord, to the glory of God the Father" (Philippians 2:10-11, NLT).

Dear Lord, At the name of Jesus, May I bow the knee and give control of myself to you. Would You lead me in the decisions I need to make, help me listen to advice, help me to trust the leading of the Spirit & not my intuition, to admit my failures and to make sure that I see the way that is best in situation / not just my way.

"When the going gets tough, the tough get going." That's how Elimelech chose to live his life. People often imagine that some-where else the grass will be greener and mistakenly think that they can run away from their problems. The reality is, their problems usually follow them because *they* are the problem. A change of scenery doesn't change the heart but turning to God can. Moses had taught the children of Israel that famine was a form of divine discipline, but repentance of their sin would restore God's blessing. Turning a famine into a feast was just a prayer away.

I've discovered that when the going gets tough, the tough should stay put. When I was a little girl and misbehaved, my dad would spank my bottom with a wooden spoon. Wiggling away from the spoon seemed like the smart thing to do. Then one day I figured out that the closer you were to Dad the less the spanking hurt because there was less momentum. And if I crawled onto his lap and apologized for my behavior, the spanking never happened. Running away from your problems or from your heavenly Father will only make things worse. Instead of running, try my philoso-phy: When the going gets tough, the tough get closer to God, because forgiveness is just a prayer away.

contemplation
Most people spend more time and energy going around problems than in trying to solve them.
Henry Ford

DAY 2 DOWN AND OUT

preparation

God, when life gets me down, help me to get back up, with Your strength, and get going in the direction You desire. Be my companion in trouble, my ever-present help in time of need. Amen.

STAYING POWER
We are pressed on every side by troubles, but we are not crushed and broken. We are perplexed, but we don't give up and quit. We are hunted down, but God never abandons us. We get knocked down, but we get up again and keep going. 2 Corinthians 4:8-9, NLT

Fidel Castro's oppressive dictatorship has forced thousands of Cubans to seek asylum in the United States. Castro has crushed his people's rights to free speech, freedom of the press, and the pursuit of economic prosperity, leaving them helpless, hopeless, and hungry. Impoverished Cuban refugees risk their lives sailing aboard unsafe boats over treacherous waters to reach the shores of America. The Cuban residents are down, and they want out.

Elian Gonzalez, a five-year-old Cuban boy, was found on November 25, 1999, clinging to an inner tube off the coast of Florida. He and several other Cuban refugees had boarded an overloaded powerboat that sank on its way to the U.S. His mother and ten others died on the tragic journey. After his rescue, the boy became the subject of a custody battle between his father in Cuba and relatives in Miami, which ended with a dramatic predawn raid during which the boy was taken at gunpoint. For Elian's mother, getting out of Cuba resulted in death. For Elian, getting out resulted in a tug-of-war between families and nations.

It would have taken the wisdom of Solomon to determine the best for this little boy. It takes God's wisdom to know what is best for you when you are in difficult circumstances. When you feel down and think you want out, stop and ask yourself two questions: *What am I running from?* and *Where am I running to?* Running to human solutions will leave you down and out. Running to God's answers will take you up and away.

exploration

Yesterday we learned that during the time of the judges Israel entered a vicious sin cycle and experienced famine as a result of

God's discipline. Elimelech chose to take his family out of the Promised Land. Now we see what happened to his family in Moab. Review Ruth 1; then focus on verses 3-7.

> *Then Elimelech, Naomi's husband, died; and she was left, and her two sons. Now they took wives of the women of Moab: the name of the one was Orpah, and the name of the other Ruth. And they dwelt there about ten years.* Ruth 1:3-4

1. How did Naomi's life suddenly change? . . . .

. . . Her husband died . . . .

2. What were the names and nationality of her sons' brides?

. . . Orpah & Ruth . . . . | Moabites . . . . .

. . . .

> *Then both Mahlon and Chilion also died; so the woman survived her two sons and her husband.* Ruth 1:5

3. How did Mahlon and Chilion's fate match that of their father?

. . . they both died . . . .

> *Then she arose with her daughters-in-law that she might return from the country of Moab, for she had heard in the country of Moab that the Lord had visited His people by giving them bread.* Ruth 1:6

4. What did Naomi decide to do after the death of her husband and sons?

. . . Return from Moab to Judah . . . .

5. What information helped motivate her to go home?

. . . The Lord had given His people Bread . . . .
(The famine was over)

> *Therefore she went out from the place where she was, and her two daughters-in-law with her; and they went on the way to return to the land of Judah.* Ruth 1:7

BAD EXAMPLE
Elimelech's sons followed their father's bad example, choosing their own way rather than God's. They married pagan women, which was strictly forbidden. God said, "Don't let your daughters and sons marry their sons and daughters. They will lead your young people away from me to worship other gods" (Deuteronomy 7:3-4, NLT).

3
CHILDLESS
Not only was Naomi a widow, she now found herself in a state of barrenness. In Old Testament times childlessness was looked upon as a great reproach as well as a punishment from God. Leviticus 20:20-21 reveals that some marriages, forbidden by God, were punished with barrenness.

5
GLIMMER OF HOPE
They left Israel to escape death—it came anyway. A decade of disobedience resulted in three widows and three graves. But God, who said, "Let there be light" (Genesis 1:3, NLT), shone a glimmer of hope by providing bread back home.

7

WIDOWS
Widows and orphans
hold a special place in
God's heart. God is
sensitive to weakness.
He loves to help those
who can't help them-
selves. "Do not exploit
widows or orphans. If
you do and they cry out
to me, then I will surely
help them" (Exodus
22:22-23, NLT).

8

FOOTSTEPS
Following in your
father's footsteps can be
good or bad, depend-
ing on the way he goes.
God warned Moses,
"I show this unfailing
love . . . by forgiv-
ing. . . . Even so I do not
leave sin unpunished,
but I punish the children
for the sins of their
parents to the third and
fourth generations"
(Exodus 34:7, NLT).

6. Who accompanied Naomi when she set out to leave Moab?
Where was she headed?

Her 2 daughters in laws

transformation

7. Naomi and her daughters-in-law had become widows. Fill
in the following chart to discover how God provides for the
widow.

SCRIPTURE	PROVISION FOR WIDOWS
Deut. 10:17-18	*Defends the Cause of the widow*
Ps. 68:5	*a defender of widows*
1 Tim. 5:3-4, 16	*give proper recognition, care for / pray* *help them*
James 1:27	*look after*

 Think of a widow you know. Journal a prayer for her,
asking God to provide for all her needs. Next write
about a way you can be God's hands and heart in
reaching out to her.

Dear Lord, please provide for all of Cathie's needs.
Help me to know when and how to reach out
to her, to minister to her physically and
spiritually

8. Elimelech's sons made the mistake of following their father's
bad example. Name two ways you have followed in your
father's footsteps, whether good or bad. (Examples: I joined
the family business. / Sometimes I talk like a sailor.)

I have my father's sense of integrity
in my work and his strength of
character. I went into teaching.
I had a reverence/awe of God and
God had a place in my family.

9. Think about the ways you have emulated your father.

Journal a prayer of thanks for those things. If your father's influence has led you to a dark place, journal a prayer asking God to shine His light on your life in new ways.

My Father's influence was a good one. He worked hard, helped others and stood up to some degree in adversity. I watched as he raised us girls. I, for a long time didn't express my feelings (much like him) but that is not a good thing (for a woman) I also got from him a sense of and reverence for God, an importance, I thank you Lord for that influence, unsickning and care as I know it made a tremendous impact on my all going the Lord.

On a foggy night, William Cowper ordered his coachman to take him to the London Bridge. Suffering from deep depression, he planned on jumping into the Thames River. However, his driver got lost and drove aimlessly for hours. Cowper left his carriage to walk to the London Bridge himself. After a short distance, he found himself back home! The coachman had driven in circles. Cowper realized that God's providential hand was guiding his way. He discovered that the way out of despair was to look to God, not jump into the river. In gratitude, he cast his cares on the Savior and experienced great peace. With renewed hope he wrote these words to the famous hymn, "God moves in a mysterious way / His wonders to perform; / He plants His footsteps in the sea, / And rides upon the storm. / Ye fearful saints, fresh courage take; / The clouds ye so much dread / Are big with mercy, and shall break / With blessing on your head."

Hard times and bad choices brought Elimelech's family so far down that it put out the light of God's truth in their hearts. However, God's faithfulness broke through the shadow of death with the promise of new life if Naomi would return home. Scripture promises us that God's faithfulness will always outshine the darkness of our doubts too. "If we are unfaithful, he remains faithful, for he cannot deny himself" (2 Timothy 2:13, NLT). If you are on the dark road of depression or doubt or death, God will faithfully lead you home.

contemplation
God is with us in darkness just as surely as he is with us in the light.
Croft Pentz

DAY 3 FORK IN THE ROAD

preparation

Dear Lord, when I reach a fork in the road of life and must decide which way to go, please lead me in Your paths of righteousness, for Your name's sake. Amen.

DIRECTION
Your ears shall hear a word behind you, saying, "This is the way, walk in it," whenever you turn to the right hand or whenever you turn to the left. Isaiah 30:21

With her head held high (and just a glimpse of a tear in her eye), a young girl kissed her mom and dad good-bye and climbed aboard a train for the first time. She was traveling alone to visit her grandmother. Along the way the train needed to cross several rivers. As they neared the first river, the girl looked out the window and saw a wide, flowing body of water. She didn't understand how the train could cross the river and imagined the train plunging into the fast-moving current and quickly sinking. Desperately she thought, *Maybe I should jump off!* As the train drew closer to the river, she spotted the bridge that would provide safe crossing. After several rivers and several bridges the young lady breathed a sigh of relief, "Someone has put bridges all the way!"

Life's journey often seems treacherous and full of hazards. There are times when we can't see the way out and just *know* we're going to crash! Then we see the bridge and know that God has provided safe passage. There comes a time when we reach a fork in the road concerning faith too. We must decide: Will we stay on the train and trust God to build the bridges, or will we jump off and try to make our own way?

exploration

As the widows began their journey, all three reached a difficult moment of decision—a fork in the road.

Review Ruth 1; then focus on verses 8-14.

> *And Naomi said to her two daughters-in-law, "Go, return each to her mother's house. The Lord deal kindly with you, as you have dealt with the dead and with me. The Lord grant that you may find rest, each in the house of her husband."* Ruth 1:8-9

1. As they started on the way to Judah, what did Naomi encourage the women to do?

...To return to their parents homes..........

2. After urging them to go home, what two things did Naomi pray for the women?

...Lord deal Kindly...................
...may find rest...................

> So she kissed them, and they lifted up their voices and wept. And they said to her, "Surely we will return with you to your people." Ruth 1:9-10

3. How did the two Moabite brides respond? ...They wanted to go with her..................

> But Naomi said, "Turn back, my daughters; why will you go with me? Are there still sons in my womb, that they may be your husbands? Turn back, my daughters, go— for I am too old to have a husband. If I should say I have hope, if I should have a husband tonight and should also bear sons, would you wait for them till they were grown? Would you restrain yourselves from having husbands?" Ruth 1:11-13

4. Explain the second argument Naomi used to convince Orpah and Ruth to turn back.

That there was nothing for them / No sons

> "No, my daughters; for it grieves me very much for your sakes that the hand of the Lord has gone out against me!" Ruth 1:13

5. How did Naomi view her losses and the consequences of her family's actions?

...As the act of the Lord against her....
...As a Consequence...................

1
TRUE HOPE
Destitute and desperate, Naomi tried to send the women home. Yet their hope wasn't in the tents of Moab but in the tabernacle of Israel. She could have echoed Moses' invitation to his foreign in-laws, "We are on our way to the Promised Land. Come with us" (Numbers 10:29, NLT).

4
PERSPECTIVE
Naomi changed tactics from the past to the future. Instead of telling Orpah and Ruth, "Go back to mother," she urged them, "Go ahead to new husbands." She could have focused on the present and offered new hope in the God of Israel. "Today is the day of salvation" (2 Corinthians 6:2, NLT).

5
GOD'S HAND
Naomi felt that the Lord's hand was causing her suffering. Instead, His hand was outstretched as a loving Father disciplining His child. "As you endure this divine discipline, remember that God is treating you as his own children" (Hebrews 12:7, NLT). Sometimes love must be tough to help us see the error of our ways.

6
TEARS
Orpah wept but withstood change, eventually returning to Moab. Ruth's tears transformed her as she moved toward the Promised Land. "Godly sorrow brings repentance that leads to salvation . . . , but worldly sorrow brings death" (2 Corinthians 7:10, NIV). Tears should not be an act, but are a symbol that we'll change our act.

How Do you use Tears?

7
BLAME SHIFTING
It's easy to blame others for problems that come our way. When Job was afflicted his wife said, "Curse God and die." But Job knew that blaming God was blasphemy and chastised her, "You talk like a godless woman. Should we accept only good things from the hand of God?" (Job 2:9-10, NLT).

8
TODAY
Worry won't empty tomorrow of its sorrows; it only robs today of its strength. Jesus said, "Don't worry about tomorrow. . . . Today's trouble is enough for today" (Matthew 6:34, NLT). The same Lord who cares for you today will take care of you tomorrow and always.

Then they lifted up their voices and wept again; and Orpah kissed her mother-in-law, but Ruth clung to her.
Ruth 1:14

6. Describe the similarities and differences between Orpah's and Ruth's responses.

lifted voices, cried . . . Both displayed affection 1 was a parting kiss, the other a clinging hug

transformation

7. When the hard times came, Naomi blamed God. Instead of seeking His ever-present help in time of need, she directed Orpah and Ruth to look to the past and future for answers.

Journal about a current circumstance in your life that concerns or unsettles you. Describe the three ways you could resolve the problem—by looking to the past, looking to the future, or looking to the present.

Andrew:
1) Past: Know he knows God / Wish I had done more
2) Present: Not worrying it . . . God can intervene
3) Future: God can intervene

8. There is no time like the present for change and growth. Many of us waste precious opportunities by regretting our past or fretting about the future. Fill in the following chart to discover the opportunities given *today*.

SCRIPTURE	OPPORTUNITY OFFERED?
Deut. 11:26-28	*Blessing + A curse* *obedience or disobedience*
Luke 23:39-43	*Salvation / punishment*
Heb. 3:12-15	*Encourage others / do not harden your heart*

9. Today we learned from Ruth's example that godly sorrow leads to repentance but the sorrow of the world is unproductive.

Journal about a time in your life when you felt sorry for yourself and reacted in the wrong way. What was the result?

When I was hurt in an interaction with someone and talked about it to others to rally them to my side, make myself feel bitter.

Journal about a time when you were grieved over your sin and responded the right way. What was the result?

Just last week when I realized that my gluttony of food nailed the Lord to the cross. He too delivered me from the bondage it held.

REPENTANCE
Repentance is a turning away from sin and a turning back to God. Repentance means a change of mind or a feeling of regret for past conduct. "True repentance is a 'godly sorrow' for sin, an act of turning around and going in the opposite direction" (*Nelson's*).

Hotel Street is the red-light district in Honolulu, Hawaii. After dusk the streets light up with neon signs promoting adult bookstores and seedy bars. The sidewalks are filled with prostitutes, transvestites, pimps, and pushers. In June of 1980 I was working on Hotel Street in a Christian coffeehouse run by Youth With A Mission.

One night I bumped into someone more glamorous than Cher in a Bob Mackie costume. "Michelle" accepted my invitation to the coffee shop, where I heard the sad story. When "Michelle" was a little boy, his father had molested him. After years of resentment and confusion little Michael had transformed himself into Michelle the transvestite, selling himself to unwitting sailors on furlough. Throughout that summer Michael would stop in to talk and cry, "I'm so miserable and empty inside." But after months of loving encouragement he refused to leave his destructive lifestyle for forgiveness and a new start. I have no doubt that Michael was suffering, but his tears did not lead him to the only One who could comfort him. Michael, like Orpah, shed tears of regret but not repentance. He felt sorry for himself, blaming his situation on his earthly father and his bitter past. As far as I know, when he came to a fork in the road, he chose to stay on the road leading to a dead end, refusing to believe that the Father in heaven had a better future in store for him.

contemplation
When something goes wrong, it is more important to decide who is going to fix it than who is to blame.
Anonymous

DAY 4 THE ROAD LESS TRAVELED

preparation

Lord, You have made all the difference in my life. Thank You for offering me the path of life. Help me to continue to walk the narrow road. Amen.

NARROW ROAD
You can enter God's Kingdom only through the narrow gate. The highway to hell is broad, and its gate is wide for the many who choose the easy way. But the gateway to life is small, and the road is narrow, and only a few ever find it. Matthew 7:13-14, NLT

Robert Frost's poem "The Road Not Taken" depicts a traveler encountering a fork in the road: "Two roads diverged in a yellow wood, / And sorry I could not travel both. . . ." The traveler is left to decide which path to choose. Life is full of little choices that can lead to great consequences. A choice repeated becomes a habit; a habit unchecked develops a character; and character determines your destiny. Like Frost's traveler, you can't have it both ways. You must choose which direction you'll take on life's journey.

During college I was traveling through a forest of life decisions: relationships, vocation, and relocation. In the summer of 1978 God's providence led me to a fork in the road. My highly successful, atheistic father became a Christian and beckoned me to follow the narrow path—the road less traveled. That summer, with reckless abandon, I packed my bags for a spiritual journey that would take me through awakening, repentance, baptism, and new life. I've never looked back—that choice determined my destiny as a follower of Jesus Christ. In Frost's words, "Two roads diverged in a wood, and I—I took the one less traveled by, and that has made all the difference."

exploration

Yesterday we saw that Naomi decided to return to Israel, the land of blessing. Her decision brought her daughters-in-law to a fork in the road: Orpah chose to stay among her people and her gods, while Ruth chose the road to the Promised Land, the road less traveled. Today we gain insight into Ruth's choice to walk forward in faith.

Review Ruth 1; then focus on verses 15-18.

And she said, "Look, your sister-in-law has gone back to her people and to her gods; return after your sister-in-law." Ruth 1:15

1. Who did Orpah, Ruth's sister-in-law, return to? *The Moabites*.

2. What did Naomi encourage Ruth to do? *To follow Orpah*

But Ruth said: "Entreat me not to leave you, or to turn back from following after you; for wherever you go, I will go; and wherever you lodge, I will lodge; your people shall be my people, and your God, my God. Where you die, I will die, and there will I be buried. The Lord do so to me, and more also, if anything but death parts you and me." Ruth 1:16-17

3. Which phrases spoken by Ruth revealed her loyalty to Naomi and her people?
Where you go I will go, where you lodge, I will lodge. Your people will be my people

4. What did she say that showed her desire to be counted with Naomi's people and her God?
Your people will be my people, & your God my God

5. Which phrase affirmed that her commitment was for a lifetime?
Where you die, I will die & there will I be buried.

When she saw that she was determined to go with her, she stopped speaking to her. Ruth 1:18

6. What did Ruth's words reveal to Naomi about her daughter-in-law?
That she was committed & determined to go with her.

7. How did Naomi respond? *She stopped trying to change her mind / she stopped speaking to her.*

15

NARROW ROAD
The narrow road is a one-way street with no U-turns allowed. By turning back to her people and her gods, Orpah turned her back on the one, true God. Jesus said, "Anyone who puts a hand to the plow and then looks back is not fit for the Kingdom of God" (Luke 9:62, NLT).

3
LOYALTY
Ruth offers the most beautiful oath of loyalty in Scripture. Loyalty is faithful allegiance to a person or country—to be steadfast in keeping one's promises. God takes oaths seriously: "If . . . a woman is a widow . . . , she must fulfill all her vows and pledges no matter what" (Numbers 30:9, NLT)

4
EMPTY HANDS
Let go and let God! Come to the Lord with empty hands and you'll leave full. Ruth let go of her nation and religion so she could take hold of Naomi's country and God. "If anyone desires to come after Me, let him deny himself, and take up his cross, and follow Me" (Matthew 16:24).

transformation

8

DECISION MAKING
Deciding which direction to take is as simple as 1, 2, 3: (1) Trust in God; (2) Don't depend on self; (3) Make God's will your own. "Trust in the Lord with all your heart; do not depend on your own understanding. Seek his will in all you do, and he will direct your paths" (Proverbs 3:5-6, NLT).

PAST
People who see the past through rose-colored glasses have selective memory disorder—remembering the good, not the bad. Are you stuck living in the past? Adopt Paul's philosophy, "I am focusing all my energies on this one thing: Forgetting the past and looking forward to what lies ahead" (Philippians 3:13, NLT).

8. Life is full of choices, both large and small. Think about a recent decision you made. Complete the following exercise to examine your decision-making process:

- In the space provided draw a large Y depicting a fork in the road.
- Below the Y describe the road you were on and the decision you faced.
- Near the fork to the left, describe how taking that road might have led you in the wrong direction.
- Near the fork to the right, describe how going another way might lead you in the right direction.

Panic
fear
discouragement
uselessness

Feelings

Faith/God

faith, security, comfort

I was given a possibility that a medical condition was potentially very serious

9. Ruth had to let go of her past to lay hold of her future. Today you can redirect your life by offering God your past problems so you can receive His promises instead. In each column check off some items that you need to release and to receive.

Release to God	**Receive from God**
___ Hate	✓ Trust
✓ Fear	✓ Humility
✓ Anxiety	✓ Faith
✓ Guilt	___ Love
✓ Pride	✓ Peace

Journal a prayer of release and receiving to God, exchanging problems for promises.

Dear Lord, take my fears, anxious thoughts, my guilt & my pride about this day and my past and ... Let me receive (accept, believe and stand on ... the promise of You Lord, Peace & Forgiveness. Let me cling to you and not those feelings

10. Ruth's declaration to Naomi is one of the most beautiful in all of Scripture.

> Take time now to journal her words into a personal prayer to the Lord, offering Him your future. "Don't ask me to leave you and turn back. I will go wherever you go and live wherever you live. Your people will be my people, and your God will be my God" (Ruth 1:16, NLT).

Lord, don't let me listen to the world and follow its urging to leave you or turn away from you. Where you tell me to go I will go., where you lead I will follow. Your people, those called by your name will be my people, Let nothing separate me from You.

Indiana Jones, the handsome adventurer of the silver screen, searched the globe to find the Holy Grail, the sacred cup of Christ, believed to give eternal life to the one who drank from it. But the quest was filled with pitfalls, leading Indy and the enemy Nazis to Jordan. In a dark cave an old Crusader knight guarded an array of chalices. Anyone entering was forced to choose which cup he would drink from. Only one goblet would give life, all others would bring excruciating death. The Nazi grasped the most ornate goblet of gold and greedily guzzled the drink. As he died a gruesome death, the knight said, "He chose poorly." Indiana Jones chose the plainest cup, one of simple clay, meekly filled it with water, and slowly drank. As Indy's strength was restored, the solemn Crusader proclaimed, "You have chosen wisely."

While the mythical grail does not offer eternal life, it does represent the crucial choice we must all make. Will we drink from the cup of blessing offered by God or the cup of sorrow offered by the world? Orpah chose poorly—she decided to accept what the world had to offer. Ruth chose wisely and followed the path to life everlasting.

10
INSEPARABLE
When you offer Christ your vow of love, you become inseparable. "Nothing can ever separate us from his love. Death can't, and life can't. The angels can't, and the demons can't. Our fears for today, our worries about tomorrow, and even the powers of hell can't keep God's love away" (Romans 8:38, NLT).

contemplation

Progress is impossible without change; and those who cannot change their minds cannot change anything.
George Bernard Shaw

DAY 5 THERE'S NO PLACE LIKE HOME

preparation

Father, thank You that there is a place in Your heart for every prodigal who desires to repent and return home. If I stray, let me hunger with a dissatisfaction of heart that compels me to come running back to You. Amen.

HOME
So he returned home to his father. And while he was still a long distance away, his father saw him coming. Filled with love and compassion, he ran to his son, embraced him, and kissed him.
Luke 15:20, NLT

When my sister Suzanne and I were young, we, like Dorothy from the *Wizard of Oz*, had hair in pigtails and imaginations that longed for "somewhere over the rainbow." Our daydreams of escape were the result of childish grievances about the way our new stepfather ran the house. He set the thermostat much too low for our liking throughout Michigan's bone-chilling winters. We resented the early curfew that put us to bed before the *Batman & Robin* show. If we were in too much of a hurry to turn off the lights or shut the back-yard gate, we were grounded for a week. We were fed up and something had to be done. Late one night we plotted our escape and agreed to run away from home. We decided to pack enough food to last a week and hide out in the bathroom of a local gas station. "We'll show them," we said. "They'll regret making our lives so miserable that we had to leave." Needless to say, we didn't get far, and we didn't last long. Once it started to get dark, we got scared and began to realize, "There's no place like home."

Naomi's family had grievances too. Like me, they decided the only answer was to run away from home. But prodigals often discover that life's hard on the road. Once you get hungry enough or scared enough, your perspective of home changes. Naomi came to her senses. She concluded, too, that there is no place like home. The prodigal daughter returned.

exploration

Today we follow Ruth and Naomi home to Bethlehem. It has been said, "You can't go home again," but with God the road home is always open, and a loving Father eagerly waits to receive His wandering children.

Review Ruth 1; then focus on verses 19-22.

Now the two of them went until they came to Bethlehem. And it happened, when they had come to Bethlehem, that all the city was excited because of them; and the women said, "Is this Naomi?" Ruth 1:19

1. What was the final destination of Ruth and Naomi's journey?

   Bethlehem . . . .

2. How did the residents of the city respond to their return?

   . Everyone seemed happy to see them . . . . . .

3. Did the women recognize Naomi? They questioned if it . . .

   was her . . . .

   But she said to them, "Do not call me Naomi; call me Mara, for the Almighty has dealt very bitterly with me." Ruth 1:20

4. What new name did Naomi give herself and why?

   Mara, She was bitter . . . .

   "I went out full, and the Lord has brought me home again empty. Why do you call me Naomi, since the Lord has testified against me, and the Almighty has afflicted me?" Ruth 1:21

5. How did Naomi leave Bethlehem, and how did she return?

   She left full of hopes and dreams/with

   Spouse + children. She returned in despair + bitterness

6. Whom did Naomi blame for the loss she suffered?

   . God . . . .

   So Naomi returned, and Ruth the Moabitess her daughter-in-law with her, who returned from the country of Moab. Now they came to Bethlehem at the beginning of barley harvest. Ruth 1:22

3

SUFFERING
The Naomi who left was not the Naomi who returned. Suffering had changed her appearance. The hopelessness and grief she experienced must have shown on her face. "A glad heart makes a happy face; a broken heart crushes the spirit" (Proverbs 15:13, NLT).

4

BITTER TRIALS
Trials can make you bitter or better. The Israelites named children after an attribute they were to display. *Naomi* means "pleasant," but her circumstances weren't. She changed her name to *Mara*, which means "bitter." "Watch out that no bitter root of unbelief rises up among you" (Hebrews 12:15, NLT).

7

HOPE OF HARVEST
After a decade of darkness, hope broke through. Our heroines returned to Bethlehem, a farming community, at the beginning of the spring barley harvest that heralded a season of fruitfulness. "Weeping may go on all night, but joy comes with the morning" (Psalm 30:5, NLT).

8

PERSPECTIVE
Two people viewed a glass filled partially with water. The optimist observed, "The glass is half full." The pessimist complained, "It's half empty." They saw the same thing but drew different conclusions. The Christian can proclaim, "My cup overflows with blessings" (Psalm 23:5, NLT).

9

TRIAL
"A trial is a temptation or adversity, . . . the means by which a person's faith is proved either true or false before God. Since many positive things come about through trials, Christians are urged to rejoice at their occurrence" (*Nelson's*).

7. What time of the year did these two women return to Bethlehem?

Beginning Hope of Harvest

transformation

8. Today we learned that Naomi left the Promised Land full and returned empty. Place a **+** by the things that have filled up your cup and a **−** by the things that at times have drained you.

Draining
- − Death
- __ Financial loss
- __ Mall shopping
- __ Romance novels
- − Demands from others
- __ Gossip
- − Strained relationships
- − Illness

Filling
- __ Birth of a child
- __ Financial gain
- + Church
- + God's Word
- + Encouragement
- + Prayer
- + Healthy friendships
- __ Health

9. As Christians we should never view God through the distorted lens of circumstances. Instead, we should view our circumstances through the lens of God's love. List five trials, big or small, you have experienced and how you viewed them.

The beginning of the ministry - Draining
new marriage - difficult but good
my job - a blessing
The death of my brother in law - a blessing + a draining (Bittersweet)
My health Bittersweet → trial of faith

10. James 1:2-4 teaches that Christians are to view their trials as blessings, knowing that they will add up to joy in the Lord.

Journal the following verses into a prayer to God, counting the trials you listed above as joy. They are meant to fill you up with faith and patience! "Count it all joy when you fall into various trials, knowing that the testing of your faith produces patience. But let patience have its perfect work, that you may be perfect and complete, lacking nothing" (James 1:2-4).

Lord, help me to view the circumstances in my life with joy. Joy that you are in control and working in my best interest. That you are using these things to mature me so that I lack nothing.

10

CONTRARY KINGDOM
God's values are contrary to the world's: The poor are rich, the weak are strong, and the humble will be exalted. For Christians, all that happens has a divine purpose. "All things work together for good to those who love God, to those who are the called according to His purpose" (Romans 8:28).

Naomi had a <u>bitter, pessimistic outlook on life</u>. She had fallen into the pit of despair. It reminds me of the story about a man who fell into a pit and couldn't get himself out. A self-pitying person wandered by and said, "That ain't nothin'. You should see *my* pit."

A Christian Scientist happened by and encouraged him, "You only *think* you're in a pit."

Confucius murmured, "If you had only listened to me, you would not be in that pit."

Buddha explained, "Your pit is only a state of mind."

A psychologist stated, "Falling into the pit is your mother's fault."

An evolutionist said, "You're a rejected mutant destined to be removed from the evolutionary cycle. It's survival of the fittest and you aren't fit—that's why you're in the pit!"

An optimist saw him and said, "Things could be worse."

The pessimist came by and predicted, "Things will get worse!"

Then Jesus walked by. When He saw the man, He took him by the hand and pulled him out of the pit.

If you've dug a pit of bitterness that you can't seem to get out of, hold out your hands to the Savior—He's ready, willing, and able to lift you up. You'll be able to say, like the psalmist, "He lifted me out of the pit of despair, out of the mud and the mire. He set my feet on solid ground and steadied me as I walked along" (Psalm 40:2, NLT).

contemplation
It is not the experience of today that drives men mad—it is remorse or bitterness for something which happened yesterday and the dread of what will happen tomorrow.
Unknown

Leaving a Trail

"Mommy, look, jelly beans!" exclaimed Nathan one Easter. We had just begun a family ritual that year to help a small adventurous boy find his basket. A trail of jelly beans began at the foot of his bed leading in a zigzag pattern throughout the house, until it ended where his basket was hidden. We heard the shuffle of slippers moving down the hall and the plunk of jelly beans dropping into his tin pail. Nathan was learning through the sweet nuggets that life's journey is a trail lined with valuable markers that can lead to great rewards.

Nathan's bountiful trail reminds me of another—the trail of grain a young widow followed through a field in ancient Bethlehem. As we continue our study, Ruth has joined her mother-in-law, Naomi, on a journey to the Promised Land. Upon their arrival she went to work in the barley fields of a local landowner named Boaz. As she gathered food following a trail of grain, we see God's providential hand once again in Ruth's and Naomi's lives. God worked behind the scenes, weaving together the lives of the main characters in this ancient love story.

God leaves a steady trail of good things for all who diligently seek Him. These markers faithfully lead all the way to His heart and home. Your heavenly Father sees your needs, as He saw Ruth's needs, and desires your company. Look beyond what you can see with your eyes to the unseen hand of God leaving bundles of goodness for you.

1 JUST COINCIDENCE?

preparation

Thank You, Lord, for leading me in the path of life. Your hand has left pleasant gifts along the way, and at the end of the trail is Your presence. Amen.

DIRECTION
You will show me the path of life; in Your presence is fullness of joy; at Your right hand are pleasures forevermore. Psalm 16:11

explanation

FAMILY RELATIONS
Relative, also translated kinsman, means "redeemer; one coming to rescue." Boaz had obligations to Naomi's family because he was a close male relative. An Israelite in debt could sell himself, his family, or his land. The nearest relative could buy back his possessions to preserve his clan (see Leviticus 25:23-28).

exploration

Today we find the poverty-stricken Ruth taking action that led to meeting a distant relative named Boaz. It is no coincidence that Boaz is featured in this Old Testament story because he foreshadows the person and work of Jesus Christ later seen in the New Testament. To foreshadow means to give an advance indication or suggestion of something so that the reader is prepared for what occurs later. Thus, the historical Boaz, through his actions and character traits, prepares readers for the coming Messiah. Just as a shadow is merely a dim representation of an actual person, Boaz dimly depicts and points to the true Redeemer, Jesus Christ.

Read Ruth 2; then focus on verses 1-3.

> ***There was a relative of Naomi's husband, a man of great wealth, of the family of Elimelech. His name was Boaz.***
> Ruth 2:1

1. What three phrases describe Boaz? *A relative of Naomi's husband, a man of great wealth of the family of Elimelech.*

2. Boaz is a picture of Christ for us. Read Revelation 1:12-16. How does this description of Jesus bring to mind a mighty man of strength and valor as Boaz was?

   robe, eyes of the blazing fire, voice like the sound of rushing waters

So Ruth the Moabitess said to Naomi, "Please let me go to the field, and glean heads of grain after him in whose sight I may find favor." And she said to her, "Go, my daughter." Ruth 2:2

3. What did Ruth ask permission to do? go to work to support her mother in law.

4. In whose fields would she glean? Him in whose sight she might find favor

5. How did Naomi respond to Ruth's request? Permission

6. What did Naomi's response reveal about their relationship?
1. Relationship had grown on the journey / Naomi had made Ruth her daughter;

Then she left, and went and gleaned in the field after the reapers. And she happened to come to the part of the field belonging to Boaz, who was of the family of Elimelech. Ruth 2:3

7. What field did Ruth "happen" to come to? Boaz

transformation

8. We've found that God often uses providence to accomplish His will in the lives of His people. Fill in the chart to discover some instances when God's providential hand orchestrated events to bring a predetermined outcome.

SCRIPTURE	PROVIDENTIAL CIRCUMSTANCE
Gen. 24:12-21	Rebekah meets the servant of Isaac
Gen. 45:4-8	Joseph re meets his brothers in Egypt
1 Sam. 14:6-14	Philistines are delivered into Jonathans hands
Phil. 1:12-14	Pauls imprisonment advances the gospel

2

BOAZ

Boaz means "in him is strength." He offered hope and strength to Ruth. He was a "man of great wealth" (Ruth 2:1), which can also be translated "man of valor," "man of war," or "man of the Law." Boaz is a type of Christ, who is all of these things—our King in shining armor.

7

PROVIDENCE

Just a coincidence? It was imperative that Ruth go to *that* field, so that God's plan could unfold. God directs all things to the ends He has chosen in His eternal plan. God orchestrates ordinary events to bring a predetermined outcome. "What has been determined will surely take place" (Daniel 11:36, NLT).

8

DIVINE DESIRES

God's providence works in hearts as well as happenstance. When you lovingly obey God, He implants His desires within your heart. You begin to want what He wants and will what He wills. "Delight yourself in the Lord and he will give you the desires of your heart" (Psalm 37:4, NIV).

NEAR RELATIVE
Not everyone has family members to help them. The brotherless are told, "a real friend sticks closer than a brother" (Proverbs 18:24, NLT). Jesus is that friend. The fatherless are promised, "When my father and my mother forsake me, then the Lord will take care of me" (Psalm 27:10). God is your closest relative.

10

HARD TIMES
Poverty prompted Ruth to take action. Providence led her to a fruitful field. God will use the hard times in your life to lead you to a place of blessing too. "He leads me beside peaceful streams. He renews my strength. He guides me along right paths" (Psalm 23:2-3, NLT).

9. Today we met the kinsman-redeemer (close male relative) of Ruth and Naomi. List a few of your close male relatives.

My Brother Mikey,

 Journal about a time one of them came to your rescue in some way. Write a prayer of blessing for him.

10. Fill in the chart listing some difficult circumstances you have experienced. Explain how God, in His providence, worked them out for your benefit.

HARD TIME	HIS GOOD WORK
(I lost my job.)	(I found a better job.)
I needed to leave my job	I got a better job
moving to New Hampshire	Growth in My Walk
Letting Andrew Go	Seeing Andrew Grow

David described God's providential care for his life in Psalm 139. Rewrite the truths of this psalm into a personal prayer to God. Praise Him for His divine intervention in your life. "O Lord, you have examined my heart and know everything about me. You know when I sit down or stand up. You know my every thought when far away. You chart the path ahead of me and tell me where to stop and rest. Every moment you know where I am. You know what I am going to say even before I say it, Lord. You both precede and follow me. You place your hand of blessing on my head. Such knowledge is too wonderful for me, too great for me to know!" (Psalm 139:1-6, NLT).

Lord, you know all about me today. Where my heart is, what I will say and what I will do. You know the places I go and the people I'll meet and have laid it out for me. You have a purpose and plan for my life. I thank you and praise you for your care for me. For going before me, being with me and picking up behind me. You do all this and then want to bless me in the midst. Such knowledge is too wonderful for me. Use my life for your glory.

In God's providence everything that comes your way can be used for your good and His glory. There are no dead ends in the will of God—only detours designed to lead you to a more fruitful place. There was once a boy who was intrigued by cameras and photographs. He ordered a book on photography from a magazine but was mistakenly sent a book about ventriloquism instead. So he began practicing the art of throwing his voice. Eventually millions of people listened to Edgar Bergen and his wooden dummy, Charlie McCarthy, on Sunday evening radio and television shows. Edgar Bergen allowed a "mistake" to become a fabulous career.

James Whistler, another renowned artist, also experienced an unwanted detour on his path. He wanted more than anything to be a soldier, so he joined West Point Academy. But he failed a chemistry examination. Later he joked about the one wrong answer that changed his life, "If silicon had been a gas, I would have been a major general instead of an artist."

Who knows what blessing awaits you at the end of your detour?

contemplation
The longer I live, the more convincing proofs I see of this truth, that God governs in the affairs of man.
Benjamin Franklin

DAY 2 DIVINE ENCOUNTERS

preparation

Father, open my eyes so that I can see how Your hand is guiding my life. Help me to recognize the divine encounters and resources You have placed in my path. Amen.

SPIRITUAL SIGHT
And God opened her eyes, and she saw a well of water; and she went, and filled the bottle with water. Genesis 21:19, KJV

We are often unaware of divine encounters until after they happen. I met my husband in such a way, at a backyard barbecue in California. I had recently met the girl having the party through a blind date I'd had with her brother. Like Ruth the Moabite, I was a new convert and felt out of place at a Christian gathering. I was attending the first party I'd been to in years that didn't have an idol—a keg of beer—as the center of attention. Skip recalls that my relaxed, friendly demeanor intrigued him and he asked to meet me. There was an immediate attraction, and we talked for hours. It was thrilling to meet a Christian man who was so alive. I noticed his long hair—still wet from surfing—his shorts, and flip-flops. I was attracted to his looks but more to his godly character and incredible wit.

Now, after twenty-plus years of marriage, I am convinced more than ever that God brought Skip and me together. That blind date with my friend's brother could have been a dead end; instead, it was a divine detour that led eventually to a match made in heaven. If I hadn't gone on the first date I never would have made my date with destiny. Providence is best seen in hindsight. We just have to have spiritual eyes to see God's handiwork. We see this principle at work as Boaz and Ruth have a divine encounter of their own.

exploration

We've seen Ruth's example of submission, industry, and hope. Today we learn more about her encounter with Boaz, Naomi's wealthy kinsman.

Review Ruth 2; then focus on verses 4-7.

Now behold, Boaz came from Bethlehem, and said to the reapers, "The Lord be with you!" And they answered him, "The Lord bless you!" Ruth 2:4

1. How did Boaz greet his workers? *The Lord be with you!*

2. How had his attitude carried over to his workers?
They blessed him in return.

Then Boaz said to his servant who was in charge of the reapers, "Whose young woman is this?" So the servant who was in charge of the reapers answered and said, "It is the young Moabite woman who came back with Naomi from the country of Moab. And she said, 'Please let me glean and gather after the reapers among the sheaves.' So she came and has continued from morning until now, though she rested a little in the house." Ruth 2:5-7

3. Who caught the attention of Boaz? *Ruth*

4. How did the servant describe this stranger to Boaz?
MOABITE woman, Hard worker / little rest

5. Boaz's servant offered a good report concerning Ruth. Which phrase lets you know she was humble (i.e., not demanding)?
Asked to glean & gather after the reapers

6. What did the servant say to let you know she was diligent?
Came + has continued all day / little rest

7. What part of the description reveals that Ruth took care of herself physically?
She needed little rest

1
CITY OF KINGS
Boaz was from Bethlehem, which became the birthplace of kings. David was born and anointed king there. The King of kings, Jesus, was also born there. "You, O Bethlehem Ephrathah, are only a small village. . . . Yet a ruler of Israel will come from you" (Micah 5:2, NLT).

4
ROMANCE
From the moment Boaz saw Ruth he took more interest in the woman than in his work. His question, "Whose young woman is this?" doesn't fully express what Boaz was feeling. Bible teacher J. Vernon McGee suggests it was more like a wolf whistle. The romance had begun.

6
APPEARANCES
You can't judge a book by its cover. Outwardly Ruth was a Moabite, a scorned minority. Yet the pages of her life were full of good works: she was submissive, polite, humble, hardworking, and balanced. Don't let labels keep you from finding beauty below the surface.

transformation

8

BLESSING
A blessing is the act of declaring or wishing God's favor upon others. Important persons blessed those with less power or influence (adapted, *Nelson's*). Jesus, the most important person who ever lived, taught us to bless friend or foe, "Bless those who curse you, and pray for those who spitefully use you" (Luke 6:28).

9

JUDGING
When you judge others unfairly you will be judged unfairly too. Jesus taught, "Stop judging others, and you will not be judged. For others will treat you as you treat them" (Matthew 7:1-2, NLT). Give blessing, and you'll be blessed; give criticism, and you'll be criticized.

8. Boaz influenced his employees through his kind greeting of blessing. How does your speech influence those around you?

   — I'm critical and sarcastic.   — I pray for others.

   ✓ season words with grace.   ✓ I exaggerate issues.

   — I gossip about others.   ✓ I sing songs of worship.

   ✓ praise the Lord.   ✓ I'm a complainer.

   — I shout with anger.   — I offer blessings.

   — I use profanity.   — I'm soft-spoken.

9. If Boaz had judged Ruth by her ethnic background or economic status, he would have missed discovering a diamond in the rough.

Journal about a time in your life when someone shortsightedly labeled you. (Example: In high school, kids called me a nerd because I wore glasses.)

. . . .

. . . .

. . . .

. . . .

Journal about a time when your lack of insight forced someone else to wear a label. (Example: I thought my new neighbor wasn't very bright because she was blonde.)

. . . .

. . . .

. . . .

. . . .

10. We've seen that you can't judge a book by its cover. The servant used three short sentences to describe Ruth's character instead of describing her appearance. If your life were a book, think about what might be written on the inside pages.

> Journal three sentences that describe who you are on the inside.

. . . .

. . . .

. . . .

. . . .

. . . .

10
CHARACTER
Character is the distinctive feature that defines an individual. The Greek word for *character* means "to scratch or engrave like an imprint." The hard times in life are meant to engrave God's imprint on our lives. Paul wrote, "Tribulation produces perseverance; and perseverance, character; and character, hope" (Romans 5:3-4).

A thirty-eight-year-old scrubwoman went to the movies and sighed, "If only I had her looks." She listened to a singer and moaned, "If only I had her voice." Then one day she stopped crying about what she didn't have and started concentrating on what she did have. She remembered that in high school she had had a reputation for being the funniest girl around. She turned her liabilities into assets and at the height of her career, Phyllis Diller made over one million dollars in one year. She wasn't good-looking and she had a scratchy voice, but she could make people laugh.

Ruth didn't have many assets either, but she was strong and unafraid of hard work. When she went to work, God went into action on her behalf. Many people sit idly by, waiting for providence to happen. However, providence is a two-sided equation: *you* plus God. Pastor Chuck Smith says, "It's easier to guide a rolling stone than it is to get a stationary one moving." You shouldn't wait for opportunity to knock. Sometimes you must knock on a few doors to see what opportunities Providence opens for you. King Solomon described the unique blend between you and God's providence like this, "Trust in the Lord with all your heart; do not depend on your own understanding. Seek his will in all you *do*, and he will direct your paths" (Proverbs 3:5-6, NLT, emphasis added). It's simple; when you *do*, God directs.

contemplation
God wishes each of us to work as hard as we can, holding nothing back but giving ourselves to the utmost, and when we can do no more, that is the moment when the hand of divine providence is stretched out to us and takes over.
Don Orione

DAY 3 FINDING FAVOR

preparation

Lord, as I grow in years let me also gain favor with You and others. Help me to recognize that the good things in my life are from Your hand. Thank You for the favorable things that come my way. Amen.

FAVOR
Meanwhile, as young Samuel grew taller, he also continued to gain favor with the Lord and with the people.
1 Samuel 2:26, NLT

For a Christian there's no such thing as luck. Believing that luck has dealt you a good *or* bad hand denies God's hand of providence in your life. Luck is impersonal; a matter of chance bringing about fortune or adversity. I do not trust my life into the hands of fate. Instead, I trust a loving God to orchestrate circumstances that are favorable or unfavorable, according to His will for me. When unfavorable situations arise, I ponder, *Am I in the will of God? Have I been obedient to His Word?* or *Is He trying to redirect my path?* When favorable circumstances come my way, I count them as God's blessings— His affirmation that I'm on the right track. Yet I know that whether good or bad things happen, God will work all things together for my good.

Paul described the process of receiving good for good or bad for bad, not as karma, but as reaping what you have sown. "Do not be deceived, . . . for whatever a man sows, that he will also reap. For he who sows to his flesh will of the flesh reap corruption, but he who sows to the Spirit will of the Spirit reap everlasting life" (Galatians 6:7-8). God will reward you according to your deeds.

Ruth had been sowing seeds of goodness toward Naomi, diligence in labor, and humility toward others. Now she is about to reap the bounty of blessing from the Lord. She will find favor from the God of Israel instead of confusion from the twisted hand of fate.

exploration

Boaz was a good master who blessed his workers and noticed the foreigner. Now we discover that Boaz's actions also provide for us a picture of Christ as our protector.

Review Ruth 2; then focus on verses 8-13.

> *Then Boaz said to Ruth, "You will listen, my daughter, will you not? Do not go to glean in another field, nor go*

from here, but stay close by my young women. Let your eyes be on the field which they reap, and go after them. Have I not commanded the young men not to touch you? And when you are thirsty, go to the vessels and drink from what the young men have drawn." Ruth 2:8-9

1. Where did Boaz instruct Ruth not to glean? to glean?

. . . .

2. How did Boaz seek to protect and provide for Ruth?

. . . .

So she fell on her face, bowed down to the ground, and said to him, "Why have I found favor in your eyes, that you should take notice of me, since I am a foreigner?" Ruth 2:10

3. How did Ruth respond, physically and verbally, to Boaz?

. . . .

And Boaz answered and said to her, "It has been fully reported to me, all that you have done for your mother-in-law since the death of your husband, and how you have left your father and your mother and the land of your birth, and have come to a people whom you did not know before. The Lord repay your work, and a full reward be given you by the Lord God of Israel, under whose wings you have come for refuge." Ruth 2:11-12

4. Explain why Ruth's reputation impressed Boaz.. . . . .

. . . .

5. What did Boaz pray for Ruth? . . . .

. . . .

Then she said, "Let me find favor in your sight, my lord; for you have comforted me, and have spoken kindly to your maidservant, though I am not like one of your maidservants." Ruth 2:13

1
GLEANING JOY
Gleaners gathered grain left behind by reapers. Spiritually, Ruth and Naomi had sown seeds of godly repentance and now would glean a season of joy from the hand of God. "He who continually goes forth weeping, bearing seed for sowing, shall doubtless come again with rejoicing, bringing his sheaves with him" (Psalm 126:6).

3
HUMILITY
Humility means "to be bowed down" or "lowliness of mind." It is not self-deprecation but instead is a lowliness of self-estimation and freedom from vanity. It can also be translated "gentleness" or "meekness." Humility conveys an attitude of willingness and obedience, a lack of resistance to God's will (adapted, *Unger's*).

RESOURCES
God has told us where
to find and where *not* to
find our resources. "Set
your mind on things
above, not on things on
the earth" (Colossians
3:2). The fields of this
world yield wax fruit—
it looks good but won't
nourish. In God's fields
one "gathers fruit for
eternal life" (John 4:36).

POSTURE
How's your posture?
As children we're taught
good posture—stand
up straight and tall. As
children of the King
we're taught good
posture too—bowed
head and bent knees.
"Come, let us worship
and bow down. Let us
kneel before the Lord
our maker, for he is our
God" (Psalm 95:6-7,
NLT).

6. How did Ruth describe herself? Boaz? . . . .

. . . .

7. What two things had Boaz done for Ruth?. . . . .

. . . .

transformation

8. Just as Boaz provided for Ruth's physical need out of his wealth,
   so God provides for our physical and spiritual needs out of His
   great resources. Fill in the chart to discover ways that God
   protects and provides for those who spiritually glean in His fields.

SCRIPTURE	WHAT GOD PROVIDES
Ps. 107:9	
Matt. 6:3-4	
John 4:14.	
John 15:16.	
2 Thess. 3:3	

9. Today we learned that Ruth humbly bowed down before Boaz
   and offered gratitude for his kindness toward her.

   Using the word *B-O-W-E-D* as an acrostic, journal
   a prayer of gratitude to God. Then bow before Him
   and offer your adoration.

   B (Example: Before I met You, I was a foreigner and You took
   me in.)

   . . . .

   O (Example: Out of the depths You have delivered my soul
   from death.)

   . . . .

W . . . .

. . . .

E . . . .

. . . .

D . . . .

. . . .

10. Boaz declared that Ruth had taken refuge under God's wing, which was a symbol of God's provision and protection. What about you? Have you found a place to nestle in the warmth and care of Jehovah?

Journal about a time you found refuge in His care.

. . . .

. . . .

. . . .

REFUGE
A *refuge* is "a place that provides shelter or protection; something to which one has recourse in difficulty" *(Webster's)*. Ruth found a safe haven when she ran to God. "The name of the Lord is a strong fortress; the godly run to him and are safe" (Proverbs 18:10, NLT).

A haughty lawyer once asked an old farmer, "Why don't you hold up your head in the world like I do? I don't let anyone push me around; I won't bow before God or man."

"See that field of grain yonder?" replied the farmer. "Only the heads that are empty stand up. Those that are well filled always bow low." The strange paradox revealed by this story is that what appears to be strong is really weak.

A paradox is a seemingly contradictory or absurd statement that is, in fact, true. Here are just a few of the paradoxical truths found in the Bible: those who are poor in spirit are truly rich; those who know they are weak are really the strongest; those who die to themselves will live forever; those who are humble will be exalted.

Ruth's life is a perfect example of God's paradoxical truths in action. Because she was filled with humility and willingly bowed down, God "lifted her up" in Boaz's sight. God has honored her throughout eternity by recording her story in the most precious of all books, the Bible. Truly Ruth understood this spiritual truth: "When you bow down before the Lord . . . , he will lift you up and give you honor" (James 4:10, NLT).

contemplation
Be humble or you'll stumble.
D. L. Moody

DAY 4 HANDFULS ON PURPOSE

preparation

Thank You, Lord, for inviting me to Your banquet table and for treating me as an honored guest. You have filled me with goodness and love. Amen.

GUEST OF HONOR
He brings me to the banquet hall, so everyone can see how much he loves me. Song of Songs 2:4, NLT

At the invitation of Princess Sharifa of Jordan, my son, Nathan, and I had the privilege of joining a team of relief volunteers to deliver gift boxes to poor children. We went to the village of Finan, where a tribe of sheepherders lived. I wouldn't have been surprised to meet Ruth and Boaz among these nomadic bedouin people, whose lives haven't changed much since Old Testament times. Men in headdresses drank Turkish coffee and discussed important village matters. Women in dark robes gleaned in the fields and tended the sheep. Each sheepskin tent was equipped with a fire pit, and the dirt floors were covered with worn handwoven rugs.

After watching the children open their gifts, we, as the honored guests, were treated to a special feast of *mansf*—an entire roasted goat, head included, served on a bed of rice with hot yogurt and broth. In true Middle Eastern style we lay on the floor around the platter, eating with our hands. The sheik was impressed with Nathan, who happily ate handfuls of goat meat. As a sign of honor, the sheik then pulled out the goat's tongue and gave it to me. In sheer panic I tossed the tongue in front of Aileen Coleman, a long-term missionary there, pleading for her to eat it before the sheik noticed!

Ruth, too, was the recipient of Middle Eastern hospitality, but she handled herself better than I did. When she was singled out and honored with extra food at a meal, she graciously accepted and left satisfied.

exploration

Boaz proved himself to be a man with godly qualities. We now examine his life in light of his treatment of Ruth.

Review Ruth 2; then focus on verses 14-17.

Now Boaz said to her at mealtime, "Come here, and eat of the bread, and dip your piece of bread in the vinegar." So she sat beside the reapers, and he passed parched grain to her; and she ate and was satisfied, and kept some back. Ruth 2:14

 1. How did Boaz show extra favor to Ruth? . . . .

. . . .

2. What impact did the meal have on Ruth? . . . .

. . . .

3. Why do you think she kept some back? . . . .

. . . .

And when she rose up to glean, Boaz commanded his young men, saying, "Let her glean even among the sheaves, and do not reproach her. Also let grain from the bundles fall purposely for her; leave it that she may glean, and do not rebuke her." Ruth 2:15-16

4. Describe what Boaz commanded his young men to do.

. . . .

. . . .

5. What did he command them not to do? . . . .

. . . .

So she gleaned in the field until evening, and beat out what she had gleaned, and it was about an ephah of barley. Ruth 2:17

6. How did Ruth prove herself to be a hard worker? . . . .

. . . .

7. How was her hard work rewarded? . . . .

. . . .

explanation

1

SPECIAL FAVORS
Webster's describes *favor* as bestowing "a token of love." It implies preference and suggests an active interest. Boaz showed an active interest in Ruth by offering her special favors that the rest of the migrant workers did not receive. His preferential treatment revealed his budding affection for her.

4

LOVE LANGUAGE
Love can be expressed in a variety of ways. *The Five Love Languages* by Gary Chapman describes five ways to communicate love: (1) quality time, (2) acts of service, (3) gift giving, (4) verbal affirmation, or (5) physical touch. If Ruth was listening, Boaz was speaking one of the many languages of love.

7

EPHAH
An ephah was equivalent to one-tenth of a homer. A homer was about 220 liters—the equivalent of the normal load a donkey could carry—and was worth fifty shekels of silver. The ephah Ruth gleaned in one day was enough to feed two women for almost a week.

transformation

Love is more than a feeling; it is a verb. A verb is an action word that expresses an act, occurrence, or state of being. People may not know of your love until you express it outwardly through word and deed. Songwriter Charlie Peacock wrote, "Love to be understood must be lived."

9

SACRIFICIAL LOVE
All the languages of love have something in common: they require sacrifice. Sacrificing your time, words, gifts, service, or touch and unselfishly offering them to another is what true love is all about. "The greatest love is shown when people lay down their lives for their friends" (John 15:13, NLT).

8. Boaz expressed his love to Ruth through one of the five love languages: gift giving. Read the following definitions, and think about which language speaks to you the most. On a scale of 1 (most) to 5 (least) rank the languages in the order that best reaches your heart.

—Quality Time: giving someone else the gift of yourself and time; undivided attention; undistracted encounters; being completely focused on another person in the moment.

—Verbal Affirmation: using words of praise and love to build another person's sense of self-worth; words of acknowledgment or appreciation.

—Gift Giving: big or small tokens of appreciation; a memento demonstrating love for another person.

—Acts of Service: using your time, energy or resources to serve someone else; doing chores; running errands; putting another's need above your own.

—Physical Touch: touching another person, whether for grooming, healing, affection, or comfort.

Journal about a time when someone spoke to you with one of these love languages, describing how it affected you.

. . . .

. . . .

. . . .

. . . .

9. Who is the most significant person in your life (husband, parent, child, sibling, friend)? To what love language does that person best respond?

Person: . . . .

Love Language: . . . .

Journal about a way you can reach out and touch someone you love in his or her own language of love.

. . . .

. . . .

. . . .

10. God speaks the language of love in gift giving too: "For God so loved the world that he gave his only Son" (John 3:16, NLT).

What handfuls of goodness has God left in your path? How have they drawn you closer to Him? Journal your thoughts.

. . . .

. . . .

. . . .

10
REWARD
Ruth learned that God rewards the diligent. He provides for those who glean in His fields, but we must do the work to reap the harvest. "For he who comes to God must believe that He is, and that He is a rewarder of those who diligently seek Him" (Hebrews 11:6).

If my mother told me once, she told me a thousand times, "I'm loving you, Lenya." I know she meant it, but her words went in one ear and out the other. When I was a freshman in high school she did something that *showed* me how much she loved me. I broke both bones in my left calf while downhill skiing in Michigan. The doctors attempted to stabilize the break with a cast from my hip to my toes. Sadly the oblique fracture slipped, and I was put in traction for nearly six weeks. Our town didn't have an orthopedic surgeon, so I was hospitalized over thirty miles from home. My angel mother drove every day, sometimes two or three times a day, to visit me. She had a husband, a household, and two other children to care for, but she sacrificed her private time of golfing or playing bridge to be with me. I have discovered that my mother's language of love is spoken through her acts of service. She is a caregiver; from preparing a meal to doing the laundry she is expressing her love.

Ruth was a caregiver too. She expressed her love to Naomi by working in the grainfields to put bread on their table. When Ruth was given a special meal of roasted grain, instead of greedily consuming it all, she kept some back for her mother-in-law. Ruth's actions spoke volumes.

contemplation
Action may not always bring happiness; but there is no happiness without action.
Benjamin Disraeli

DAY 5 TAKING NOTICE

preparation

Lord, I'm amazed that You take notice of me. Help me to live my life in such a way that when You notice what I'm doing, You will be pleased. Amen.

NOTICED
Your prayers have been heard, and your gifts to the poor have been noticed by God! Acts 10:31, NLT

A husband and wife were celebrating their golden wedding anniversary. After attending a big party given in their honor, they returned home and decided to have a snack of tea with bread and butter. The husband opened up a new loaf of bread and handed the heel to his wife. She unexpectedly exploded saying, "For fifty years you have been dumping the heel of the bread on me. I won't take your lack of concern for me and what I like!" The husband was wounded by her cutting words and said quietly, "But it's my favorite piece."

By sacrificing his own needs and wants, this man had been showing his wife how much he loved her. But for most of their marriage she had read his message all wrong. He had faithfully left her a trail of bread crumbs that led to his heart, but she had not even noticed. Similarly, Boaz left a trail of love for Ruth. He revealed his deep affection for her through verbal affirmation and meeting her needs with his gifts. As Naomi realized what was happening, she didn't want Ruth to miss the message. She pointed to the trail left by Boaz and made sure that Ruth took notice.

exploration

Today we examine Naomi and her response to the goodness of Boaz. We find Naomi's hope revived after a period of bitterness.

Review Ruth 2; then focus on verses 18-23.

> *Then [Ruth] took it up and went into the city, and her mother-in-law saw what she had gleaned. So she brought out and gave to her what she had kept back after she had been satisfied.* Ruth 2:18

1. How did Ruth provide for her widowed mother-in-law?

. . . .

> *And her mother-in-law said to her, "Where have you gleaned today? And where did you work? Blessed be the one who took notice of you." So she told her mother-in-law with whom she had worked, and said, "The man's name with whom I worked today is Boaz."* Ruth 2:19

2. How did Naomi react when she saw all the grain Ruth had brought?

. . . .

> *Then Naomi said to her daughter-in-law, "Blessed be he of the Lord, who has not forsaken His kindness to the living and the dead!" And Naomi said to her, "This man is a relation of ours, one of our close relatives."* Ruth 2:20

3. What was Naomi's response upon learning who had taken notice of Ruth?

. . . .

4. What did she reveal about Boaz? . . . .

. . . .

> *Ruth the Moabitess said, "He also said to me, 'You shall stay close by my young men until they have finished all my harvest.'" And Naomi said to Ruth her daughter-in-law, "It is good, my daughter, that you go out with his young women, and that people do not meet you in any other field."* Ruth 2:21-22

5. Explain how Boaz would continue to provide for them.

. . . .

6. Where did Naomi instruct Ruth to go? Not to go? . . . .

. . . .

1

SHARING
Sharing is caring. Love that does not bear with, care for, and share is not love at all. The early church shared and cared: "All the believers were of one heart and mind, and they felt that what they owned was not their own; they shared everything they had" (Acts 4:32, NLT).

4

CLOSE RELATIVE
The close relative (kinsman-redeemer) could rescue a widow through marriage. "If brothers dwell together, and one of them dies and has no son, the widow of the dead man shall not be married to a stranger outside the family; her husband's brother shall . . . take her as his wife" (Deuteronomy 25:5).

6

GOOD ADVICE
Was Boaz's recommendation for Ruth to stay in his fields good advice? Ruth wisely sought a second opinion from Naomi, who agreed, "It is good." Not sure you've received good advice? Ask for a second opinion. "Plans go wrong for lack of advice; many counselors bring success" (Proverbs 15:22, NLT).

8

GIVING
You can't outgive God. "Give, and it will be given to you: good measure, pressed down, shaken together, and running over will be put into your bosom. For with the same measure that you use, it will be measured back to you" (Luke 6:38). God turns givers into getters.

9

WISE COUNSEL
Heeding unbiblical advice can take you places you don't want to go. You may end up standing where you don't belong. "Oh, the joys of those who do not follow the advice of the wicked, or stand around with sinners. . . . But they delight in doing everything the Lord wants" (Psalm 1:1-2, NLT).

So she stayed close by the young women of Boaz, to glean until the end of barley harvest and wheat harvest; and she dwelt with her mother-in-law.
Ruth 2:23

7. How did Ruth follow these instructions? For how long?

. . . .

. . . .

transformation

8. Today we discovered that sharing what we have is a way of caring. Write a list of your personal and material assets. (Example: money, time, transportation, house, etc.)

. . . .

. . . .

. . . .

Journal about a way you can show your care for someone this week by sharing out of your resources.

. . . .

. . . .

. . . .

. . . .

9. When Ruth received advice, she sought a second opinion. Check the boxes that indicate what you usually do with advice you are given.

__ Pray about it.   __ Resist.
__ Do the opposite.   __ Buckle to peer presure.
__ Read a self-help book.   __ Act impulsively.
__ Search the Scriptures.   __ Seek godly advice.
__ Wait and see.

Journal about a time when you followed good advice and saw good results. How did you know it was good advice?

. . . .

. . . .

. . . .

. . . .

10. Naomi's hope was renewed because of her close relative and kinsman-redeemer. According to Matthew 12:48-50, as believers, whose close relative are we?

. . . .

11. According to Ephesians 1:7, how has Jesus redeemed His family?

. . . .

10
RELATIVE
Relatives are generally connected by blood or marriage. Believers become blood relatives because Jesus "has freed us from our sins by shedding his blood for us" (Revelation 1:5, NLT). We're related through marriage as His bride. "I promised you as a pure bride to one husband, Christ" (2 Corinthians 11:2, NLT).

The men in my life have a few cherished articles of clothing. I can't wash them fast enough for them to wear again. My son's favorite shirts come from Abercrombie & Fitch. He had only two because they don't come cheap. So when he went to his buddy's sleepover, he wore one and packed the other to wear the next day. When I picked up Nathan, I saw his friend wearing one of my son's Abercrombie shirts. I was suspicious, and when we got in the car asked, "What is he doing with your expensive shirt?"

Nathan replied, "When I was getting dressed, he said, 'Those are the coolest shirts I've ever seen.' I knew I had two, so I gave him one. It seemed like the right thing to do."

I told Nathan I was so pleased with his kind heart and reminded him what John the Baptist said, "He who has two tunics, let him give to him who has none" (Luke 3:11). I assured him that God would notice and bless him for it. Nathan was discovering that givers are getters. When he gave, he not only got the gratitude of a friend but also honored God. (And later his proud grandpa took him out to get another shirt!)

When Ruth was willing to share with Naomi, she received not only the gratitude of her mother-in-law but also the love and admiration of Boaz. God honors giving hearts.

contemplation
The secret of being loved is in being lovely; and the secret of being lovely is in being unselfish.
J. G. Holland

Matchmaker, Matchmaker

From the time Skip picked me up for our first date, my father was confident that Skip was the man I would marry. "There's something special about Skip," he said, "God's going to use him." The problem was that after we had dated for a year, ministry pulled us in different directions: Skip to Israel to live on a kibbutz, me to Hawaii to join Youth With A Mission. Providentially, Skip and I bumped into one another a year later and had dinner. We both regretted moving past our relationship, but we left our thoughts unspoken.

Dad knew I was at the point of making some crucial life decisions, and like Naomi, he decided to play matchmaker. Without my knowledge he called Skip and boldly said, "Lenya has some difficult decisions to make. If she could have her dream come true, you would be her knight in shining armor. Let her know if you're interested or not, so she can move on." Skip sent me twelve beautiful roses to show his intentions. God had a plan for Skip and me, and He used my dad to bring us together.

Naomi had seen Boaz's favorable response to Ruth. She remembered the law that a kinsman should marry the widow of a near relative to preserve the family name and reclaim the family property. Without Ruth's knowledge, Naomi played matchmaker to bring Ruth and Boaz together. Behind the scenes, however, we know that God inspired her plans and prepared two hearts for romance.

DAY 1
Matchmaker

DAY 2
Risk Taker

DAY 3
Promise Maker

DAY 4
Gift Giver

DAY 5
Promise Keeper

preparation

God, I know that Your plans for my future are good. Thank You for using the people in my life to accomplish Your plans for me. Use me in the lives of my loved ones too. Amen.

FUTURE

"For I know the plans I have for you," says the Lord. "They are plans for good and not for disaster, to give you a future and a hope."
Jeremiah 29:11, NLT

explanation

1

SECURITY

In Hebrew, the word *security* means "to settle down; establish a permanent dwelling." Naomi knew that true security did not come from a barn filled with grain but from a home filled with love. "My people will dwell in a peaceful habitation, in secure dwellings, and in quiet resting places" (Isaiah 32:18).

exploration

Ruth had become a beloved daughter to Naomi. We see this week how God used Naomi to bring Ruth and Boaz together.

Read Ruth 3; then focus on verses 1-4.

> *Then Naomi her mother-in-law said to her, "My daughter, shall I not seek security for you, that it may be well with you? Now Boaz, whose young women you were with, is he not our relative? In fact, he is winnowing barley tonight at the threshing floor."*
> Ruth 3:1-2

1. What did Naomi desire for her daughter-in-law?

. . . .

. . . .

2. What did Naomi remind Ruth of? . . . .

. . . .

3. Where could Boaz be found? . . . .

. . . .

> *"Therefore wash yourself and anoint yourself, put on your best garment and go down to the threshing floor; but do not make yourself known to the man until he has finished eating and drinking."* Ruth 3:3

4. Name three things Naomi instructed Ruth to do before she presented herself to Boaz.

. . . .

. . . .

. . . .

5. What one thing did Naomi instruct Ruth not to do?

. . . .

6. Why do you think Naomi gave this instruction? . . . .

. . . .

> *"Then it shall be, when he lies down, that you shall notice the place where he lies; and you shall go in, uncover his feet, and lie down; and he will tell you what you should do."* Ruth 3:4

7. Once Ruth had noticed where Boaz slept, what three things was she to do?

. . . .

. . . .

. . . .

8. What was Ruth told to wait for? . . . .

. . . .

. . . .

transformation

9. The steps Naomi, the matchmaker, told Ruth to take in preparation for her relationship with Boaz are similar to the steps that God, our heavenly matchmaker, requires us to take in preparation for our relationship with Jesus. Fill in the following chart to discover these steps.

4
MOURNING ENDS
Widows wore sackcloth and threw ashes on their heads. Naomi told Ruth to take off her widow's garb and put on her best garment, what commentators believe was a wedding dress. God promises to give mourners "beauty for ashes, the oil of joy for mourning, the garment of praise for the spirit of heaviness" (Isaiah 61:3).

7
AT HIS FEET
Biblically, falling at someone's feet showed respect; kissing another's feet showed reverence; licking dust from the feet signified subjection; uncovering the feet displayed adoration (*Unger's*).

9
MATCHMAKER
God is our divine matchmaker. He sent His only begotten Son to become our heavenly Bridegroom (see Matthew 9:14-15). Then God chose a bride, His church, and drew us unto His Son. "People can't come to me unless the Father who sent me draws them to me" (John 6:44, NLT).

SCRIPTURE   STEPS TO CHRIST

CLEANSING
Uncleanness starts inwardly with the motives of the heart and is manifested outwardly by our actions. Jesus taught, "You are defiled by what you say and do!" (Mark 7:15, NLT). Cleansing is achieved by obeying His Word. "You are already clean because of the word which I have spoken to you" (John 15:3).

Isa. 61:10. . . . .

2 Cor. 7:1 . . . .

Eph. 5:25-27 . . . .

1 John 2:20 . . . .

2 Cor. 1:21-22. . . . .

Have you taken these steps? If you have, journal your thoughts about how you have experienced them. If you have not, journal about what might be keeping you from taking these steps to a more intimate relationship with Christ.

. . . .

. . . .

. . . .

10. To prepare for her relationship with Boaz, Ruth cleansed herself physically. This world can defile a believer spiritually, but we are cleansed from sin through the blood of Christ. Check off any of the following items that have had a corrupting influence on you and need to be cleansed from your life.

___ TV programs   ___ Movies
___ Books   ___ Thoughts
___ Magazines   ___ Medicines
___ CDs and cassettes   ___ Food
___ Clothes   ___ Other_____

Journal a prayer of confession, asking God to cleanse you from the sin of this world.

. . . .

. . . .

. . . .

11. After cleansing, Ruth anointed herself with sweet-smelling oil to make herself appealing. What kind of fragrance do you anoint yourself with and why? Luke 7:38 tells us that a woman once anointed Jesus' feet to honor him: "She knelt behind [Jesus] at his feet, weeping. Her tears fell on his feet, and she wiped them off with her hair. Then she kept kissing his feet and putting perfume on them" (NLT).

> Anoint this page with your favorite scent. Then journal a prayer of adoration to Jesus, your Lord of the harvest.

. . . .

. . . .

. . . .

. . . .

ANOINTING
Middle Eastern people anointed themselves with oil for protection and healing. Fragrant oils were used as perfume to appeal to others. "Who is this coming out of the wilderness like pillars of smoke, perfumed with myrrh and frankincense, with all the merchant's fragrant powders?" (Song of Solomon 3:6).

"Do you have a minute? I want to tell you something I've never told anyone else." Eleanor, a vivacious senior citizen, had my undivided attention. She began her story nervously, "My husband loves me, but he doesn't always like me to come to church. So I've made my bedroom a sanctuary to the Lord. Whenever I can't go to worship services, I get on my knees at the foot of my bed and worship the Lord at home." Such devotion in the midst of opposition made me admire Eleanor. She went on, "Sometimes when I'm praying, the room becomes filled with the most wonderful scent. It's so sweet and distinctive, like nothing I've ever smelled before. Do you think I'm crazy?"

I told her that I couldn't be sure what the origin of the scent was, but the Bible teaches that the name of Jesus is as fragrant ointment poured forth. The psalmist said of the Messiah, "God . . . has anointed you, pouring out the oil of joy on you more than on anyone else. Your robes are perfumed with myrrh, aloes, and cassia" (Psalm 45:7-8, NLT). I think the aroma my friend enjoyed during her devotions was the fragrance of Jesus. She wasn't crazy. She was incredibly blessed!

Eleanor had a choice: she could whine when she didn't get her way, or she could worship God. When things didn't go Ruth and Naomi's way, they didn't wallow in self-pity either. They trusted God and were anointed with the oil of joy.

contemplation
The crushed rose gives off the sweetest fragrance.
Tony Corzine

49

DAY 2 RISK TAKER

preparation

God, I want to be a risk taker for Your kingdom. Please give me the faith to take chances in my life. I want to please You with all I say and do. I trust You to reward me as You see fit. Amen.

REWARDS

So, you see, it is impossible to please God without faith. Anyone who wants to come to him must believe that there is a God and that he rewards those who sincerely seek him.
Hebrews 11:6, NLT

A survey was taken of people over the age of ninety-five, asking, "If you could live your life over again, what would you do differently?" The top three answers were: (1) Reflect more; (2) Risk more; (3) Do more things that had a lasting reward. God rewards risk takers. Noah risked his reputation to build an ark and was rescued by God. Moses risked losing the riches of Egypt and received intimacy with God. The apostle Paul risked imprisonment to preach the gospel, and God used him to revolutionize the church.

What was true for the people of the Bible is still true for believers in the twenty-first century. My times of greatest blessing have always been preceded by risk taking. I risked leaving college and a career in Michigan to pursue my faith in Christ in California. There I heard the call of God to full-time ministry and risked leaving my secure job and Christian community to join Youth With A Mission. There I obtained a passion for the lost that compels me to this day. My greatest leap of faith was to leave that established ministry to marry Skip and together build a new church in New Mexico. God has greatly rewarded our risks. Our church, Calvary of Albuquerque, currently ministers to close to twelve thousand people weekly.

What about you? Do you want to end your life with regrets or rewards? Ruth risked her past to reach for a future in the Promised Land. Perhaps it's time for *you* to take some risks.

exploration

Yesterday we learned about Naomi's plan to obtain a husband for Ruth. Today we see that Ruth was willing to take the risk of following Naomi's plans and trusted God to work things out.

Review Ruth 3; then focus on verses 5-9.

And she said to her, "All that you say to me I will do."
So she went down to the threshing floor and did according
to all that her mother-in-law instructed her. Ruth 3:5-6

1. How do you know that Ruth was willing to act in complete obedience to Naomi's instructions?

. . . .

2. By going to the threshing floor, what risks do you think Ruth faced?

   a. Physical risks _____

   b. Emotional risks _____

   c. Reputation risks _____

And after Boaz had eaten and drunk, and his heart was
cheerful, he went to lie down at the end of the heap of
grain; and she came softly, uncovered his feet, and lay
down. Ruth 3:7

3. What effect did eating and drinking have on Boaz?

. . . .

4. How did Ruth approach Boaz, and what did she do?

. . . .

Now it happened at midnight that the man was startled,
and turned himself; and there, a woman was lying at
his feet. And he said, "Who are you?" So she answered,
"I am Ruth, your maidservant. Take your maidservant
under your wing, for you are a close relative." Ruth 3:8-9

5. What happened to Boaz at midnight? . . . .

. . . .

6. How did Ruth describe herself? . . . .

. . . .

explanation

1

OBEDIENCE
True obedience is immediate, complete, and cheerful. Ruth demonstrated all three attributes by acting on what Naomi asked her to do as soon as she was asked, with a good attitude and by thoroughly completing every detail. Jesus said, "If you love me, obey my commandments" (John 14:15, NLT).

4

QUIET BEAUTY
True beauty is more than skin deep. For Boaz, Ruth's outward appearance caught his eye, but her quiet spirit captured his heart. "The unfading beauty of a gentle and quiet spirit . . . is so precious to God" (1 Peter 3:4, NLT).

UNDER YOUR WING
Wing here refers to the skirt of a garment or corner of a bedspread. Ruth's request could be translated: "Spread your covering around me." By placing herself under Boaz's wing, Ruth was asking him to marry her. "So I wrapped my cloak around you . . . and declared my marriage vows" (Ezekiel 16:8, NLT).

OBEDIENCE IS BEST
What do you give a God who has everything? He doesn't want your dollars or your offerings as much as your devotion and obedience. "What is more pleasing to the Lord: your burnt offerings and sacrifices or your obedience to his voice? Obedience is far better than sacrifice" (1 Samuel 15:22, NLT).

APPEARANCES
People look at the body beautiful; God looks into the heart. "The Lord does not see as man sees; for man looks at the outward appearance, but the Lord looks at the heart" (1 Samuel 16:7). In God's eyes you'll never have a bad hair day—only a bad heart day.

7. Explain what Ruth asked of Boaz and why. . . . .

. . . .

transformation

8. Ruth's obedience to Naomi was immediate, complete, and cheerful. Rank your general obedience response to God on the following scale:

Immediately:
never   1   2   3   4   5   6   7   8   9   10   always

Completely:
never   1   2   3   4   5   6   7   8   9   10   always

Cheerfully:
never   1   2   3   4   5   6   7   8   9   10   always

9. Ruth was beautiful inside and out. Place the following items in the appropriate column: makeup, love, hairstyle, accessories, humility, kindness, jewelry, faith, patience, clothing, quiet spirit, peace, pride, self-control.

Inward Adornment   **Outward Adornment**

Choose one fruit of the Spirit with which you would like to be adorned inwardly: "love, joy, peace, patience, kindness, goodness, faithfulness, gentleness, and self-control" (Galatians 5:22-23, NLT). Journal a prayer to God asking Him to give you a heart makeover.

. . . .

. . . .

. . . .

10. Ruth was a risk taker; therefore she could live her life with no regrets. She would not have to look back at her life and say, "I wish I would have . . . " Take some time to think about how you approach taking risks in your life.

Prayerfully journal through the following exercise by filling in the blanks.

I wish I would have . . . .

. . . .

I'll never regret . . . .

. . . .

I'm going to risk . . . .

. . . .

To laugh is to risk appearing the fool.
To weep is to risk appearing sentimental.
To expose feelings is to risk exposing our true self.
To love is to risk not being loved in return.
To live is to risk dying. To hope is to risk despair.
To try at all is to risk failure.
But risk we must, because the greatest hazard in life
   is to risk nothing.
The man, the woman, who risks nothing does nothing,
   has nothing, is nothing.

(Anonymous)

Ruth was a risk taker who took a step of faith by asking Boaz to take her under his wing of protection. Today we also must take the risk of faith to come under God's wing for safekeeping. We risk embarrassment from the world; we may risk the loss of our reputation or the loss of a job. Some people risk physical harm by coming to Christ. However, the benefits of belonging to Christ far outweigh the risks. Under God's protective wing was the best place for Ruth, and it is the best place for you and me.

TAKING RISKS
A *risk* is a "possibility of loss or injury; peril; a dangerous element or factor" *(Webster's)*. It means to expose to hazard or danger. Jesus was the greatest risk taker of all! He incurred the loss of heaven, was cruelly injured at the hands of humanity, and hazarded death to save our lives.

contemplation
Man is God's risk.
Philip Yancey

DAY 3 PROMISE MAKER

preparation

Lord, thank You that You are a promise maker and never a promise breaker. I have full confidence that You will fulfill everything promised in Your Word. Amen.

PROMISE MAKER
For all the promises of God in Him are Yes, and in Him Amen, to the glory of God through us. 2 Corinthians 1:20

On a romantic cruise from Mexico to Hawaii, lawyer John Peckham and his wife placed a note in a bottle and tossed it into the Pacific Ocean. Three years and nine thousand miles later, Vietnamese refugee Nguyen Van Hoa reached down from a tiny, crowded boat and plucked the bottle from the South China Sea. He found a name and address, a dollar for postage, and the promise of a reward. "It gave me hope," said Hoa, who had escaped from a prison camp in Vietnam. Safe in a refugee camp in Thailand, Hoa wrote the surprised Peckhams. For two years they corresponded. During that time Hoa married and had a son. Recently the Peckhams sponsored the emigration of Hoa and his family. They arrived for an emotional meeting with the Peckhams and a new life from an old bottle.

At Naomi's instruction, Ruth had plucked grain from the fields of Boaz. Then Naomi showed Ruth how to pluck a promise from the law that provided redemption through a near kinsman. Ruth and Naomi found hope in God's promise and anxiously waited to see if Boaz would become their promise maker too.

exploration

We have seen Naomi the matchmaker and Ruth the risk taker. Today we examine Boaz, the promise maker.

Review Ruth 3; then focus on verses 10-13.

> *Then he said, "Blessed are you of the Lord, my daughter! For you have shown more kindness at the end than at the beginning, in that you did not go after young men, whether poor or rich." Ruth 3:10*

1. How did Boaz describe Ruth? . . . .

. . . .

2. What two things did Boaz commend Ruth for? . . . .

. . . .

. . . .

> *"And now, my daughter, do not fear. I will do for you all that you request, for all the people of my town know that you are a virtuous woman."* Ruth 3:11

3. How did Boaz comfort Ruth? . . . .

. . . .

4. What did Boaz promise Ruth? . . . .

. . . .

. . . .

5. What was Ruth's reputation among the townspeople?

. . . .

> *"Now it is true that I am a close relative; however, there is a relative closer than I. Stay this night, and in the morning it shall be that if he will perform the duty of a close relative for you—good; let him do it. But if he does not want to perform the duty for you, then I will perform the duty for you, as the Lord lives! Lie down until morning. "* Ruth 3:12-13

6. Describe the complication that might have hindered Boaz from marrying Ruth.

. . . .

7. What action would Boaz take in the morning? . . . .

. . . .

2

KINDNESS
Ruth's kindness was not fleeting but constant. It began when she left home to assist her grieving mother-in-law. In the end her kindness increased when her decision of a marriage partner was based not on fancy or outward appearance but on family commitments and scriptural obedience.

4

SAY AND DO
The Bible teaches to say what you mean and mean what you say. You don't have to "cross your heart and hope to die" to make people believe you'll keep your word. Simply do what you say. "Let your 'Yes,' be 'Yes,' and your 'No,' 'No,' lest you fall into judgment" (James 5:12).

7

DO HIS DUTY
Duty implies obligation. In the Old Testament the word *duty* is literally translated "kinsman-redeemer," the obligation a man had to the wife of his dead brother's widow. It was Boaz's way of saying, "On my honor I will do my duty to God and my family."

transformation

8

VIRTUE

Virtue means "moral excellence or goodness." Virtue is considered a necessary ingredient in the exercise of faith. The Greek word for *virtue* is sometimes used to express the idea of power or strength (adapted, *Nelson's*). "Giving all diligence, add to your faith virtue" (2 Peter 1:5).

9

PROMISE

A promise is a solemn assertion, a pledge to do or refrain from doing something specified. Some promises are predictions, as the promise of the Messiah and the blessings of the gospel (adapted, *Unger's*). All true believers in Christ are called "heirs of promise" (Hebrews 6:17).

8. Ruth's reputation among the townspeople was that she was a virtuous woman. The only other biblical reference to a virtuous woman is found in Proverbs 31:10-31. Read this homage to a godly wife, then after each of the following categories write the activities she was engaged in.

Relational Duties: . . . .
. . . .

Household Duties:. . . . .
. . . .

Business Duties: . . . .
. . . .

Devotional Duties:. . . . .
. . . .

The passage concludes by saying this kind of woman "shall be praised." Journal about a woman you know who is virtuous. What qualities have you observed in her life? Contact her this week and offer her praise for a life well lived.

. . . .

. . . .

. . . .

9. Throughout this study we have seen that Boaz foreshadows Jesus, our "kinsman-redeemer." Today we saw that Boaz was a promise maker. Fill in the chart to discover some of the precious promises Jesus *will* keep.

SCRIPTURE	PROMISES OF JESUS
John 14:3.	
John 14:12-14	
John 14:16-18	

John 14:21. . . . .

John 14:23. . . . .

10. Boaz realized his duty to Ruth and Naomi and became a promise maker.

Journal about a time when someone made a promise to you. Did he or she keep the promise or break it? How did it make you feel?

. . . .

. . . .

. . . .

. . . .

10
PROMISE BREAKERS
God takes our promises seriously. Promise breakers in the Old Testament suffered serious consequences of God's wrath (2 Chronicles 34:21), even captivity (Jeremiah 16:11-13). If you're a promise breaker, God says, "You have gone away from My ordinances and have not kept them. Return to Me, and I will return to you" (Malachi 3:7).

Before founding the commonwealth of Pennsylvania, William Penn made friends with the Native Americans in that area. One day they offered to give him as much of their land as he could stake out on foot in a single day. Early the next morning he started out and walked until late at night. When he went to claim his gift, the Native Americans were completely surprised that he had taken them seriously. But they kept their promise and gave him a large area of land, which became part of the city of Philadelphia. William Penn simply believed the promise his friends made to him.

Ruth believed God's promise to care for helpless widows, so she walked the long road to the threshing floor to claim a promise from Boaz. Although he was completely surprised at her request, he vowed to fulfill his duty to her. If the Native Americans were true to their word, and Boaz was faithful to keep his promise, how much more will your heavenly Father do what He says? "If you sinful people know how to give good gifts to your children, how much more will your heavenly Father give good gifts to those who ask him" (Matthew 7:11, NLT).

contemplation
He who is slow in making a promise is most likely to be faithful in the performance of it.
Jean Jacques Rousseau

DAY 4 GIFT GIVER

preparation

Lord, every good thing in my life is a gift from You. Your gifts come with no strings attached because they spring from Your heart of love. Thank You for being a gift giver. Amen.

GIFT
Every good gift and every perfect gift is from above, and comes down from the Father of lights, with whom there is no variation or shadow of turning. James 1:17

"What NOT to Buy Your Wife" is a great article on gift giving written by Herb Frost. He says, "Although the only person a man usually shops for is his wife, the whole experience is a stressful one. Many a man has felt extreme frigid temperatures for a long period based on a poor present decision. As a veteran of these wars, I'm still not sure what to buy my wife, but I'll pass on what not to buy her.

1. Don't buy anything that plugs in. Anything that requires electricity is seen as utilitarian.

2. Don't buy clothing that involves sizes. The chances are one in seven thousand that you will get her size right, and your wife will be offended the other 6,999 times.

3. Don't buy jewelry. The jewelry your wife wants, you can't afford. And the jewelry you can afford, she doesn't want.

4. Don't buy anything that involves weight loss or self-improvement. She'll perceive a six-month membership to a diet center as a suggestion that she's overweight.

5. Do not fall into the traditional trap of buying her frilly underwear. Your idea of the kind your wife should wear and what she actually will wear are light-years apart."

Perhaps Boaz could have used some advice in choosing the perfect gift for his future wife. But as a man of his times, he presented an unusual gift to Ruth as a sign of his love and devotion—a bundle of grain.

exploration

Ruth and Boaz must have spent a long, sleepless night wondering how things would work out between them. It was their hearts' desire to marry one another—but what if the nearer kinsman chose to exercise his rights? Finally the long night ended. Ruth and Boaz moved forward to meet the future.

Review Ruth 3; then focus on verses 14-17.

> *So she lay at his feet until morning, and she arose before one could recognize another. Then he said, "Do not let it be known that the woman came to the threshing floor."* Ruth 3:14

 1. How long did Ruth lie at the feet of Boaz? . . . .

. . . .

2. When did she arise? . . . .

. . . .

 3. If nothing scandalous had happened between them, why do you think Boaz wanted to keep Ruth's presence on the threshing floor secret?

. . . .

> *Also he said, "Bring the shawl that is on you and hold it." And when she held it, he measured six ephahs of barley, and laid it on her. Then she went into the city.* Ruth 3:15

4. Why did Boaz ask for her shawl? . . . .

. . . .

5. Before she left, what did Boaz give Ruth? . . . .

. . . .

> *When she came to her mother-in-law, she said, "Is that you, my daughter?" Then she told her all that the man had done for her.* Ruth 3:16

6. What do you think Naomi's greeting to Ruth meant?

. . . .

---

explanation

1

NEW DAWN
God is the God of endless second chances. The dawning sun rises every morning, offering the earth a fresh start. Likewise, God's mercy faithfully dawns day after day, offering hope to weary hearts. "The Lord's mercies . . . are new every morning; great is Your faithfulness" (Lamentations 3:22-23).

3

BUSYBODIES
A busybody is a gossipy, meddlesome person. Boaz was protecting Ruth's reputation. Nothing had happened, but gossipers are not careful with facts. Gossip is a sin. "Let none of you suffer as a murderer, a thief, an evildoer, or as a busybody in other people's matters" (1 Peter 4:15).

5

SEED PROMISE
Instead of a diamond Boaz gave Ruth grain, signifying hope for a fruitful future. Nothing would hinder their faith or future. "Faith as small as a mustard seed . . . could say to this mountain, 'Move from here to there,' and it would move. Nothing would be impossible" (Matthew 17:20, NLT).

FIRM HOPE
"In the New Testament, *hope* is the expectation of good, . . . of eternal salvation. In the Old Testament, *hope* means safety or security, . . . a firm expectation" *(Unger's)*. "So be strong and take courage, all you who put your hope in the Lord!" (Psalm 31:24, NLT).

REFLECTING LIGHT
Jesus said, "I am the light of the world. If you follow me, . . . you will have the light that leads to life" (John 8:12, NLT). The moon reflects the glory of the sun. The Christian reflects the light of Christ. "You are the light of the world" (Matthew 5:14, NLT).

7. How did Ruth report the night's events to her mother-in-law?

. . . .

transformation

8. Ruth and Naomi had lived through many dark nights. But with the dawn of a new day and the promise from the Lord of the harvest came bright hope for these two widows.

> Journal about a season of darkness in your life. This could be a time when you felt hopeless, overwhelmed, defeated, or spiritually down. How did the "Sonshine" break through?

. . . .

. . . .

. . . .

. . . .

9. Name someone you know who is experiencing a dark season right now.

. . . .

> Rewrite the following verses into a prayer for that person's deliverance from darkness and hopelessness. "'Lord, help!' they cried in their trouble, and he saved them from their distress. He led them from the darkness and deepest gloom; he snapped their chains. Let them praise the Lord for his great love and for all his wonderful deeds to them" (Psalm 107:13-15, NLT).

. . . .

. . . .

. . . .

. . . .

10. Boaz gave Ruth a handful of grain as a token of hope and his promise to her. Take the time now to write and mail a letter of hope to your friend, reminding him or her of God's promises. What small gift could you give as a token of your love? (Example: Perhaps you could include a packet of seeds, with instructions on how to plant them in faith, water them in prayer, place them in the "Sonshine," and wait to see a harvest of hope spring forth.)

. . . .

. . . .

. . . .

. . . .

. . . .

. . . .

. . . .

10

LOVING LETTERS
Solomon knew that letters of encouragement could refresh those who are out of sight but not out of mind. "As cold water to a weary soul, so is good news from a far country" (Proverbs 25:25). Paul received good news from afar. "Timothy has come to us from you, and brought us good news of your . . . love" (1 Thessalonians 3:6).

In a low-rent district of New York City, a boy in hand-me-down clothes was playing with a broken mirror. Lifting it high in the air, he tilted it slowly back and forth to catch the light of the sun and reflect the beam on passersby. At last he reflected a ray of light into a window two stories above him. Just then a man grabbed him saying, "What are you doing? You're up to some sort of mischief, aren't you?" The startled boy looked up into the gruff face of his captor and said, "See that window up there? That's my little brother's room. He can't come out in the sunshine and play because he's handicapped. The only sunlight he ever sees is what I shine up to him with my mirror."

Appearances can be deceiving, from boys at play to a couple on a midnight rendezvous on a threshing floor. It's possible that others may misinterpret your gifts and acts of kindness. But that should never stop you from taking the risk of reaching out and offering hope to others. A mirror in a boy's hand offered the gift of light to the dark corner of a brother's room. A handful of grain from Boaz gave Ruth hope for a bright future. Gift givers light up the face and help lighten the load.

contemplation
The grand essentials of happiness are: something to do, something to love, and something to hope for.
Allan K. Chalmers

preparation

Father, I don't know what my future holds but I'm grateful that You hold my future. Help me to trust You even when I can't see Your hand at work in my life. Amen.

TRUST
Trust in the Lord with all your heart; do not depend on your own understanding. Seek his will in all you do, and he will direct your paths. Proverbs 3:5-6, NLT

Hunting enthusiast Scott Harrison tells in a *Guidepost* article about his best bird dog, Sam. Sam found birds with contagious enthusiasm. If his point said a bird was hiding in a clump of bushes, it was there. He was more than just a bird dog though. Often they would share lazy lunches together in an abandoned apple orchard and then snooze afterwards. Late one afternoon Sam and Scott became separated. Scott called and whistled. No sign of Sam. He had to get back to town for an important appointment, but how could he leave Sam? Then he remembered an old trick a dog trainer had passed on. Scott unbuttoned his jacket, removed his shirt and laid it on the ground under the branches of a small bush, and then left. When Scott returned the next morning, there was Sam, curled up with his nose under the sleeve of Scott's shirt. He looked up and wagged his tail as if to say, "I've been waiting for you all night. But I knew you'd come back."

Scott left Sam a promise—his shirt as a safe place to curl up. Sam could rest throughout the night because he knew his friend would not rest until he found him. Boaz gave Ruth and Naomi a promise they could rest in—six ephahs of barley. The grain gave them a message: Boaz would not rest until he kept his promise and returned with good news.

exploration

Ruth and Naomi took the necessary steps to ensure their future. They had called upon the kinsman-redeemer, and he promised them action. Now came the tough part—they had to wait!

Review Ruth 3; then focus on verses 17-18.

And she said, "These six ephahs of barley he gave me;

for he said to me, 'Do not go empty-handed to your mother-in-law.'" Ruth 3:17

1. Why did Boaz give Ruth the barley? . . . .

. . . .

2. Why were Boaz's words so meaningful? (See Ruth 1:21.)

. . . .

Then she said, "Sit still, my daughter, until you know how the matter will turn out; for the man will not rest until he has concluded the matter this day." Ruth 3:18

3. What gives you the impression that Ruth was restless?

. . . .

4. Put in your own words the advice Naomi gave to Ruth.

. . . .

5. When would Boaz rest? . . . .

. . . .

6. How do Naomi's words show confidence in Boaz's character?

. . . .

7. Ruth had to wait for her promise keeper to act. In our Christian walk we often have to wait on God. Complete the following chart. What do the verses reveal to you about how to wait on the Lord? What do they say about the blessings of waiting on Him?

SCRIPTURE	BLESSING FROM WAITING
Ps. 40:1 . . . .
Ps. 62:1 . . . .
Isa. 40:31 . . . .
Lam. 3:25-26 . . . .

2
EMPTY AND FILLED
Naomi had returned empty-handed from Moab. Boaz's gift signified that her empty days were over. Sometimes God allows our lives to be emptied so He can fill them with His grace. "And of His fullness we have all received, and grace for grace" (John 1:16).

5
REST
Ruth could now rest because Boaz would *not* rest until his work was finished. Jesus said, "Take my yoke upon you, . . . and you will find rest for your souls" (Matthew 11:29, NLT). *You* can find rest in the finished work of Christ.

7
WAITING
Waiting on the Lord is not passive, it is active. It doesn't mean giving up but holding on to God. In the Bible *waiting* means to remain in readiness, . . . the confident expectation . . . that the Lord will intervene (adapted, *Nelson's*).

SATISFIED?

The well of human resources cannot satisfy your soul. Only the well of living water can quench humanity's thirst. "My people have committed two evils: They have forsaken Me, the fountain of living waters, and hewn themselves . . . broken cisterns that can hold no water" (Jeremiah 2:13).

SEEKING GOD

You're not waiting *for* something, you're waiting *on Someone*—God. Sometimes we become so obsessed with what *we* want that we forget what *He* wants—prayer, praise, and the pursuit of righteousness. "But seek first the kingdom of God and His righteousness, and all these things shall be added to you" (Matthew 6:33).

transformation

8. As Boaz filled Ruth's shawl with grain, so God loves to fill empty hands and empty lives. Sometimes we try to fill our lives with things that do not satisfy. There are things we must let go of before God can fill us with His goodness. Draw a line connecting items in the first column we must release before we can receive those of God's provision in the second column.

Release Worry	Receive His Providence
bitterness	forgiveness
earthly treasure	peace
new wardrobe	humility
pride	robes of righteousness
my plans	treasure in heaven

9. God wants you to wait to receive all He has for you. We learned that waiting is not passive; it's active.

> Think about one hope or promise or answer to prayer you are waiting for right now. Then journal through the following exercise to discover some practical steps for waiting on the Lord.

Step One: Find a promise in the Bible that fits your situation.

. . . .

. . . .

Step Two: Write a prayer claiming this promise.

. . . .

. . . .

Step Three: Write praises to God thanking Him for His promise.

. . . .

. . . .

Step Four: Write a promise to pursue righteousness while you wait.

. . . .

10. In this busy world it's difficult to find the time to be still and wait on God. Curl up in the promise you found today in God's Word. Set a timer for five minutes and take time to "be still, and know that I am God" (Psalm 46:10).

   Journal about what God spoke to you in your quiet place.

. . . .

. . . .

. . . .

10
STILLNESS
The bustle of modern life can drain away strength and serenity. God's remedy: "Be still." Are you running on empty? "The Sovereign Lord, the Holy One of Israel, says, 'Only in returning to me and waiting for me will you be saved. In quietness and confidence is your strength'" (Isaiah 30:15, NLT).

Ruth learned valuable lessons in waiting. For most of us waiting is hard. The most difficult waiting I've experienced was in childbearing. After five years of marriage Skip and I finally conceived. We announced the news on Sunday, but by the next week I had miscarried. God provided a gift in my time of disappointment—two ladies who promised to pray weekly for God's blessing in my womb. Within three months I was pregnant again. Our son, Nathan, whose name means "a gift," was given to us.

Soon we began trying for another child. Again my friends arrived to pray and wait. After three years no pregnancy had occurred. God prompted Skip and me to go through the painful road of artificial insemination. After six months of treatment we conceived again. After we saw our baby's flickering heartbeat on an ultrasound, we told everyone a baby was on the way. A month later the tiny heart stopped, and I needed surgery.

Years have passed, and I continue to wait on the promise God gave me during my time of loss, "A kernel of wheat must be planted in the soil. Unless it dies it will be alone—a single seed. But its death will produce many new kernels—a plentiful harvest of new lives" (John 12:24, NLT). God comforts me with the knowledge that although I won't see fruit from my physical womb again, He will make sure that my spiritual womb is bountiful. I live today in the hope and joy of seeing new lives birthed into the kingdom of God.

contemplation
Second only to suffering, waiting may be the greatest teacher and trainer in godliness, maturity, and genuine spirituality most of us ever encounter.
Richard Hendrix

Happily Ever After

Are you a hopeless romantic? Do you love stories that end with a passionate kiss and the words "And they lived happily ever after"? One of the most romantic movies is *The Princess Bride* because it follows the classic fairy-tale formula. Beautiful Buttercup, the damsel in distress, is kidnapped by evil Prince Humperdink, the rival for her affections. She is rescued by Westley, her true love and hero. After a swashbuckling sword fight, they escape, good triumphing over evil. The princess and her dashing savior are seen galloping through a lush field on a pair of pure white steeds. The music crescendos as the narrator says, "They rode to freedom. As dawn arose Westley and Buttercup knew they were safe. A wave of love swept over them and as they reached for each other. . . . Since the invention of the kiss there have been five kisses that were rated the most passionate, the most pure. This one left them all behind." The viewers sigh with complete satisfaction because they know Buttercup and Westley lived happily ever after.

Over the past few weeks the biblical narrator has told us the romantic story of Ruth and Boaz, which is better than a fairy tale because it's true. In this section the hero, Boaz, completes his rescue of the damsel in distress, Ruth, from shame and poverty. Their happily-ever-after ending once again shows God's love and providence at work in situations that seem hopeless.

THE PLOT THICKENS

preparation

God, thank You for making a happy ending possible in my life. You are my helper, my hero. I know I can trust You to rescue me from sin. Amen.

HAPPINESS
Happy are those who have the God of Israel as their helper, whose hope is in the Lord their God. He is the one who made heaven and earth, the sea, and everything in them. He is the one who keeps every promise forever. Psalm 146:5-6, NLT

explanation

GATES
City gates were the place where elders of the city met to exchange news and settle disputes. Boaz was known in the city gates, and centuries later his ancestors could still be found there. "Her husband is known in the gates, when he sits among the elders of the land" (Proverbs 31:23).

exploration

Boaz revealed to Ruth that he would gladly redeem her and the family property if the nearer relative would not. Thus Boaz went to the city gate to secure the redemption of Ruth, Naomi, and their family land.

Read Ruth 4; then focus on verses 1-6.

> *Now Boaz went up to the gate and sat down there; and behold, the close relative of whom Boaz had spoken came by. So Boaz said, "Come aside, friend, sit down here." So he came aside and sat down. And he took ten men of the elders of the city, and said, "Sit down here." So they sat down. Ruth 4:1-2*

1. Whom did Boaz encounter at the city gate? . . . .

. . . .

2. Remembering previous lessons about how God has worked throughout the book of Ruth, what word could be used to describe this meeting? Write a definition of this word.

. . . .

3. Whom did Boaz ask to witness the transaction? . . . .

. . . .

> *Then he said to the close relative, "Naomi, who has come back from the country of Moab, sold the piece of land which belonged to our brother Elimelech. And I thought to inform you, saying, 'Buy it back in the presence of the*

inhabitants and the elders of my people. If you will redeem it, redeem it; but if you will not redeem it, then tell me, that I may know; for there is no one but you to redeem it, and I am next after you."' And he said, "I will redeem it." Ruth 4:3-4

4. What had Naomi done with the land belonging to Elimelech?

. . . .

5. Explain the offer Boaz made to the close relative.

. . . .

6. How did the relative respond to this offer? . . . .

. . . .

Then Boaz said, "On the day you buy the field from the hand of Naomi, you must also buy it from Ruth the Moabitess, the wife of the dead, to perpetuate the name of the dead through his inheritance." Ruth 4:5

7. What condition went along with redeeming the land?

. . . .

And the close relative said, "I cannot redeem it for myself, lest I ruin my own inheritance. You redeem my right of redemption for yourself, for I cannot redeem it." Ruth 4:6

8. Upon learning of his complete responsibilities, how did the close relative respond? What reason did he give?

. . . .

. . . .

transformation

9. The nearer kinsman rejected Ruth. Rejection for a believer should not be a surprise because Jesus, our Redeemer, was rejected first. Fill in the chart to discover who rejected our Redeemer.

TO REDEEM

To *redeem* means to release by paying a ransom price; to buy, as in purchasing a slave's freedom. Old Testament redemption refers to a financial payment by a kinsman to rescue people or property. New Testament redemption refers to salvation from the bondage of sin through the payment of Christ's blood.

REJECTION

To *reject* means to refuse to acknowledge; to decline to hear, receive, or admit. Those who reject Christ will find themselves rejected in the end. Jesus said, "All who reject me and my message will be judged at the day of judgment by the truth I have spoken" (John 12:48, NLT).

GOOD COMPANY
If the world has rejected you, you're in good company. Jesus said, "Anyone who rejects you is rejecting me. And anyone who rejects me is rejecting God who sent me" (Luke 10:16, NLT). Take heart, the world's rejection proves your acceptance in heaven.

ACCEPTED
Accepted means "to receive favor; to be welcomed." Biblically, a person is accepted by the grace, mercy, or covenant-love of God, through faith and repentance, on the merits of Christ (adapted, *Nelson's*). "There is only one way of being accepted by him. He makes people right with himself only by faith" (Romans 3:30, NLT).

SCRIPTURE	REJECTED BY
Isa. 53:3-5	
Mark 8:31	
Luke 17:25	
1 Pet. 2:4	

10. We have seen that Ruth is an Old Testament picture of the New Testament church. Boaz is symbolic of Jesus, our Redeemer. The closer relative can represent the world, which rejects Christ.

> Journal about a time when you have experienced some form of rejection by others for your faith. How did God use it for your good? How did He use it for the good of others?

. . . .

. . . .

. . . .

. . . .

. . . .

11. Although the world may reject you, Jesus will always accept you: "To the praise of the glory of His grace, by which He has made us accepted in the Beloved" (Ephesians 1:6).

> Take time to praise God for His love and acceptance through Jesus, the Beloved. Journal a prayer, affirming your desire to never reject Him in word or deed.

. . . .

. . . .

. . . .

. . . .

For Ruth, being turned down by the nearer kinsman turned out to be the best thing that could have happened to her. Because of his rejection she was able to marry the man of her dreams. As Christians, we suffer rejection and persecution from the world, and that's a blessing—it means we're accepted in the Beloved. We have a Savior who completely accepts us, because He knows what it means to be rejected. Jesus was not always accepted: He was not well liked. In fact, after one of His sermons, all of His followers deserted Him except for the twelve apostles.

Did He have political power? No. He was a political failure. All levels of government rejected Him, then conspired to kill Him.

Did He have lots of friends? No. His friends hurt Him, abandoned Him, and denied Him. One of them betrayed Him to death.

Was He respected by His peers? No. His professional peers (the Pharisees and Sadducees) rejected His work.

Despite His rejection by the world, Jesus has changed the lives of millions of men and women across the centuries who have accepted Him into their hearts. How about you? Have you accepted your Kinsman-Redeemer? He's waiting to welcome you into the family.

contemplation
You are not accepted by God because you deserve to be or because you have worked hard for him, but because Jesus died for you.
Colin Urquhart

DAY 2 THE DUEL

preparation

Jesus, sometimes it feels like the world is bigger than I am. I need Your help to be an overcomer. Please give me victory in You, by helping me to win the battle I face today. Amen.

VICTORY

For every child of God defeats this evil world by trusting Christ to give the victory. And the ones who win this battle against the world are the ones who believe that Jesus is the Son of God. 1 John 5:4-5, NLT

Every good story includes an antagonist (bad guy) and a protagonist (good guy). Books and movies are filled with the classic conflict between good and evil, whether it's Dudley Do-Right of the Canadian Mounties foiling the plans of Snidely Whiplash, cowboys dressed in white hats shooting it out with villains in black hats, or the Star Trek Federation fighting intergalactic battles with the dreaded Klingons.

To become a hero you've got to vanquish a villain or two. Good guys without bad guys are just plain old guys. Think about it. Luke Skywalker would be an annoying adolescent if it weren't for Darth Vader. Superman could hang up the phone (and his cape for that matter) if Lex Luthor stopped threatening the world. And Robin Hood would be just another merry man in green tights if the Sheriff of Nottingham quit oppressing the poor.

Today we see an ordinary man, Boaz, become a great man when he goes toe-to-toe with his rival. In their duel for the fair Ruth, one walked away a winner and the other a loser.

exploration

Boaz had accomplished his goal. Because the nearer kinsman was unwilling to risk his inheritance, Boaz secured the right to redeem Ruth, Naomi, and the land. Today we see Boaz willingly and graciously assume his responsibilities as kinsman-redeemer.

Review Ruth 4; then focus on verses 7-10.

> *Now this was the custom in former times in Israel concerning redeeming and exchanging, to confirm anything: one man took off his sandal and gave it to the other, and this was a confirmation in Israel. Therefore*

*the close relative said to Boaz, "Buy it for yourself."
So he took off his sandal.* Ruth 4:7-8

1. Explain the custom in Israel concerning redeeming and exchanging.

. . . .

2. What did the nearer kinsman do and say to follow the custom?

. . . .

3. Read Deuteronomy 25:7-10. What was supposed to happen to one who refused the right of redemption?

. . . .

And Boaz said to the elders and all the people, "You are witnesses this day that I have bought all that was Elimelech's, and all that was Chilion's and Mahlon's, from the hand of Naomi. Moreover, Ruth the Moabitess, the widow of Mahlon, I have acquired as my wife, to perpetuate the name of the dead through his inheritance, that the name of the dead may not be cut off from among his brethren and from his position at the gate. You are witnesses this day." Ruth 4:9-10

4. Who witnessed this legal transaction? . . . .

. . . .

5. What did Boaz acquire as kinsman-redeemer? How did he acquire it?

. . . .

6. Boaz's actions again remind us of Christ's actions. According to 1 Corinthians 6:19-20, what did the greater Kinsman-Redeemer, Jesus Christ, acquire?

. . . .

7. Explain the reason Boaz gave for marrying Ruth.

. . . .

explanation

1

CONFIRMATION

In ancient Israel, instead of a written contract transferring rights or confirming an agreement, a symbolic act occurred: A sandal was removed and presented to another. Like signing on the dotted line, this signified a "done deal." By handing over the sandal, the kinsman relinquished his right to redeem the land and widow.

3

SHOELESS

Boaz graciously dealt with the nearer kinsman. He could have allowed the man to be humiliated in the city gate. Boaz could have spat upon him, and his name could have been changed to "Shoeless." Instead, Boaz allowed the man to remove his own sandal and walk away with his dignity.

6

QUALIFIED

Redeemers must be ready, willing, and able. Boaz was *ready* because he was related, he was *willing* to marry Ruth, and he was *able* since he had the finances. Jesus our Redeemer was *ready* through the Incarnation, *willing* at Gethsemane, the only sinless one *able* to pay the price for sin.

transformation

8.
KEEPING PROMISES
God keeps His prom-
ises, and He expects
and enables us to be
promise keepers like
Him. "As we know Jesus
better, his divine power
gives us everything we
need for living a godly
life. . . . He has given
us all of his rich and
wonderful promises"
(2 Peter 1:3-4, NLT).

9.
MY REDEEMER
Ruth and Boaz are long
gone; the traditions of
a kinsman-redeemer are
obsolete. But Jesus is
alive! The Redeemer still
offers deliverance and
eternal life to you and
me, his near relatives.
"I know that my
Redeemer lives" (Job
19:25, NLT).

8. The transfer of the nearer kinsman's shoe was like signing on the dotted line. As Christians, our word is our bond. We shouldn't need a signature or a contract to do what we have promised. Put a *C* in the blanks where you have *completed* your promised obligations. Place an *N* in the blanks where you have *neglected* your duty.

__ Home mortgage	__ Home/auto insurance
__ Voter registration	__ Rental agreement
__ PTA obligations	__ Legal contracts
__ Church membership	__ Marriage license
__ Driver's license	__ Employment duties
__ Income tax return	__ Verbal promises

9. Boaz redeemed Ruth from a life of poverty by paying the redemption price for Elimelech's land. Fill in the chart to discover what believers have been redeemed *from* and *by* what price.

SCRIPTURE	REDEEMED FROM/REDEEMED BY
Ps. 103:4	
Ps. 107:2-3	
Rom. 3:23-24	
Gal. 3:13	
Titus 2:13-14.	

Journal about a few things you've been redeemed from; then write a prayer of thanksgiving to your Redeemer.

. . . .

. . . .

. . . .

. . . .

. . . .

10. When Ruth was rejected by her nearer kinsman, Boaz could have shamed him publicly by spitting in his face and calling him a name that would stick. Instead of returning insult for insult, he turned the other cheek and let his adversary walk away in dignity. What about you? When have you been humiliated publicly by another?

. . . .

Journal a prayer of repentance to God if you have retaliated against your adversary through your actions or words. Ask God to help you speak blessing to that person instead of a curse, to turn the other cheek and be gracious as Boaz was.

. . . .

. . . .

. . . .

. . . .

REVENGE
Revenge is never sweet; it perpetuates an endless cycle of pain. Taking an "eye for an eye and a tooth for a tooth" would leave the world blind and toothless. Jesus' remedy? "Whoever slaps you on your right cheek, turn the other to him also" (Matthew 5:38-39). Turning your cheek can turn your enemy into your friend.

The emotional pain of rejection stings as surely as a physical slap on the face. It's human nature to want to strike back. Boaz emulated the nature of God in letting the insult to his bride go and letting God take care of the rest. God uses people and circumstances to teach us His ways. We've learned from Boaz to turn the other cheek as Jesus taught in the Sermon on the Mount.

Sir Walter Scott had difficulty with the idea of "turning the other cheek." But Jesus' words took on special meaning one day when Scott threw a rock at a stray dog to chase it away. His aim was straighter and his delivery stronger than he had intended, for he hit the animal and broke its leg. Instead of running off, the dog limped over to him and licked his hand. Sir Walter never forgot that touching response. He said, "That dog preached the Sermon on the Mount to me as few ministers have ever presented it." Scott said he had not found human beings so ready to forgive their enemies.

If sticks, stones or name-calling have hurt you, maybe it's time you learned how to turn the other cheek.

contemplation
Forgiveness is the fragrance that the flower leaves on the heel of the one who crushed it.
Mark Twain

DAY 3 THE BLESSING

preparation

God, thank You for blessing my life in so many ways. Teach me to use my words to encourage and uplift others, offering blessings to those I meet. Amen.

BLESSING
May the Lord bless you and protect you. May the Lord smile on you and be gracious to you. May the Lord show you his favor and give you his peace. Numbers 6:24-26, NLT

"God bless you" we often respond after someone sneezes. This tradition began in the Middle Ages when Gregory the Great instigated a short prayer, or blessing, to be said by someone sneezing. During that superstitious era it was believed that people who sneezed violently were in danger of expelling their souls and that a proper prayer could prevent this danger.

Scripture does not support superstition. In the Bible the "blessing" is a very special gift. It is the act of announcing or predicting God's favor upon another. A blessing was not only kind words of encouragement; it was also prophetic, possessing the power to bring those words spoken to pass. Usually an influential person offered a blessing to someone of less importance. Toward the end of their lives, the patriarchs would give prophetic blessings that pronounced benefits upon their children. Leaders frequently blessed their people before departing. Priests blessed their congregations in the name of the Lord in the form of a benediction.

The townspeople in Bethlehem had observed the budding romance between Ruth and Boaz and witnessed the legal transaction between the kinsmen. As a special wedding gift to the couple, the crowd rejoiced and proclaimed words of blessing. Their words were prophetic and powerful, just as a blessing ought to be.

exploration

In most fairy tales, the townspeople gather to shower the prince and his bride with love and good wishes. So, too, in this true "fairy tale" the people bless the happy couple.

Review Ruth 4; then focus on verses 11-12.

> *And all the people who were at the gate, and the elders, said, "We are witnesses. The Lord make the woman who*

is coming to your house like Rachel and Leah, the two who built the house of Israel; and may you prosper in Ephrathah and be famous in Bethlehem." Ruth 4:11

1. Describe the other people at the city gate with Boaz and the nearer kinsman.

. . . .

2. What was their purpose for watching the transaction?

. . . .

3. What was the first blessing the townspeople offered for Ruth?

. . . .

4. What did they pray for Boaz in verse 11? . . . .

. . . .

"May your house be like the house of Perez, whom Tamar bore to Judah, because of the offspring which the Lord will give you from this young woman." Ruth 4:12

5. Whose house did the townspeople pray would be the model for Ruth and Boaz?

. . . .

6. According to Genesis 38:24-26, what is Tamar remembered for? Why would it be odd to use her name as a source of blessing?

. . . .

. . . .

. . . .

7. What did the people pray the Lord would give Boaz through Ruth?

. . . .

explanation

1

WEDDING
This scene demonstrates that marriage is not a private but a public affair. Marriages are sacred to God and ought to be upheld by society and accompanied by prayer and blessing. Couples should desire the blessing of God and His people. Support the marriages you attend with prayer and a blessing.

3

FRUITFUL
Rachel and Leah were Jacob's two wives who bore eight of his twelve sons, founding the nation of Israel. Their blessing acknowledges that fruitfulness, prosperity, and prominence are gifts from God. Give Him credit when you are blessed with prosperity.

6

FUTURE
Although Tamar had a blemished reputation and Ruth was a foreigner, their names appear in Matthew's genealogy of Christ. Although your past may be tarnished, you can be included in the Lamb's Book of Life. "Help these women, . . . whose names are written in the Book of Life" (Philippians 4:3, NLT).

transformation

9.

FROM THE HEART
A blessing or a curse comes straight from the heart. Jesus taught that words reveal the soul. "Whatever is in your heart determines what you say. A good person produces good words from a good heart, and an evil person produces evil words from an evil heart" (Matthew 12:34-35, NLT).

10

BLESSING GOD
When we bless God, we acknowledge His great attributes, offering praise and adoration for who He is. "Bless the Lord your God forever and ever! Blessed be Your glorious name, which is exalted above all blessing and praise! You alone are the Lord" (Nehemiah 9:5-6).

8. Today we discovered what a blessing it is to receive a blessing. Fill in the chart to learn some of the blessings offered in Scripture.

SCRIPTURE	BLESSING GIVEN
Gen. 1:22, 28	
Gen. 24:59-60	
Num. 6:22-27	
Heb. 11:21	

9. Follow the model of the people of Bethlehem, and pray blessings on the couples in your community. Fill in your own personal chart of blessing.

NAME OF COUPLE	PRAYER FOR BLESSING
Pastor:	
Relative:	
Neighbor:	
Friend:	

10. List several ways God has blessed you with prosperity, prominence, or fruitfulness.

. . . .

. . . .

. . . .

Journal a blessing to God, thanking Him for His goodness to you.

. . . .

. . . .

. . . .

Bad times are rarely seen as a blessing. Yet for Ruth, the death of her husband resulted in her devotion to God, which changed her destiny forever. Hard work led her to handfuls of grain, which was God's provision. Rejection was turned into redemption.

People in the southern town of Enterprise, Alabama, know something about bad times turning into blessings. There the citizens have erected a monument to an insect—the Mexican boll weevil. In 1895 the boll weevil began to destroy the cotton, the county's major crop. In desperation the farmers decided to plant something not appealing to the weevil—peanuts. By 1919 the county's peanut crop was many times more plentiful than cotton had ever been. In that year of prosperity a fountain and monument were built. The inscription reads: "In profound appreciation of the boll weevil and what it has done as the herald of prosperity this monument was erected by the citizens of Enterprise, Coffee County, Alabama." As with Ruth's experience, growth and success came from struggle and crisis. Adversity can be transformed into blessing.

contemplation
Reflect upon your present blessings of which every man has many; not on your past misfortunes of which all men have some.
Charles Dickens

DAY 4 THE GRANDCHILD

preparation

Father, thank You for giving me the right to become one of Your children. Help me to live up to Your name. I want to be a child You can be proud of. Amen.

CHILD OF GOD
But to all who believed him and accepted him, he gave the right to become children of God. John 1:12, NLT

I'm named after two wonderful women in my family. My first name, Lenya, comes from my famous aunt, Lotte Lenya, a German vaudevillian actress. Her famous husband, Kurt Weill, wrote *The Three Penny Opera* and *The Seven Deadly Sins* to showcase her haunting voice and talents. I inherited my middle name from my grandmother, May Farley, who was of Scottish descent and temperament. She was a feisty, petite woman who was fiercely loyal to her family.

Grandparents are notoriously proud of their grandchildren, happy to tell you the latest accomplishments and show you the newest pictures at the slightest hint of interest. My granny was no exception to the rule. After she and my grandpa died, we discovered a scrapbook of memories chronicling the lives of their precious grandchildren. Several pages were dedicated to each grandchild. School pictures, wedding invitations, and newspaper clippings were carefully glued into the treasured keepsake. Even though Granny is gone, I carry on her family name. My best friends don't just call me Lenya; they call me Lenya May.

Naomi had suffered much loss, but she remained extremely loyal to her family. She had done everything she could to preserve the family line and had waited a long time for a grandchild to carry on the family name. At long last God made her a proud grandmother.

exploration

Yesterday we saw the crowd bless Ruth and Boaz. Today we see them offer their blessings to Naomi and her new grandchild.

Review Ruth 4; then focus on verses 13-17.

So Boaz took Ruth and she became his wife; and when he went in to her, the Lord gave her conception, and she bore a son. Ruth 4:13

1. Following their marriage, what did God give Ruth and Boaz?

. . . .

Then the women said to Naomi, "Blessed be the Lord, who has not left you this day without a close relative; and may his name be famous in Israel! And may he be to you a restorer of life and a nourisher of your old age; for your daughter-in-law, who loves you, who is better to you than seven sons, has borne him." Ruth 4:14-15

2. According to the women of the town, how had the Lord blessed Naomi?

. . . .

3. Describe the things the women prayed for this baby and how they would affect Naomi.

. . . .

. . . .

4. What tribute did they pay Ruth?

. . . .

Then Naomi took the child and laid him on her bosom, and became a nurse to him. Also the neighbor women gave him a name, saying, "There is a son born to Naomi." And they called his name Obed. He is the father of Jesse, the father of David. Ruth 4:16-17

5. What special relationship did Naomi form with the baby?

. . . .

6. What name was given to the baby? . . . .

. . . .

explanation

1

CONCEPTION
Conception is a gift from God—He opens or closes the womb. An open womb indicated God's blessing. "Then God remembered Rachel, and . . . opened her womb" (Genesis 30:22). A barren womb was evidence of God's sovereignty. "He loved Hannah, although the Lord had closed her womb" (1 Samuel 1:5).

4

WOMEN
Women were not valued in Hebrew society. Pious Jews often began their daily prayers saying, "Thank you, God, that I have not been born a Gentile or a woman." The tribute paid to Ruth was high praise indeed. She—a woman and a Gentile—was better than seven native sons.

5

LINEAGE
Hebrew law declared that Ruth's firstborn became the foster son of Naomi, carrying on the lineage of Elimelech. "Judah said to Er's brother Onan, 'You must marry Tamar, as our law requires of the brother of a man who has died. Her first son from you will be your brother's heir'" (Genesis 38:8, NLT).

· ·

transformation

8. We saw that Boaz and Ruth had a healthy marriage, which included the intimacy of a sexual relationship resulting in offspring. Fill in the chart to discover some truths about sex in a marital relationship.

SCRIPTURE	LESSON ON INTIMACY
Gen. 1:27-28	· ·
Gen. 2:24-25	· ·
Prov. 5:18-19	· ·
1 Cor. 7:3-5	· ·
Heb. 13:4	· ·

9. We saw that Ruth overcame the prejudice of her day against foreigners and women. To Naomi she became more valuable than many native sons.

Journal about a time when you were demeaned, diminished, demoted, or denied opportunities because of your race or gender. How did you overcome this?

· ·

· ·

· ·

10. It was clear that Naomi treasured her grandson Obed.

Name some ways your grandparents have shown they treasure you.

· ·

· ·

8

UNASHAMED

Sex isn't a dirty word. Sex is good if it is practiced in marriage between a man and a woman. God created male and female bodies to please as well as to procreate.

9

EMANCIPATION

Prejudice is an irrational attitude of hostility directed against one who's different. Jesus was the great emancipator, breaking down walls of prejudice. "There is no longer Jew or Gentile, slave or free, male or female. . . . You are one in Christ Jesus" (Galatians 3:28, NLT).

10

LEGACY

It has been said that the best things in life are not things. Not everyone has land or riches to pass on to children and grandchildren, but everyone has lessons learned along life's journey to bestow. Let your legacy to your descendants be the things that money can't buy.

. . . .

. . . .

What spiritual truths will you pass on to your children, grandchildren, and/or nieces and nephews from the book of Ruth?

. . . .

. . . .

. . . .

. . . .

My (Penny's) grandmother didn't leave many earthly posses-sions—a few pieces of jewelry, some family crystal, a Bible—but she left a rich spiritual legacy. Whenever I visited her small, immaculate house, Mima welcomed me with open arms and home-baked goodies. She spoiled me by letting me stay up late. When I went to her room to kiss her good-night, I always found her reading her well-worn Bible. She would look up with her gentle, brown eyes and murmur, "This way I know I'll get a good night's rest." Later, when she lay dying in the cancer ward of the hospital, she continued to read her Bible and pray for her chil-dren and grandchildren. I know she prayed especially hard for me because I had walked away from the Lord.

The night before she died, I sat in Mima's sterile hospital room listlessly thumbing through a magazine. Suddenly she sat up and looked at someone in the room I couldn't see. A serene smile transformed her pain-racked face, her eyes lit up, and she nodded her head as if to say, "I'm ready to go home." One of my deepest regrets is that my grandmother didn't live to see me recommit my life to the Lord.

It's been said that with God there are no grandchildren, only sons and daughters. We each must come to God on our own. But largely because of the example, prayers, and lessons bequeathed to me by my godly grandmother, I am one of His children.

contemplation

When I approach a child, he inspires in me two sentiments: tenderness for what he is, and a respect for what he may become.
Louis Pasteur

DAY 5 THE SEQUEL

preparation

Lord God, thank You that You know the entire story of my life and that You have given me a preview of coming attractions—eternity with You. Help me show my unsaved loved ones the script of the love story written by You. Amen.

LIFE STORY
You saw me before I was born. Every day of my life was recorded in your book. Every moment was laid out before a single day had passed. Psalm 139:16, NLT

Hollywood producers love sequels. They make movies using familiar characters and reworked plots to lure moviegoers back to the theater with films such as *Back to the Future 2* or *Rocky 3*. But sequels usually aren't as good as the original movie because they're not—well—original. Did anyone see *Scarlett*, the sequel to *Gone with the Wind*? It was a desperate attempt to recapture the movie magic of Scarlett O'Hara and Rhett Butler's love story. But the on-screen chemistry fizzled, and the movie was a dud.

God in His providence supplied the sequel to Ruth and Boaz's love story before time began. He used the story of Ruth and Boaz as a prequel—a preview of coming attractions. God's sequel to the story of the kinsman-redeemer and his bride is the story of Jesus, the true Kinsman-Redeemer, who came to save the world and redeem His bride, the church. This story has captured the hearts and minds of millions of people worldwide. This is one sequel worth seeing!

exploration

The final paragraph in the book of Ruth is a genealogy leading to King David. We get a glimpse of God's plan, not only for Ruth and Boaz to live happily ever after, but also for all people to discover their own happy ending in a relationship with Jesus Christ.

Review Ruth 4; then focus on verses 18-21.

> *Now this is the genealogy of Perez: Perez begot Hezron; Hezron begot Ram, and Ram begot Amminadab; Amminadab begot Nahshon, and Nahshon begot Salmon; Salmon begot Boaz, and Boaz begot Obed; Obed begot Jesse, and Jesse begot David.* Ruth 4:18-22

1. Looking back to Ruth 4:12, who was the father of Perez?

. . . .

2. According to Revelation 5:5, who is the Lion of the tribe of Judah?

. . . .

3. How does Revelation 19:16 confirm the prophecy of Genesis 49: 8-10?

. . . .

4. How many ancestors are recorded in the genealogy from Perez to Boaz?

. . . .

5. Record the genealogy from Boaz to King David.

. . . .

6. The genealogy in Ruth 4 agrees with Jesus' genealogy in Matthew 1. Salmon was Boaz's father. According to Matthew 1:5, who was Boaz's mother?

. . . .

7. What do you learn about Rahab from Joshua 2?

. . . .

transformation

8. Jesus was a descendant of Ruth and Boaz through their son Obed. In the space provided, draw or write a genealogy of your own family tree.

explanation

1

JUDAH
Judah was the son of Jacob and founder of the messianic line. Judah received Jacob's blessing, which foretold the rise of this kingly tribe (adapted, *Nelson's*). "The scepter will not depart from Judah, . . . until the coming of the one to whom it belongs" (Genesis 49:10, NLT).

4

GENEALOGY
A genealogy is a list of ancestors—the members of each generation in succession. This was vital for verifying the royal succession in the kingdom of Judah because Old Testament prophets proclaimed that Messiah would come from the line of Jesse, the father of David (adapted, *Nelson's*).

7

GENTILE
Gentile is a term used by Jewish people to refer to anyone not part of the Jewish race. Boaz's mother was not Jewish. Two non-Jewish women, Rahab and Ruth, were included in Jesus' genealogy—the messianic line. This may explain why Boaz was not prejudiced against Ruth, a Gentile (adapted, *Nelson's*).

9

BLACK SHEEP
Jesus' family tree has
some surprising
branches: Tamar, a
seductress; Rahab,
a harlot; Manasseh, an
idolater. The genealogy
of Jesus branches out
to adopt all kinds of men
and women. "I bow my
knees to the Father of
our Lord Jesus Christ,
from whom the whole
family in heaven and
earth is named" (Ephe-
sians 3:14-15).

10

BORN AGAIN
Believers have been
"begotten" twice: once
on earth, again in
heaven. "You have been
born again. Your new
life did not come from
your earthly parents. . . .
[That life] will end in
death. But this new life
will last forever because
it comes from the eter-
nal, living word of God"
(1 Peter 1:23, NLT).

11

HAPPY ENDING
Ruth's journey from futil-
ity to faithfulness fore-
shadows every believer's
story. All begin as
sinners. "All have
sinned" (Romans 3:23,
NLT). Through faith,
believers are rescued
by the Redeemer to a
happy ending. "Through
Christ Jesus, [God] has
freed us by taking away
our sins" (Romans 3:24,
NLT).

9. Jesus' family tree included some "black sheep."

> Journal about how you were a black sheep until Jesus washed you white as snow and included you in His family tree.

. . . .

. . . .

. . . .

. . . .

10. God uses many different ways and means to "beget" new members into His spiritual family. Write out a personal spiritual genealogy that includes the people God used to help birth you into His family. Include the people who prayed for you, witnessed to you, and showed you the love of God through their lives.

. . . .

. . . .

. . . .

> Journal a prayer asking God to beget into His family the unsaved people you know and love. Ask Him to reveal how you can participate in this birthing process.

. . . .

. . . .

. . . .

. . . .

11. Ruth's story had a happy ending, not only for her family, but also for everyone blessed by her lineage to the Messiah. Throughout the generations she continues to serve as a model for women of faith. Check the boxes that indicate which attributes you most admire in Ruth. Circle the attributes you would like to exhibit in your life.

— Loyal   — Humble
— Hardworking   — Faithful
— Brave   — Obedient
— Loving   — Other _____

Journal a prayer asking God to help you exhibit the attributes of Ruth that are lacking in your life. Ask Him to make you a model of faith for generations to come.

. . . .

. . . .

. . . .

. . . .

. . . .

What do people today consider the greatest source of pleasure in their lives? According to a 1989 study reported in *USA Today*, an overwhelming 63 percent of respondents answered "family." Family is a great source of pleasure to God, too, and the story of Ruth and Boaz shows us how important one family can be. Their descendants were the heirs to the throne of Israel, and they paved the way for our Kinsman-Redeemer and King, Jesus Christ.

God wants to include *your* story in His genealogy. We can be His daughters and heirs. "But when the right time came, God sent his Son, born of a woman, subject to the law. God sent him to buy freedom for us who were slaves to the law, so that he could adopt us as his very own children. And because you Gentiles have become his children, God has sent the Spirit of his Son into your hearts, and now you can call God your dear Father. Now you are no longer a slave but God's own child. And since you are his child, everything he has belongs to you" (Galatians 4:4-7, NLT). God has written a happily-ever-after ending for your life story by adopting you into His family and making *you* one of His heirs. It's a fairy tale come true.

A Distant Kingdom

The lion strutted up to the rhinoceros and asked, "Who's the king of the jungle?"

"You are, O Lion," came the answer.

The lion stalked to the hippopotamus and asked, "Who's the king of the jungle?"

The hippo said, "You are, O Lion."

The lion sauntered up to the elephant and asked, "Who's the king of the jungle?"

The elephant seized the lion with his trunk, threw him high into the air, caught him on the way down, and slammed him hard against a tree. The lion arose, half dazed, shook himself, and said weakly, "Just because you don't know the right answer, you don't have to get sore."

The book of Esther moves forward in time over 800 years to the days of the Persian Empire and King Ahasuerus, who was ruler of the known civilized world. He truly believed he was king of the jungle. But he would discover that there was a greater king to reckon with. Although God's name is not mentioned in the book of Esther, His invisible power permeates the story. The great king of Persia was powerless in his dealings with the King of the universe. As you study the book of Esther, look for the unseen hand of God providentially protecting and providing for His people.

DAY ONE
A Powerful King

DAY TWO
A Rich King

DAY THREE
An Angry King

DAY FOUR
A King's Counselors

DAY FIVE
A Vindictive King

DAY **1** A POWERFUL KING

preparation

Father, though earthly kings often seek revenge, You desire mercy. Help me to be merciful because of the mercy You have shown to me. Amen.

MERCY
The Lord is merciful and gracious; he is slow to get angry and full of unfailing love. Psalm 103:8, NLT

explanation

HIGH KING
Ahasuerus means "high father" or "venerable king." Known as Xerxes the Great, he ruled over a vast empire that extended through the Fertile Crescent, making him sovereign ruler over the known world. At this time in history he was probably the most powerful man alive.

exploration

Much happened in Israel in the years between Ruth and Esther. Through the line of Ruth and Boaz the Jewish monarchy was established with a succession of kings. The nation of Israel experienced civil war and divided into the two kingdoms of Israel and Judah. Because they continued to disobey God's commands, Judah was taken captive by the Babylonians in 586 B.C. Later Cyrus, king of Persia, conquered Babylon and freed the Israelite captives in 538 B.C. Fewer than sixty thousand Jews returned to the Promised Land.

The book of Esther is a record of the millions of Israelites who chose to remain in Persia. This book shows that God, in His providence, continued to care for His children, even in a distant land.

Read Esther 1; then focus on verses 1-4.

> *Now it came to pass in the days of Ahasuerus (this was the Ahasuerus who reigned over one hundred and twenty-seven provinces, from India to Ethiopia), . . .*
> Esther 1:1

1. When did this story take place? . . . .

. . . .

2. Describe King Ahasuerus and his kingdom. . . . .

. . . .

> *. . . in those days when King Ahasuerus sat on the throne of his kingdom, which was in Shushan the citadel, that in the third year of his reign he made a feast for all his*

officials and servants—the powers of Persia and Media, the nobles, and the princes of the provinces being before him— . . . Esther 1:2-3

3. Where was King Ahasuerus holding court? . . . .

. . . .

4. What special event did Ahasuerus hold during the third year of his reign?

. . . .

5. Identify the people he invited. . . . .

. . . .

. . . when he showed the riches of his glorious kingdom and the splendor of his excellent majesty for many days, one hundred and eighty days in all. Esther 1:4

6. What was Ahasuerus's goal in hosting a feast for his officials and servants?

. . . .

7. How long did this elaborate feast last? . . . .

. . . .

transformation

8. Ahasuerus was a powerful king, but in his heart he harbored bitterness for past atrocities committed against his people and his father.

Journal about a time when you felt bitter toward someone who treated you or your family badly.

. . . .

. . . .

. . . .

SHUSHAN
Shushan (or Susa) was the royal residence and capital of the Persian Empire. When Cyrus established the empire, he made Shushan its capital. Darius I built a magnificent palace there. Ahasuerus and other Persian kings occupied the royal palace. Daniel and Nehemiah both served kings in Shushan.

FEAST FOR REVENGE
Ahasuerus's ulterior motive was to gain support for a war against the Greeks. Scholars believe he wanted to obtain vengeance from the Athenians for the wrongs committed by them against the Persians and against his father.

BITTERNESS
Ill-treatment is a bitter pill to swallow. It is even worse to let bitterness consume you. Unchecked bitterness will poison you. "Watch out that no bitter root of unbelief rises up among you, for whenever it springs up, many are corrupted by its poison" (Hebrews 12:15, NLT).

10

MERCY

Mercy is compassion toward an offender. Mercy implies kindness that withholds punishment even when justice demands it. It shows tolerance toward others, a generous overlooking of their faults. Jesus said, "Now go and learn the meaning of this Scripture: 'I want you to be merciful'" (Matthew 9:13, NLT).

11

VENGEANCE

Taking revenge into our own hands may result in injustice and overreaction. Give it to God. "O Lord Almighty, you are just, and you examine the deepest thoughts of hearts and minds. Let me see your vengeance against them, for I have committed my cause to you" (Jeremiah 11:20, NLT).

9. Because Ahasuerus was poisoned by bitterness, he developed a strong desire for revenge.

> Reflect on the situation you wrote about in question 8, then journal your responses to these questions: How did your bitterness lead to a desire for revenge? How did you act vengefully in the situation? Did taking vengeance make you feel better or worse?

· ·

· ·

· ·

10. It is a natural human response to feel revengeful toward those we think have wronged us. It takes a supernatural grace to respond with mercy. Fill in the chart to discover the benefits of responding with supernatural mercy and compassion.

SCRIPTURE	BLESSING OF SHOWING MERCY
Matt. 5:7	
Rom. 9:23	
Phil. 2:1-2	
James 2:13	

11. Those who are merciful respond not only with tender hearts but also outward actions. Read the following Scripture passage and answer the questions. "Dear friends, never avenge yourselves. Leave that to God. For it is written, 'I will take vengeance; I will repay those who deserve it,' says the Lord. Instead, do what the Scriptures say: 'If your enemies are hungry, feed them. If they are thirsty, give them something to drink, and they will be ashamed of what they have done to you.' Don't let evil get the best of you, but conquer evil by doing good" (Romans 12:19-21, NLT).

a. Why does God tell you to withhold taking vengeance on others?

· ·

b. Describe what you should do instead and what the results will be.

. . . .

Journal about how and when you will show mercy in a tangible way to the person you wrote about in questions 8 and 9.

. . . .

. . . .

. . . .

. . . .

Hissy fits between preschoolers can get ugly fast. The blowout began with a tug-of-war over the Batmobile. My son, Nathan, was the Caped Crusader and his cousin Lenya Elizabeth was Catwoman. Whoever controlled the car would be victorious in the battle for Gotham City. Nathan yanked hard as Lenya's grip slipped, catapulting her off the bed. In a fury she bit Nathan so hard a full imprint of her teeth was left on his leg. The scream was deafening; something had gone terribly wrong in Gotham City.

After binding up wounds and wiping tears, God inspired me to go beyond a lecture on sharing to teaching them about grace and mercy instead. I said, "Mercy means not getting what you two deserve, like a spanking. So you're off the hook. Grace goes way beyond mercy; it's getting what you don't deserve, like a reward." I loaded the wounded warriors into my car for a shopping spree at Target and bought them each a new superhero figure.

Ahasuerus did not believe in extending mercy. He was a rich, vengeful, and decadent king. We know from history that he failed in his efforts to conquer Greece—he is known as the king who fought the Greeks and was humiliated by them. Eventually he failed as a ruler and was assassinated by trusted colleagues. Because he was unwilling to offer mercy, he didn't receive mercy either.

contemplation
Doing an injury puts you below your enemy; revenging one makes you even with him; forgiving it sets you above him.
Anonymous

DAY 2 A RICH KING

preparation

Lord, thank You that You are more precious than any possessions. All blessing, glory, power, and honor be Yours!

GLORY AND POWER
"Silver and gold I do not have, but what I do have I give you: In the name of Jesus Christ of Nazareth, rise up and walk." Acts 3:6

For my (Penny's) fortieth birthday my mother wanted to give me the perfect gift. One day she called and said excitedly, "I've decided to take some of my old jewelry and have it remade into a diamond necklace for your birthday present!" Who could say no to that? I could just picture the little black dress I would wear to show off my beautiful diamond necklace. I couldn't wait for my friends to ooh and aah! We began to look for the perfect setting and a jeweler to make the necklace.

Not long after, I received another call from my mother. Her voice was no longer excited but sounded devastated, "Someone's stolen all my jewelry, including the things I wanted you to have!" I was so disappointed. At that moment God had to give me a perspective check. His Word echoed in my heart: "Do not lay up for yourselves treasures on earth, where moth and rust destroy and where thieves break in and steal; but lay up for yourselves treasures in heaven" (Matthew 6:19-20). I was reminded that my mother was the true treasure, not her jewelry. Our common faith in Jesus and our close bond would be the ornaments I would display to others.

King Ahasuerus was a rich show-off who expected the world to ooh and aah over his lavish possessions. He didn't have the heavenly perspective that things don't matter, people do.

exploration

Yesterday we met the ruler of the world, King Ahasuerus. We found him to be vengeful and power hungry. Today we learn of Ahasuerus's incredible earthly wealth and how he used it.

Review Esther 1; then focus on verses 5-9.

And when these days were completed, the king made a feast lasting seven days for all the people who were present in Shushan the citadel, from great to small, in the court of the garden of the king's palace. Esther 1:5

1. After the feast for the nobles, what kind of feast did Ahasuerus hold?

. . . .

2. Identify those who were invited. . . . .

. . . .

There were white and blue linen curtains fastened with cords of fine linen and purple on silver rods and marble pillars; and the couches were of gold and silver on a mosaic pavement of alabaster, turquoise, and white and black marble. Esther 1:6

3. Describe how the palace gardens were decorated.

. . . .

And they served drinks in golden vessels, each vessel being different from the other, with royal wine in abundance, according to the generosity of the king. In accordance with the law, the drinking was not compulsory; for so the king had ordered all the officers of his household, that they should do according to each man's pleasure. Esther 1:7-8

4. In what were the drinks served? Were any limits set?

. . . .

5. Explain the law concerning drinking. . . . .

. . . .

Queen Vashti also made a feast for the women in the royal palace which belonged to King Ahasuerus. Esther 1:9

explanation

1

FEASTS
For the Israelites, feasts were regular assemblies for worshiping the Lord. For the Persians, feasts were an opportunity to set political agendas and display royal wealth and power. The feasts of the Israelites led to spiritual fullness; the feasts of the Persians led to personal decadence.

3

OPULENCE
Ahasuerus held a feast to end all feasts, sparing no expense to prove that he had the resources to wage war against Greece. White and purple were royal colors. Marble, gold, silver, and semiprecious stones added to the splendor. His opulent garden party paved the way for a vicious war party.

QUEEN VASHTI
The name *Vashti* means "one who is desired" or "beloved." She was the beautiful queen of King Ahasuerus, believed by many to be Amestris, the mother of Artaxerxes, who ruled from 465 to 425 B.C.

WEALTH
Having money is not a sin. Many godly people were wealthy like Abraham, Job, and Joseph of Arimathea. Making money an idol *is* a sin. "The love of money is at the root of all kinds of evil. And some people, craving money, have wandered from the faith" (1 Timothy 6:10, NLT).

GOOD INVESTMENT
A financial investment uses money to purchase assets in order to make a profit. A spiritual investment is a commitment of money, time, or resources to profit God's kingdom, resulting in eternal reward. "Be diligent so that you will receive your full reward" (2 John 1:8, NLT).

6. What was Queen Vashti doing while the men had their drinking party?

. . . .

transformation

7. King Ahasuerus used wealth to manipulate his people into fighting a losing war. The Bible describes how earthly wealth ought to be used. From the following verses, list in one column God's plan for wealth. In the other column, contrast Ahasuerus's worldly use of wealth. "Command those who are rich in this present age not to be haughty, nor to trust in uncertain riches but in the living God, who gives us richly all things to enjoy. Let them do good, that they be rich in good works, ready to give, willing to share, storing up for themselves a good foundation for the time to come, that they may lay hold on eternal life" (1 Timothy 6:17-19).

Godly Use of Wealth	**Worldly Use of Wealth**
Do not be haughty	Proudly showed off wealth

8. Examine your personal view of wealth based on the chart in question 7.

Journal about a time when you trusted in earthly wealth to fulfill or accomplish a selfish desire. How did it make you feel?

. . . .

. . . .

. . . .

. . . .

Now journal about a time when God allowed you to invest your finances to do a good work for His kingdom. How did it make you feel?

. . . .

. . . .

. . . .

. . . .

9. King Ahasuerus used alcohol to manipulate the nobility by dulling their senses. God's plan is to fill us with His Spirit in order to heighten our senses so that we can accomplish His will.

Journal Ephesians 5:17-18 into a personal prayer that you will be filled with the Spirit. "Don't act thoughtlessly, but try to understand what the Lord wants you to do. Don't be drunk with wine, because that will ruin your life. Instead, let the Holy Spirit fill and control you" (Ephesians 5:17-18, NLT).

. . . .

. . . .

. . . .

Corrie ten Boom was a Holocaust survivor who, through the filling of the Holy Spirit, learned to forgive her captors. She explained the filling of the Spirit in this simple yet profound way: "I have a glove here in my hand. The glove cannot do anything by itself, but when my hand is in it, it can do many things. True, it is not the glove, but my hand in the glove that acts. We are gloves. It is the Holy Spirit in us who is the hand, who does the job. We have to make room for the hand so that every finger is filled."

This saintly woman could have been filled with anger, revealing the fruit of bitterness. She could have filled her body with alcohol or drugs to dull the memories of her years in the Nazi concentration camp. Instead, she chose to be filled with the Spirit of God and let His unseen hand guide her through life.

9

DRUNKENNESS
Like a salesman wining and dining clients, Ahasuerus used an abundance of wine to sell his plan for world domination. Solomon warned, "When dining with a ruler, pay attention to what is put before you. . . . Don't desire all the delicacies—deception may be involved" (Proverbs 23:1-3, NLT).

contemplation

There is the drunkenness of pride, of anger, and of vengeance; and there is another kind altogether, of zeal and fervor. It was with this latter that the apostles were filled when they received the Holy Spirit.
François Fénelon

DAY 3 AN ANGRY
KING

preparation

Father, I want to have a childlike faith, yet I don't want to be childish. Please help me to grow up and become a mature Christian. Amen.

GROWN UP
When I was a child, I spoke and thought and reasoned as a child does. But when I grew up, I put away childish things. 1 Corinthians 13:11, NLT

I've often wondered what I would do if I were a queen. The 1950s television program *Queen for a Day* promised new potentates many lavish prizes. When Lady Diana married Prince Charles, she gained not only royalty but also an awesome wardrobe. But it's not the perks that come with being a queen that would allure me; it's the power and control that I would find most intoxicating. I'd probably use the power for good: ending world hunger, educating the masses, and bringing about lasting peace. But being in absolute control could get me into trouble. I like to drive fast so there would be no speed limits in my kingdom. I would appoint a Czar of Good Taste, banishing "all you can eat" buffets and replacing them with pastry shops full of decadent delicacies. My motto would be "Let them eat cake!"

Lord Acton said, "Power tends to corrupt and absolute power corrupts absolutely." Power can turn a timid human into a tyrant. The kings of the East were despots who held absolute sway over their subjects. Their words and whims became the letter of the law. Ahasuerus was intoxicated by power and displayed erratic behavior similar to a tyrannical two-year-old on a sugar high. One minute he was up, and the next he was down, and the people around him were along for the roller-coaster ride.

exploration

King Ahasuerus and his cronies partied for six months. On the last day of the feast he decided to stage a beauty pageant with his wife Vashti as the main attraction.

Review Esther 1; then focus on verses 10-12.

On the seventh day, when the heart of the king was merry with wine, he commanded Mehuman, Biztha, Harbona, Bigtha, Abagtha, Zethar, and Carcas, seven eunuchs who served in the presence of King Ahasuerus, to bring Queen Vashti before the king, wearing her royal crown, in order to show her beauty to the people and the officials, for she was beautiful to behold.
Esther 1:10-11

1. Describe the king's condition as the feast drew to a close.

. . . .

2. What did he command his eunuchs to do? . . . .

. . . .

3. What did he want Vashti to wear? . . . .

. . . .

4. Why did he want to parade Vashti before the people and officials?

. . . .

But Queen Vashti refused to come at the king's command brought by his eunuchs; therefore the king was furious, and his anger burned within him.
Esther 1:12

5. How did Vashti respond to the summons? . . . .

. . . .

6. What was the king's reaction? . . . .

. . . .

7. How did his anger affect him inwardly?. . . . .

. . . .

explanation

4

CROWN JEWELS
Ahasuerus viewed Vashti like just another one of his possessions, wanting to use her beauty to showcase the crown jewels. The king should have known that the true jewel was his wife. "Who can find a virtuous and capable wife? She is worth more than precious rubies" (Proverbs 31:10, NLT).

5

OFFENDED
Vashti's refusal was a triple offense: (1) a woman challenging a man; (2) a wife disobeying her husband; (3) a subject defying her king. However, Vashti had received a triple offense herself: (1) he violated the custom keeping men and women segregated; 2) the king affronted her modesty; 3) the command interrupted her royal duties.

transformation

8

GENTLENESS
Gentle means goodness of heart, meekness in dealing with others, or sweet reasonableness. Gentleness displays an equitable fairness that does not insist on the letter of the law. "But the wisdom that comes from heaven is . . . peace loving, gentle at all times, and willing to yield to others" (James 3:17, NLT).

9

CHILDISH
Ahasuerus wanted what he wanted when he wanted it. If he had truly loved Vashti, he would have protected her rather than expose her. True love acts maturely not childishly. "Love is not jealous or boastful or proud or rude. Love does not demand its own way" (1 Corinthians 13:4-5, NLT).

11

MATURITY
Mature Christians exhibit a "trinity" of godly attributes: faith, hope, and love. *Faith* is a belief in God and commitment to His will. *Hope* is a confident expectancy that God is in control of future events. *Love* is the high esteem we should have for God and other people.

8. King Ahasuerus responded in anger. According to Proverbs 15:1, how could the king have responded?

. . . .

9. We see in this passage that the man who ruled the world could not control his own heart.

Journal about a time when you responded childishly because you didn't get your way.

. . . .

. . . .

. . . .

. . . .

. . . .

10. Our Scripture promise for today (1 Corinthians 13:11) reveals that growing Christians are willing to put away childish things in order to grow into spiritual maturity. From the list, check the childish characteristics you need to put away.

— temper tantrums   — manipulating

— pouting   — teasing

— demanding   — whining

— begging   — other_____

11. The apostle Paul wrote: "When I was a child, I spoke as a child, I understood as a child, I thought as a child; but when I became a man, I put away childish things. For now we see in a mirror, dimly, but then face to face. Now I know in part, but then I shall know just as I also am known. And now abide faith, hope, love, these three; but the greatest of these is love" (1 Corinthians 13:11-13).

Journal this Scripture passage into a prayer, asking God to help you put away childish things and put on faith, hope, and love.

. . . .

. . . .

. . . .

. . . .

. . . .

. . . .

. . . .

. . . .

Two lessons I learned the hard way are "Never get drunk" and "Never take a dare." I was living in Hadely Hall at Western Michigan University during the long, cold winter of 1977. Boredom induced our dorm to have a kegger party. During a beer-chugging contest I was determined to keep up with the best of them. Sometime past midnight Stu, the party animal, snickered and said, "I dare you to pull the fire alarm." My impaired mind thought, *His challenge must not go unmet.* In a stupor I staggered down the hallway to the stairwell, opened the red box, pulled the lever, and ran for cover. Stu found me in the bathroom laughing as the entire building of students was evacuated into the snowy night, while three emergency vehicles came screaming down the street.

Weeks later, when my friends found out who the culprit was, they were furious with me. I discovered that sounding a false fire alarm was a felony. I could have gone to jail or paid a hefty fine. I lived in fear of being exposed to the authorities for the rest of the semester. Drinking resulted in childish behavior and some very bad judgment on my part.

Ahasuerus, though ruler of a vast empire, was ruled by wine and childish emotions. If you are a mature Christian, you will be ruled by a gracious God, who enables you to be self-controlled; you won't give in to the dares made by the world.

contemplation
A big part of Christian maturity is learning to let God keep you steady and to be ruled less and less by your emotions and circumstances.
Twila Paris

DAY 4 — A KING'S COUNSELORS

preparation

God, help me to be discerning when seeking counsel. Keep my ears clear from the cluttered advice of ungodly sources and open to You and Your Word. Amen.

WISE COUNSEL
Oh, the joys of those who do not follow the advice of the wicked, or stand around with sinners, or join in with scoffers. But they delight in doing everything the Lord wants.
Psalm 1:1-2, NLT

Where do you go when you want advice? Millions of people today turn to astrology. "A [recent] poll reported that 47 percent of people believe astrology has some scientific truth," Conan O'Brien noted on his *Late Night* show. "I don't believe in astrology because I'm an Aries, and we're really skeptical." We found well over a million astrology Web sites on the Internet and learned that astrology is big business. One site offered an astrology shopping mall, complete with an international currency converter so people can spend any kind of money. The astrologers to celebrities charge up to two hundred dollars per reading. People are willing to pay big bucks to find out who they are compatible with, what their job prospects are, and what the future holds. These people are looking to the stars for help when they should seek the Star worth gazing at: Jesus, "the Bright and Morning Star" (Revelation 22:16).

King Ahasuerus was looking for advice too, so he turned to seven wise guys—his personal astrologers who consulted the stars and used various forms of divination. They overreacted to the situation to inflate their own importance. They encouraged the king to act rashly instead of rationally. He would live to regret heeding their counsel.

exploration

We have seen the worldly king Ahasuerus at his worst. Today we find that he sought poor counsel to help him deal with his marital problems.

Review Esther 1; then focus on verses 13-18.

> **Then the king said to the wise men who understood the times (for this was the king's manner toward all who**

*knew law and justice, those closest to him being
Carshena, Shethar, Admatha, Tarshish, Meres, Marsena,
and Memucan, the seven princes of Persia and Media,
who had access to the king's presence, and who ranked
highest in the kingdom): . . . Esther 1:13-14*

1. Describe the men whose advice the king sought.

. . . .

2. Why did he seek their counsel? . . . .

. . . .

*"What shall we do to Queen Vashti, according to law,
because she did not obey the command of King
Ahasuerus brought to her by the eunuchs?" Esther 1:15*

3. How did the king turn a domestic matter into a legal matter?

. . . .

*And Memucan answered before the king and the princes:
"Queen Vashti has not only wronged the king, but also
all the princes, and all the people who are in all the
provinces of King Ahasuerus. For the queen's behavior
will become known to all women, so that they will
despise their husbands in their eyes, when they report,
'King Ahasuerus commanded Queen Vashti to be brought
in before him, but she did not come.'" Esther 1:16-17*

4. According to Memucan, who would be affected by the queen's
behavior?

. . . .

5. What repeated word reveals that Memucan was exaggerating?

. . . .

*"This very day the noble ladies of Persia and Media will
say to all the king's officials that they have heard of the
behavior of the queen. Thus there will be excessive
contempt and wrath." Esther 1:18*

---

explanation

1

WISE MEN
Wise men served as
astrologers, magicians,
and soothsayers. God's
prophets confounded
the counsel of pagan
"wise men." Moses
vanquished Pharaoh's
magicians. God gave
Joseph, not the sooth-
sayers, the interpreta-
tion to Pharaoh's
dream. Daniel was wiser
than Nebuchadnezzar's
astrologers. "Your
commands make me
wiser than my enemies"
(Psalm 119:98, NLT).

5

EXAGGERATION
Exaggeration means to
enlarge beyond the
truth or to misrepresent
by overstating. Exag-
geration is a form of
manipulation. A good
rule of thumb: Never
say *all, every,* or *always*
when trying to make
your point. *Every* time
you do, you will *always*
get into trouble of *all*
kinds.

6

CHAUVINISM
Does one bad woman spoil the whole bunch? The king and his wise men thought so, and judged all women unfairly. Just because one woman makes an unpopular choice doesn't mean that all others will follow mindlessly. "You husbands must love your wives with the same love Christ showed the church" (Ephesians 5:25, NLT).

8

MANIPULATION
Ahasuerus and his queen were in conflict. He blamed Vashti and went to biased friends to manipulate the situation in his favor. Perhaps some soul-searching and conflict resolution might have repaired their marriage. "God blesses those who work for peace, for they will be called the children of God" (Matthew 5:9, NLT).

9

COUNSEL
A wise person pursues a variety of counselors. A foolish one listens to it all. How do you discern bad counsel? If it is contrary to Scripture or God's character, it is unreliable. "The counsel of the Lord stands forever, the plans of His heart to all generations" (Psalm 33:11).

6. What did Memucan fear the Medo-Persian women would do?

. . . .

transformation

7. You cannot have a relationship without encountering some conflicts. It has been said that if two people always agree on everything, one of them is not thinking.

> Journal about a situation in your life when you were in conflict with another person. What caused the conflict? How did you seek to resolve it?

. . . .

. . . .

. . . .

8. Real conflict resolution must avoid trying to manipulate others and instead honestly represent the truth. Place an *M* in front of the different forms of manipulative behaviors you've used trying to end conflict, and put an *H* in front of the honest attempts you've used to reconcile with others.

— exaggeration   — forgiveness

— repentance   — bringing up the past

— gossip   — prayer

— silent treatment   — false accusations

— pastoral advice   — turning the other cheek

— power tripping   — admitting your faults

9. Our Scripture promise for today (Psalm 1:1-2) encouraged us not to seek the counsel of the ungodly but to seek God's solutions in life. Make a list of people and/or places you have sought for advice. Which are godly? Which are ungodly?

. . . .

. . . .

. . . .

10. The best counsel is God's counsel. Proverbs 2:2-5 says: "Tune your ears to wisdom, and concentrate on understanding. Cry out for insight and understanding. Search for them as you would for lost money or hidden treasure. Then you will understand what it means to fear the Lord, and you will gain knowledge of God" (NLT).

Journal a prayer crying out for understanding and asking God to advise you with wisdom from above.

. . . .

. . . .

. . . .

. . . .

WISDOM
Wisdom is the ability to judge correctly and to follow the best course of action, based on knowledge. The biblical concept of wisdom is different from the world's. Biblical wisdom is humility, reverence, and obedience toward God. "If any of you lacks wisdom, let him ask of God" (James 1:5).

Surfing the television with a remote control in your living room or hanging ten off the shores of Waikiki can be dangerous. Either way, you could get carried away by a riptide or be attacked by a shark. Recently I was surfing the ocean of cable television when I encountered a steely eyed predator. A man named John Edward, dressed like a model from Banana Republic, was standing in the middle of a circular auditorium. The audience waited anxiously for him to make contact with a loved one who had "crossed over." He would stop abruptly, cock his head, and stare into space. Then he began to spew ambiguous information that could be construed to fit almost anybody's experience. He was a master manipulator. Listening to people's sad stories, he would adjust his vision to deceive them with false hope about the well-being of their dearly departed.

He reminded me of the traveling medicine man Dorothy in the *Wizard of Oz* encountered when running away from home. While the gullible girl closed her eyes, he snatched Auntie Em's photograph out of her knapsack and placed it under his mystical crystal ball. A little mumbo jumbo, and Dorothy was putty in his hands.

There's nothing new under the sun. From astrologers in the court of Ahasuerus to late-night infomercials, there are people willing to exploit others for riches and reputation. Don't let these modern mystics take you for a ride. Next time you need advice make sure you ask Jesus first. He is the way, *the truth*, and the life.

contemplation
He who builds according to every man's advice will have a crooked house.
Danish proverb

105

DAY 5 A VINDICTIVE KING

preparation

God, thank You that You make all things beautiful in Your time. Help me to be patient when circumstances are not going the way I planned, and I wait on You to make my future bright. Amen.

FUTURE

"For I know the plans I have for you," says the Lord. "They are plans for good and not for disaster, to give you a future and a hope." Jeremiah 29:11, NLT

It's easy to believe in God's providence when it works to our advantage. But if things get shaky, we mistakenly think God has fallen asleep at the wheel. Charles West observed, "We turn to God when our foundations are shaking, only to learn that it is God who is shaking them." In the book of Esther, we see that providence can be a double-edged sword. In order for Esther to be *in*, Vashti had to go *out*. Providence can seem harmful in the moment, but God promises His children that things will always turn out for the best in eternity. Paul said, "God causes everything to work together for the good of those who love God" (Romans 8:28, NLT). Only time will tell the whole story of God's providential care.

When Joseph was betrayed by his brothers and sold into slavery, it seemed the hand of Providence was against him. But it led Joseph to Egypt where he was made second in command to Pharaoh. Through Joseph's interpretation of a prophetic dream and his wise counsel, Egypt was sustained through a terrible famine. Years after his brothers' betrayal Joseph told them, "You meant evil against me; but God meant it for good, in order to bring it about as it is this day, to save many people alive" (Genesis 50:20). What Memucan meant for evil against Vashti, God meant for good for His chosen people. God wasn't finished with His people in exile.

exploration

Yesterday we saw how King Ahasuerus sought the counsel of men who exaggerated the impact of what Vashti had done and told him what he wanted to hear. Now we learn how these advisors encouraged the king to vent his anger rather than control it.

Review Esther 1; then focus on verses 19-22.

"If it pleases the king, let a royal decree go out from him, and let it be recorded in the laws of the Persians and the Medes, so that it will not be altered, that Vashti shall come no more before King Ahasuerus; and let the king give her royal position to another who is better than she." Esther 1:19

1. Describe the action Memucan encouraged the king to take.

. . . .

2. How would the decree make way for a new queen? Could the decree be changed?

. . . .

"When the king's decree which he will make is proclaimed throughout all his empire (for it is great), all wives will honor their husbands, both great and small." Esther 1:20

3. How far-reaching would the decree be?. . . . .

. . . .

4. What was the desired result of the royal decree? . . . .

. . . .

And the reply pleased the king and the princes, and the king did according to the word of Memucan. Then he sent letters to all the king's provinces, to each province in its own script, and to every people in their own language, that each man should be master in his own house, and speak in the language of his own people. Esther 1:21-22

5. How did the king and princes respond to Memucan's advice?

. . . .

6. How did he ensure that his entire kingdom received the decree?

. . . .

explanation

1

DIVORCE
One scriptural basis for divorce is infidelity. All other excuses reveal hard hearts. "Jesus replied, 'Moses permitted divorce as a concession to your hard-hearted wickedness, but it was not what God had originally intended. . . . A man who divorces his wife and marries another commits adultery—unless his wife has been unfaithful'" (Matthew 19:8-9, NLT).

4

HONOR
Honor means "to esteem or respect." Men aren't better than women, but they hold a God-given position as head of the family. A president isn't a better man than a resident, but we esteem his position. Honor relates to God's order so that a country or a home will run smoothly.

**MASTER OF
THE HOUSE**
The king fooled himself
into believing that his
law could enforce
submission of wives to
their husbands. True
submission begins with
the fear of the Lord,
not the fear of others.
"Submit to one another
out of reverence for
Christ" (Ephesians 5:21,
NLT).

MODERN DIVORCE
In the U.S., divorce has
risen 700 percent in the
last century. In 1920
one in seven marriages
ended in divorce; today,
close to one in two
marriages end in
divorce. "'I hate
divorce!' says the
Lord. . . . 'So guard
yourself; always remain
loyal to your wife'"
(Malachi 2:16, NLT).

7. What information about the husband's role did Ahasuerus include in his royal decree?

. . . .

transformation

8. Because of bad advice and a hard heart, Ahasuerus divorced his wife. We, too, live in an age of careless counsel and calloused hearts.

> Journal about a time when your life was influenced by a divorce: parents, siblings, friends, or yourself. Who was involved? Why did the relationship crumble? How did the split tear you and others apart?

. . . .

. . . .

. . . .

9. Fill in the chart to discover some biblical teaching on marriage and divorce.

SCRIPTURE	LESSON ON DIVORCE
Deut. 24:1-4	. . . .
Mal. 2:15-16	. . . .
Matt. 5:31-32	. . . .
Matt. 19:3-9	. . . .
1 Cor. 7:10-11	. . . .

10. Jesus said that when two people marry, they become united as one. As an experiment, glue two pieces of paper together and let them dry. Then try to tear the pieces apart. What is the result? Can the damage be repaired?

. . . .

. . . .

11. God can make tough hearts tender through the touch of His Spirit and can bring reconciliation. List one person or couple who is currently pursuing a divorce.

. . . .

Journal a prayer, rewriting Ezekiel 11:19-20 into a petition to God on their behalf. "I will give them single-ness of heart and put a new spirit within them. I will take away their hearts of stone and give them tender hearts instead, so they will obey my laws and regulations. Then they will truly be my people, and I will be their God" (NLT).

. . . .

. . . .

. . . .

. . . .

RECONCILIATION
Reconciliation is the restoration of friendship and fellowship after estrangement. In the Old Testament recon-ciliation contains the idea of an "atonement" or covering for sin. In the New Testament it possesses the idea "to change thoroughly from one position to another" (adapted, Unger's).

Had Ahasuerus consulted the true God about his marriage, he would have received counsel that was completely different from the advice seven wise guys gave him. The king was angry. Instead of offering a gentle answer to turn away his wrath, the counselors agitated him further. By taking their advice, Ahasuerus shattered his marriage. All the king's horses and all the king's men would not be able to put it back together again.

Jesus said, "God blesses those who work for peace, for they will be called the children of God" (Matthew 5:9, NLT). In his book on the Beatitudes titled *The Heavenly Octave*, F. W. Boreham wrote, "The ideal peacemaker is the man who prevents the peace from being broken. To prevent a battle is the best way of winning a battle. I once said to a Jewish rabbi, 'I have heard that at a Jewish wedding a glass is broken as part of the symbolism of the cere-mony. Is that a fact?' 'It certainly is,' he replied. 'We hold aloft a glass, let it fall and be shattered to atoms, and then, pointing to its fragments, we exhort the young people to guard jealously the sacred relationship into which they have entered since, once it is fractured, it can never be restored.'"

contemplation
Reconciliation is not weakness or cowardice. It demands courage, nobility, generosity, sometimes heroism, an overcoming of oneself rather than of one's adversary.
Pope Paul VI

Persia's Beauty Pageant

What's more American than baseball and apple pie? Miss America. Little girls all over the U.S. dream that one day they might wear the crown and parade down the runway. Contestants from all fifty states line up, flashing their bleached-white smiles at an audience inflicted with temporary blindness. These beauties are judged in four categories: talent, interview, on-stage personality in evening wear, and physical fitness in swimsuit.

Many contestants have participated in pageants since they were children, taking one high-heeled step after another toward the runway. A 1995 *Time* magazine article revealed how the women grow more savvy with each contest: "Many wear Firm Grip, a sports adhesive, to keep their swimsuits from riding up. Miss Vermont eats bananas to steady her nerves. Miss Indiana confides, 'I have really fine hair, so I fill in my hairline with dark eye shadow.'"

Beauty contests are nothing new. King Ahasuerus's servants encouraged him to hold his own Miss Persia pageant. Contestants were recruited from every province in the empire. The girls underwent extensive beauty preparations for the spectacle. They were judged in two categories: beauty and personal interview. There was only one judge: King Ahasuerus. The girls who didn't win would be doomed to a life of oblivion, but the winner would be crowned queen of Persia.

DAY 1
The Contestants

DAY 2
Least Likely to Succeed

DAY 3
The Runners-Up

DAY 4
The Winner

DAY 5
Mr. Congeniality

DAY 1 THE CONTESTANTS

preparation

Father, thank You that I don't have to compete for Your affection. You chose me, not because of the way I look, but because You love me. Your love is better than any earthly crown. Amen.

CHOSEN
You didn't choose me. I chose you. I appointed you to go and produce fruit that will last. John 15:16, NLT

explanation

TIME MARCHES
Three years had passed since Ahasuerus banished his wife, during which time he had launched a disastrous attack against the Greeks. After he had been defeated, it was time to rebuild his life and his kingdom. "There is a time for every-thing. . . . A time to kill and a time to heal" (Ecclesiastes 3:1-3, NLT).

exploration

Last week we met Ahasuerus, the most powerful man in the world. He was a vengeful and prideful pagan king who lived a decadent life. He took the advice of self-serving men to dethrone his wife, the beautiful Queen Vashti, making way for God's choice for queen of Persia. This week we will see God providentially working behind the scenes in Ahasuerus's court, promoting Esther and her cousin Mordecai to positions of prominence. This chapter shows that God works in even the most carnal and secular of places to accomplish His purposes.

Read Esther 2; then focus on verses 1-4.

> *After these things, when the wrath of King Ahasuerus subsided, he remembered Vashti, what she had done, and what had been decreed against her.* Esther 2:1

1. Reviewing last week's lesson, what does "After these things" refer to?

. . . .

2. What gives you the impression that Ahasuerus regretted his rash decision to depose Queen Vashti?

. . . .

3. Why could the king now remember Vashti fondly?

. . . .

Then the king's servants who attended him said: "Let beautiful young virgins be sought for the king; and let the king appoint officers in all the provinces of his kingdom, that they may gather all the beautiful young virgins to Shushan the citadel, into the women's quarters, under the custody of Hegai the king's eunuch, custodian of the women. And let beauty preparations be given them. Then let the young woman who pleases the king be queen instead of Vashti." This thing pleased the king, and he did so. Esther 2:2-4

4. Describe the suggestion the king's servants made.

. . . .

5. Into whose care would the girls be placed? . . . .

. . . .

6. How would the girls be prepared to meet the king?

. . . .

. . . .

7. What would become of the young woman who pleased the king?

. . . .

. . . .

8. How did the king respond to this suggestion? . . . .

. . . .

transformation

9. There are times and seasons in every life. The king had gone from a season of war to a time of peace. He also wanted to move from a time of loneliness to a time for a new queen. Review Ecclesiastes 3:1-8 below. Underline the seasons you are presently experiencing. Then circle the seasons for which you are anxiously waiting.

3

ANGER SUBSIDES
Ahasuerus couldn't move forward until he let go of his anger. When he finally did, it was too late. His wife was in exile, and he was trapped by his own legislation. "Get rid of all bitterness, rage, anger, harsh words. . . . Instead, be kind to each other" (Ephesians 4:31-32, NLT).

5

EUNUCH
A *eunuch* was a male servant of a royal household, often castrated as a precautionary measure to serve among the ruler's wives (adapted, *Nelson's*). "Some are born as eunuchs, some have been made that way by others, and some choose not to marry for the sake of the Kingdom" (Matthew 19:12, NLT).

9

SEASONS
Winter's cold is chilling, while summer's sun brings warmth. However, all sunshine and no rain make a desert. Each season has a purpose. "Let us not grow weary while doing good, for in due season we shall reap if we do not lose heart" (Galatians 6:9).

FORGIVENESS
Forgiveness goes beyond pardoning someone for a wrong he or she committed. It must also lead to an end of feeling resentment toward the offender. "When you are praying, first forgive anyone you are holding a grudge against, so that your Father in heaven will forgive your sins, too" (Mark 11:25, NLT).

To everything there is a season,
A time for every purpose under heaven:
A time to be born, and a time to die;
A time to plant, and a time to pluck what is planted;
A time to kill, and a time to heal;
A time to break down, and a time to build up;
A time to weep, and a time to laugh;
A time to mourn, and a time to dance;
A time to cast away stones, and a time to gather stones;
A time to embrace, and a time to refrain from embracing;
A time to gain, and a time to lose;
A time to keep, and a time to throw away;
A time to tear, and a time to sew;
A time to keep silence, and a time to speak;
A time to love, and a time to hate;
A time of war, and a time of peace.

> Journal a prayer asking God to give you grace and hope through all the seasons of your life.

. . . .
. . . .
. . . .
. . . .

10. Sadly, it took King Ahasuerus three years and defeat in a battle to get over his anger toward his ex-wife.

> Journal about someone you've been angry with, the length of time your anger lasted, and the reason for it. Have you forgiven those who provoked you?

. . . .
. . . .
. . . .
. . . .
. . . .

11. Read the following verse and answer the questions. "'Don't sin by letting anger gain control over you.' Don't let the sun go down while you are still angry, for anger gives a mighty foothold to the Devil" (Ephesians 4:26-27, NLT).

a. When does anger become a sin?. . . . .

. . . .

b. How long should your anger last? . . . .

. . . .

c. What is the consequence of anger that lasts longer than a day?

. . . .

RIGHTEOUS ANGER
All anger is not wrong. Even "[God] is angry with the wicked" (Psalm 7:11, NLT). Aristotle said, "To be angry with the right person, and to the right degree, and at the right time, and for the right purpose, and in the right way . . . is not easy."

If a rattlesnake is cornered, it becomes so frenzied that it will accidentally bite itself with its own deadly fangs. In the same way, when people harbor anger, the poison of their own wrath often hurts them.

I remember a time when taunting my younger brother, Scott, made him spittin' mad. I was a scrawny ten-year-old equipped with a sharp tongue, and Scott was powerless against my constant mocking. My favorite subject of ridicule included a freckle-faced girl with glasses named Melissa. I knew he couldn't stand her, so I would chide, "Kissy, kissy, kissy, Melissy, lissy, lissy." When he reached the boiling point he jumped off the kitchen counter and tackled me to the floor with his fists flailing. I should have apologized, but all I could do was laugh, making him madder still. When Mom walked in, boy did Scott get it! In high school he still harbored resentment toward me. My immaturity provoked Scott to anger and I regretted it, but it was too late to take back my biting words.

It seems that Ahasuerus regretted his ugly words and actions in dethroning Vashti. But it was too late to make amends. She was dethroned, and God had a plan to put a new woman in the palace.

As a Christian, I've worked hard to make amends with my brother. Today our friendship flourishes with words that build up rather than tear down.

contemplation
He that would be angry and sin not must not be angry with anything but sin.
Thomas Secker

DAY 2 LEAST LIKELY TO SUCCEED

preparation

Lord, thank You for viewing me differently than the world does. You see the potential in me and have elevated me to a place in Your kingdom despite my flaws. Amen.

GOD'S CHOICE
Remember, dear brothers and sisters, that few of you were wise in the world's eyes, or powerful, or wealthy when God called you. Instead, God deliberately chose things the world considers foolish in order to shame those who think they are wise. 1 Corinthians 1:26-27, NLT

Most high schools have mock elections where the graduating class votes for their fellow students in such categories as: Class Clown, Most Spirited, and Most Likely to Succeed. I come from a long line of women voted Best Dressed. My mother won this award in the '50s; my sister and I won in '74 and '76 respectively. I eventually attended Western Michigan University to study fashion merchandising.

However, everyone pities the people who win Least Likely to Succeed. They must battle to prove their classmates wrong. Adolescence was agonizing for one five-foot-two-inch high school sophomore. He had only one date in four years. Today actor Kevin Costner has no problems getting a date.

Those observing the beauty pageant for queen of Persia could have voted Esther Least Likely to Succeed. She was from a minority race. Her ancestors were slaves. She was an orphan adopted into a single-parent family. Yet despite her shortcomings Esther had great potential. She was like a tiny bud waiting to blossom. God shone the light of His favor upon her so that the palace officials took notice of her. When they did, she was plucked from obscurity and transplanted into a prominent position in the king's household.

exploration

The author now takes us back in time before Ahasuerus's reign to the period when the Jews were taken into captivity. In this way we are introduced to the hero and heroine of our story: Mordecai and Esther.

Review Esther 2; then focus on verses 5-10.

In Shushan the citadel there was a certain Jew whose name was Mordecai the son of Jair, the son of Shimei, the son of Kish, a Benjamite. Kish had been carried away from Jerusalem with the captives who had been captured with Jeconiah king of Judah, whom Nebuchadnezzar the king of Babylon had carried away. Esther 2:5-6

1. Identify Mordecai's ancestors and explain how they came to be in Shushan.

. . . .

And Mordecai had brought up Hadassah, that is, Esther, his uncle's daughter, for she had neither father nor mother. The young woman was lovely and beautiful. When her father and mother died, Mordecai took her as his own daughter. Esther 2:7

2. Describe whom Mordecai adopted.

. . . .

3. What was the girl's Hebrew name? What was her Persian name?

. . . .

. . . .

4. Why would Esther attract the attention of those seeking women for the king?

. . . .

So it was, when the king's command and decree were heard, and when many young women were gathered at Shushan the citadel, under the custody of Hegai, that Esther also was taken to the king's palace, into the care of Hegai the custodian of the women. Now the young woman pleased him, and she obtained his favor; so he readily gave beauty preparations to her, besides her allowance. Then seven choice maidservants were provided for her from the king's palace, and he moved her and her maidservants to the best place in the house of the women. Esther 2:8-9

1

BENJAMITES
Mordecai hailed from the tribe of Benjamin, the smallest tribe of Israel. Israel's first king, Saul, was a Benjamite. Kish was called a mighty man of power. Shimei, out of loyalty to Saul, cursed David as he fled Jerusalem. The apostle Paul was of the tribe of Benjamin too.

3

NAME-CALLING
Hadassah is a Hebrew name that means "myrtle." The myrtle tree produced white flowers used for perfume and was a symbol of peace and joy. *Esther,* her Persian name, means "star." Her names were prophetic since she would rise as a star among her people, bringing them peace and joy.

DISCRETION
Not only did Esther possess outward beauty, she also possessed "the incorruptible beauty of a gentle and quiet spirit, which is very precious in the sight of God" (1 Peter 3:4). Her discretion and obedience were qualities that enhanced her physical beauty.

CAPTIVITY
Captivity was living in bondage to one's enemies, usually after being deported to a foreign land. It commonly described two periods when the nations of Israel (722–721 B.C.) and Judah (586 B.C. and later) were taken from their native lands and exiled. Captivity was a humiliating punishment for disobedient, idolatrous people (adapted, *Nelson's*).

GOD'S FAVOR
Esther received favor from a man, the king's eunuch. However, all blessing and favor originate from the hand of God. Another captive of Persia also received the favor of God and his colleagues: "Now God had brought Daniel into the favor and goodwill of the chief of the eunuchs" (Daniel 1:9).

5. Who was Esther's supervisor at the citadel? How and why did he show her special favor?

. . . .

Esther had not revealed her people or family, for Mordecai had charged her not to reveal it. Esther 2:10

6. How did Esther act discreetly and obediently while at the citadel?

. . . .

transformation

7. The Israelites in Persia had been taken captive by their enemy Nebuchadnezzar and carried away to Babylon. Christians can be taken captive by their enemy, the devil, and be carried away by sin. Read the following verse and answer the questions. "Then they will come to their senses and escape from the Devil's trap. For they have been held captive by him to do whatever he wants" (2 Timothy 2:26, NLT).

Journal about a time when you were caught in the devil's snare. How did God bring you to your senses? How did you escape the trap?

. . . .

. . . .

. . . .

. . . .

8. Esther found favor in the king's court. Fill in the chart to discover other men and women in the Bible who found favor in the eyes of God and others.

SCRIPTURE	WHO FOUND FAVOR?	WITH WHOM?
Gen. 39:2-4; 21-22		
Exod. 12:35-36		

Luke 1:29-31. . . . .

Luke 2:52 . . . .

9. Check the blessings that you have received from God's favor.

    — Mercy (Isa. 60:10)
    — Good wife/spouse (Prov. 18:22)
    — Life (Job 10:12)
    — Stability (Ps. 30:7)
    — Protection (Ps. 5:12)
    — Physical healing (1 Kings 13:6)

Journal a prayer to God, thanking Him for His favor in the past and asking Him for new favor in the future.

. . . .

. . . .

. . . .

UNFAVORABLE
God gives favor and God can take it away if you turn your back on Him and His Word. "Because your fathers have forsaken Me . . . and not kept My law . . . I will not show you favor" (Jeremiah 16:11-13).

An underdog is the victim of injustice or persecution, the predicted loser in a contest. Think of the movies *Bad News Bears, Rocky,* or *The Mighty Ducks.* These are classic examples of the struggle between the haves and the have-nots, the highly esteemed and the under-estimated. There's no satisfaction like seeing the top dogs get their comeuppance while the underdog beats the odds.

Maybe we love to see the underdogs on top because at one time or another we have been the people no one thought would make it. Perhaps you applied to an Ivy League university when you came from a minor league school, or developed a crush on an uptown boy when you lived downtown. The good news is that God backs underdogs too. He helped the Israelite slaves against the power-tripping Pharaoh, the sheepherder David against the sword-wielding Goliath, and Esther the foreigner competing against Persian beauties who had the hometown advantage. God's divine hand can elevate saints, both past and present, above the worst of circumstances. If you've found yourself in a no-win situation, remember, "with God everything is possible" (Matthew 19:26, NLT).

contemplation
God looks with favor at pure, not full, hands.
Latin Proverb

DAY 3 THE RUNNERS-UP

preparation

Lord, the world often makes me feel like an anonymous, nameless number. Thank You for calling me by name and leading me out of the world. Amen.

PROMISE
He calls his own sheep by name and leads them out. John 10:3

Brainteasers challenge our mental acumen, testing our knowledge of the trivial. Put on your thinking cap, and take the following quiz:

1. Name the second wealthiest person in the world.
2. Name the teams that lost the last three World Series.
3. Name the women nominated with Gwyneth Paltrow for the Academy Award.
4. Name the runners-up for last year's Miss America contest.

How did you do? None of us remember the nameless runners-up in competitions, unless of course, *we* were the runner-up. I (Penny) will never forget being a runner-up. I had been a cheerleader throughout high school. I thought I was a shoo-in to make the varsity squad my senior year. I had already looked through the uniform catalogues and chosen my favorite letter sweater. I added two new jumps to my cheer and threw in splits at the end. Naturally I'd be chosen, right? Wrong! I came in a few votes shy of the coveted position. My mother called it a "character-building experience"; I was humiliated to be labeled "the alternate."

The women who tried out for queen of Persia dedicated a year to preparing for their tryout, but they didn't quite make the cut. Only one could be the winner; the rest would have to settle for runners-up.

exploration

At this point in the story our attention shifts to the young women who competed for the king's affections. Once again we are reminded of how much greater God's kingdom is than the kingdoms of this world.

Review Esther 2; then focus on verses 11-14.

And every day Mordecai paced in front of the court of the women's quarters, to learn of Esther's welfare and what was happening to her. Esther 2:11

1. How did Mordecai continue to watch after his adopted daughter?

. . . .

Each young woman's turn came to go in to King Ahasuerus after she had completed twelve months' preparation, according to the regulations for the women, for thus were the days of their preparation apportioned: six months with oil of myrrh, and six months with perfumes and preparations for beautifying women. Thus prepared, each young woman went to the king, and she was given whatever she desired to take with her from the women's quarters to the king's palace. Esther 2:12-13

2. Describe the beauty treatments the young women underwent to prepare for their time with the king.

. . . .

3. How long did these beauty preparations take?. . . . .

. . . .

4. When the time came for a young woman to go to the king, what was she allowed to take with her?

. . . .

In the evening she went, and in the morning she returned to the second house of the women, to the custody of Shaashgaz, the king's eunuch who kept the concubines. She would not go in to the king again unless the king delighted in her and called for her by name. Esther 2:14

5. How long did the women have to make a good impression on the king?

. . . .

explanation

1

GUARDIAN
Guardians are lookouts who protect and defend. Mordecai paced outside Esther's room. As our faithful guardian, God's eyes do the pacing. "The eyes of the Lord run to and fro throughout the whole earth, to show Himself strong on behalf of those whose heart is loyal to Him" (2 Chronicles 16:9).

3

PRIMPING
Extensive beauty preparations revealed the tremendous emphasis placed on physical appearance in Persia. Women used their looks to gain position and status. It is not much different today. If we would spend this kind of time and our resources to cultivate inner beauty, the world would be a better place.

CONCUBINES

Once these women had been with King Ahasuerus, they belonged to him and couldn't marry. They became concubines, not wives. In Old Testament times a concubine was a female with whom a man was legally permitted to have sexual relations (adapted, *Nelson's*).

STAND GUARD

The most vulnerable part of a person is the heart. Drugs and alcohol or peer pressure and persuasion can destroy vital defense mechanisms. Once your guard is down your life is vulnerable to a hostile takeover. "Above all else, guard your heart, for it affects everything you do" (Proverbs 4:23, NLT).

INWARD BEAUTY

Outward beauty will fade away. Time and gravity eventually take their toll. Inward beauty lasts for eternity. God's Word and His Spirit will revitalize our souls. "We do not lose heart. Even though our outward man is perishing, yet the inward man is being renewed day by day" (2 Corinthians 4:16).

6. Explain the fate of the women after they visited the king.

. . . .

transformation

7. Just as Mordecai guarded Esther, God guards His people. Fill in the chart to discover what God will guard.

SCRIPTURE	GUARDED BY GOD
1 Sam. 2:9	
Ps. 127:1	
Prov. 2:8	
Phil. 4:7	

Journal about an area in your life in which you feel vulnerable, and write a prayer asking God to "stand guard" where your defenses are weak.

. . . .

. . . .

. . . .

. . . .

8. It took a year of beauty preparations for the women to meet the king. Think of your own inner and outer beauty preparations. In the space provided, write a list of things you do in the course of a year to make yourself beautiful physically (outwardly), and then write a list of the things you do to make yourself beautiful spiritually (inwardly).

Outward Treatments	**Inward Treatments**
1.	1.
2.	2.
3.	3.
4.	4.

9. Examine your lists of beauty treatments. Do you spend the most time on outer or inner beauty?

> Journal a prayer asking God to help you make His standard of beauty your own by rewriting this verse: "Charm is deceptive, and beauty does not last; but a woman who fears the Lord will be greatly praised" (Proverbs 31:30, NLT).

. . . .

. . . .

. . . .

. . . .

. . . .

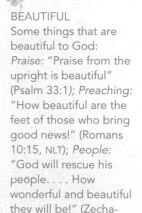

9

BEAUTIFUL
Some things that are beautiful to God: *Praise:* "Praise from the upright is beautiful" (Psalm 33:1); *Preaching:* "How beautiful are the feet of those who bring good news!" (Romans 10:15, NLT); *People:* "God will rescue his people. . . . How wonderful and beautiful they will be!" (Zechariah 9:16-17, NLT).

As I (Penny) was walking in the Sandia Mountains one spring day, I stumbled across a cluster of fragrant flowers thriving among the rocks and weeds, unnoticed and untended. I breathed in their sweet scent. It made me think about some of the women attending our women's Bible study who live beautiful and fragrant lives but often go unnoticed.

I thought of Minnie, who comes in every Monday morning to make hundreds of copies of homework for women who don't even know her name. And Olive who is easily overlooked because she's small and fragile, but she greets everyone she meets with a kiss. And the child-care workers who faithfully show up every week to watch the kids. These fragrant lives may seem obscure, but they faithfully fulfill God's calling. When God brings us to heaven, He won't ask, "Did anyone notice you?" I believe His question will be, "Did you serve Me with all your heart where I placed you?"

We don't know the fate of the obscure women in Ahasuerus's kingdom. Yet they serve as a poignant reminder that any situation has possibilities. We can bloom where God has planted us, whether in a hothouse or on a hillside.

contemplation
Beauty without virtue is a flower without perfume.
French proverb

DAY 4 THE WINNER

preparation

Lord, Your love is incomparable. You loved me before I was even born. Though I cannot see You, I love You. I long to see You face-to-face. Amen.

PROMISE
"I have loved you, my people, with an everlasting love. With unfailing love I have drawn you to myself."
Jeremiah 31:3, NLT

Love at first sight, the phenomenon of the heart, happens when a wistful glance from a distance sparks the eternal flames of love. Poets and historians throughout the ages have recorded the stories of young lovers whose hearts were ignited by the mere sight of one another. When Shakespeare's Romeo spotted the fair Juliet across a crowded ballroom, he was compelled to seek her bedroom window, regardless of the danger, for just one sight of her. When she appeared on the balcony, he sighed, "But, soft! What light through yonder window breaks? It is the east, and Juliet is the sun. . . . It is my lady; O! it is my love."

Playing the flirt, Josephine caught young General Napoleon's attention, and he was instantly mesmerized. A letter written by Napoleon to his love in 1796 reads, "I wake filled with thoughts of you. Your portrait and the intoxicating evening which we spent yesterday have left my senses in turmoil. Sweet, incomparable Josephine, what a strange effect you have on my heart!"

Love at first sight is possible, and it is powerful. It has changed the fate of people and the course of history. In Persia, love turned the heart of King Ahasuerus. He had seen a pageant of beautiful women, but none had won his heart—until he saw the incomparable Esther. When he did, he couldn't live without her and made her his queen.

exploration

Esther risked great disappointment in becoming just another member of the king's harem. Yet God, in His providence, had great plans for her.

Review Esther 2; then focus on verses 15-18.

Now when the turn came for Esther the daughter of Abihail the uncle of Mordecai, who had taken her as his daughter, to go in to the king, she requested nothing but what Hegai the king's eunuch, the custodian of the women, advised. And Esther obtained favor in the sight of all who saw her. So Esther was taken to King Ahasuerus, into his royal palace, in the tenth month, which is the month of Tebeth, in the seventh year of his reign. Esther 2:15-16

1. How was Esther described in verse 15? . . . .

   . . . .

2. Explain what Esther asked for when her turn came to visit the king.

   . . . .

3. What was the people's response to Esther? . . . .

   . . . .

The king loved Esther more than all the other women, and she obtained grace and favor in his sight more than all the virgins; so he set the royal crown upon her head and made her queen instead of Vashti. Then the king made a great feast, the Feast of Esther, for all his officials and servants; and he proclaimed a holiday in the provinces and gave gifts according to the generosity of a king. Esther 2:17-18

4. How did the king feel about Esther? . . . .

   . . . .

5. How did the king reveal that Esther was chosen to be his wife?

   . . . .

6. Describe the celebration held for the king's new bride.

   . . . .

explanation

2

ADVICE
Esther would have had no way of knowing what would please a Persian king. She placed herself in the hands of Hegai who had inside knowledge of what would please Ahasuerus. God said, "Good advice and success belong to me. Insight and strength are mine" (Proverbs 8:14, NLT).

4

MARITAL LOVE
Love in this instance means a strong emotional attachment and desire either to possess or to be in the presence of the person. Such love is rooted in sexual desire, although as a rule, it is desire within the bounds of lawful relationships (adapted, *Vine's*).

6

HOLIDAY
Persian kings liked to party. This was the fourth celebration mentioned in this book. Ahasuerus wanted his subjects to love his queen as he did. The holiday the king proclaimed probably included: (1) taxes and debt canceled, (2) vacation time from work, and (3) servants or captives to be set free.

transformation

God's clothing advice? Modesty is the best policy! "I want women to be modest. . . . They should . . . not draw attention to themselves by the way they fix their hair or by wearing gold or pearls or expensive clothes. [They] should make themselves attractive by the good things they do" (1 Timothy 2:9-10, NLT).

8

BRIDE OF CHRIST
The church is described in Scripture as the bride of Christ. Paul told Christians, "For I promised you as a pure bride to one husband, Christ" (2 Corinthians 11:2, NLT). John the Baptist referred to Jesus as the bridegroom (see John 3:29). Jesus called Himself the bridegroom (see Matthew 9:15).

7. Esther didn't stress out about her clothing, instead she took Hegai's advice. Read the following verses, and answer the questions to discover Jesus' fashion advice. "And why worry about your clothes? Look at the lilies and how they grow. They don't work or make their clothing, yet Solomon in all his glory was not dressed as beautifully as they are. And if God cares so wonderfully for flowers that are here today and gone tomorrow, won't he more surely care for you?" (Matthew 6:28-30, NLT).

a. What example did Jesus give of dressing without stressing?

. . . .

b. What is the moral of this story? . . . .

. . . .

8. Ahasuerus threw a great feast to celebrate his marriage. God will throw a feast to beat all feasts at the marriage supper of the Lamb. Jesus is our heavenly bridegroom and we (the church) are His bride. Read Revelation 19:7-9, then fill in the chart to determine whether you're prepared for your heavenly wedding day.

GROOM'S QUESTIONS	BRIDE'S ANSWERS
Are you ready? (v. 7)	
Are you dressed? (v. 8)	
Are you blessed? (v. 9)	

Journal a love letter to your heavenly Bridegroom, extolling His virtues and exalting His value. Tell Him how you are preparing for your wedding day.

. . . .

. . . .

. . . .

. . . .

9. Ahasuerus gave his people remission from debt, rest from labor, and freedom from captivity. As our greater King, Jesus acts with the same benevolence.

Look up the following verses. Then journal three short prayers of thanksgiving for the gracious gifts these Scriptures impart.

Matthew 11:28 . . . .

. . . .

John 8:36 . . . .

. . . .

Acts 10:43 . . . .

. . . .

9
REMISSION
"*Remission* means to be released or set free from sin. The word in Greek indicates that forgiveness is more than a passive act on God's part" (*Nelson's*). Through the death of His Son, God has taken the initiative to break the grip of sin and set man free for a new way of life in God's Spirit.

What does America think about love at first sight? In a Gallup poll conducted in February 2000, just over half of American adults (52 percent) said they believed in "love at first sight," while 47 percent of the public said they did not. The poll also revealed that four in ten Americans said they have actually fallen in love at first sight.

What does God think about love at first sight? There are several instances in the Bible when God took advantage of the human propensity to fall in love fast. In the Garden of Eden, once Adam saw Eve, his heart began to go pitter-patter, and the rest is history. In ancient Israel, Samson spotted a woman from Timnah and fell head over heels for her and demanded his parents get her for him as a wife. His mother and father were horrified and begged him to find an Israelite wife. What Samson's parents didn't understand was God, in His providence, was pulling on the strings of their son's heart. In Persia, God used love at first sight to transform Esther, a young Jewish woman least likely to succeed, into the winner of the king's heart, a queen's crown, and the country's affection.

contemplation
Women fall in love through their ears and men through their eyes.
Woodrow Wyatt

DAY 5 MR. CONGENIALITY

preparation

Dear Lord, I want to be the kind of friend whom others can trust. Give me a pure heart and gracious lips that are pleasing to You, my King. Amen.

PROMISE

He who loves purity of heart and has grace on his lips, the king will be his friend. Proverbs 22:11

No beauty pageant would be complete without the winner of the congeniality contest: an honor that's given by fellow contestants to the most sociable and harmonious personality in the bunch. The congeniality winner doesn't usually make it to the top-ten finals. She's not always the prettiest or the most talented contender. What she lacks in outward appearance she more than makes up for in personality and social graces. A likely candidate for this title is the contestant who immediately becomes your "new best friend"—the one you can trust with all your deep, dark secrets. She would never stab you in the back or put you down in order to climb up the ladder of success. She remains anonymous until her peers acknowledge her worth and usher her into the limelight.

Behind the scenes of Persia's beauty pageant there was a person with the qualities necessary to win the congeniality contest. There was just one small problem: He was a man. Of course Mordecai didn't make the top-ten list, but he made sure that Esther did. He was her trustworthy advisor who guarded her secret past. He had willingly lived a life of obscurity, literally pacing in the wings, while Esther received the opportunity to become queen. When he discovered a secret that threatened the king, he risked his own life to expose some very dangerous conspirators. It was time for Mordecai to come out of the shadows and into the limelight.

exploration

This week we have seen how God worked behind the scenes to place Esther on the throne of Persia. Today we discover that Mordecai, Esther's guardian, also rose to a position of influence. Review Esther 2; then focus on verses 19-23.

When virgins were gathered together a second time, Mordecai sat within the king's gate. Now Esther had not revealed her family and her people, just as Mordecai had charged her, for Esther obeyed the command of Mordecai as when she was brought up by him. Esther 2:19-20

1. Where could Mordecai be found, and what does that reveal about the position he occupied?

. . . .

2. How do you know that Mordecai didn't obtain this position because of his relationship to the queen?

. . . .

3. Who made sure Mordecai's history was kept a secret and why?

. . . .

. . . .

In those days, while Mordecai sat within the king's gate, two of the king's eunuchs, Bigthan and Teresh, doorkeepers, became furious and sought to lay hands on King Ahasuerus. So the matter became known to Mordecai, who told Queen Esther, and Esther informed the king in Mordecai's name. And when an inquiry was made into the matter, it was confirmed, and both were hanged on a gallows; and it was written in the book of the chronicles in the presence of the king. Esther 2:21-23

4. Describe what Mordecai overheard in the king's gate.

. . . .

5. When Mordecai discovered the threat, how did he protect the king?

. . . .

6. What punishment did the would-be assassins receive?

. . . .

explanation

1
KING'S GATE
To sit in the king's gate meant that Mordecai, a Jewish exile, had obtained a post in the empire's judicial system, most likely serving as a judge or a palace official of some sort. He was on duty in the palace on this occasion.

3
OBEDIENCE
Obedience is carrying out the word and will of another person. In the Bible, obedience is a positive, active response to what a person hears (adapted, *Nelson's*). "Children, obey your parents because you belong to the Lord, for this is the right thing to do" (Ephesians 6:1, NLT).

GOOD DEED
Mordecai's good deed, though recorded, went unrewarded. He didn't act in order to receive a reward but from a sense of duty. Later we will learn that God makes sure this good deed is not wasted. Proverbs 13:21 assures us, "Evil pursues sinners, but to the righteous, good shall be repaid."

PEARLY GATES
Heaven's gates are made of pearl and open wide to those who obey God. "Blessed are those who do His commandments, that they . . . may enter through the gates into the city" (Revelation 22:14).

HONOR
The biblical meaning of the word *honor* is the esteem due another person of virtue, wisdom, and reputation. It is respect paid to superiors, such as God, parents, and kings. It includes submission, obedience, and service (adapted, *Unger's*). Honoring your parents is intended to last a lifetime.

7. How was Mordecai's good deed remembered?

. . . .

transformation

8. Mordecai, like Boaz, was known for sitting in the city gate, a kind of ancient courthouse. Fill in the chart to discover other activities that occurred in the city gates.

SCRIPTURE	LESSON ABOUT THE CITY GATES
Deut. 17:2-5	. . . .
2 Kings 23:8	. . . .
2 Chron. 31:2	. . . .
Neh. 12:25	. . . .

9. Esther was obedient to Mordecai, her adoptive father. She remained submissive throughout her adult years, even after becoming the wife of Ahasuerus.

Using the word *H-O-N-O-R* as an acrostic, journal about some creative ways you can show your parents the respect they are due.

Help . . . .

. . . .

Offer . . . .

. . . .

Nurture . . . .

. . . .

Observe . . . .

. . . .

LESSON 6 - DAY 5

Respect . . . .

. . . .

10. The good deed that Mordecai did for the king was noticed but not rewarded.

> Journal about a good deed you have done for someone on behalf of your King, Jesus Christ. Have you seen a reward for your efforts? When will God set the record straight?

. . . .

. . . .

. . . .

. . . .

TIMELY REWARD
Sometimes it seems as if God doesn't see or remember our good deeds. But God is never late! His rewards will come at just the right time. "The Son of Man will come, . . . and then He will reward each according to his works" (Matthew 16:27).

A missionary couple was returning home from Africa after decades of service. With no retirement fund, they were uncertain of their future. They happened to be booked on the same ship as President Teddy Roosevelt, who was returning from a safari in Africa. When the ship safely reached the New York harbor, a marching band announced the president's arrival. The mayor and all the city officials stood in a reception line. But no one was there to welcome this missionary couple home. They quietly scurried off unnoticed.

Feeling sorry for himself, the man said, "God is not treating us fairly. The president receives a tremendous homecoming for returning from a vacation, yet not one person was here to acknowledge us after years of sacrifice."

His wife interrupted him saying, "But we're not *home* yet!"

Sometimes life just isn't fair, is it? Especially when your focus is on the moment, the right here and now of life. Thankfully, Mordecai's story doesn't end here. In an upcoming lesson, Providence will perform a balancing act in the circumstances of his life. God has a way of making sure that many nice guys who finish last today will end up being first tomorrow or in eternity. Jesus said, "Many who are first will be last, and the last first" (Mark 10:31, NIV). If you're feeling neglected, remember, "You're not home yet!" A wonderful welcome and reward await you in heaven, your true home.

contemplation
He that does good
for God's sake seeks
neither praise nor
reward; he is sure
of both in the end.
William Penn

Haman's Holocaust

The Holocaust conjures up visions of a living nightmare: emaciated human beings reduced to skin and bones, mass graves layered with bullet-ridden corpses, gas chambers emitting toxic fumes of death, and crematoriums billowing the ashes of doomed people. Adolf Hitler instigated these atrocities in Nazi Germany during World War II against the Jewish nation, God's chosen people.

Hitler's holocaust began in Germany when he rose to power in 1933. Jews were disenfranchised, terrorized in anti-Jewish riots, forced into ghettos, stripped of property, and were finally sent to concentration camps. Hitler established these death camps to implement what he called "the final solution of the Jewish question." By the time World War II ended, 6 million Jews had been exterminated by Hitler's anti-Semitic reign of terror.

Centuries before Hitler, another holocaust plan was formulated when Haman rose to power under King Ahasuerus in the Persian Empire. Haman's diabolical scheme also evolved from intense anti-Semitism. Hatred of the Jews is nothing new. It began in the heart of Satan, who has spread his propaganda of racism and prejudice throughout the ages. In the Old Testament the Egyptians enslaved the Israelites. When they were freed and entered the Promised Land, many surrounding nations became their bitter enemies. Haman's ancestors had been tainted by Satan's racist lies, and they passed the poison on to him.

1 RISING TO POWER

preparation

*God, help me to love
Your chosen people,
Israel, the way You do.
You have called them
Your special treasure
above all others. May
You grant Israel peace
and prosperity. Amen.*

PEACE
*For you [Israel] are a
holy people, who
belong to the Lord your
God. Of all the people
on earth, the Lord your
God has chosen you
to be his own special
treasure. Deuteronomy
7:6, NLT*

exploration

Last week we met Esther and Mordecai, the heroine and hero of our story, and saw God's providential hand at work placing them in positions of prominence in Ahasuerus's kingdom. Now we encounter a powerful man named Haman.

If this story were a melodrama instead of a true story, Haman would be the villain in the black cape and large mustache, the man who plots all kinds of evil against the damsel in distress. In fact, much like a melodrama, whenever the book of Esther is read aloud by Jews today during the Feast of Purim, upon hearing the villainous name Haman, the audience boos, hisses, and shouts, "May his name be blotted out!"

Read Esther 3; then focus on verse 1.

> **After these things King Ahasuerus promoted Haman,
> the son of Hammedatha the Agagite, and advanced him
> and set his seat above all the princes who were with him.**
> Esther 3:1

1. Review the previous lessons on the book of Esther and briefly list what events "after these things" refers to.

   . . . .

   . . . .

   . . . .

2. Whom did the king promote? . . . .

   . . . .

3. Describe the position he received. . . . .

. . . .

4. What was Haman's ancestry?. . . . .

. . . .

5. Read 1 Samuel 15:7-8, then answer the following questions.
   a. From whom did the Agagites descend? . . . .

   . . . .

   b. Over what people did this king rule? . . . .

   . . . .

6. Read Deuteronomy 25:17-18. Explain why God declared war
   on Amalek and his descendants.

   . . . .

7. What promise did God give Israel concerning the Amalekites
   in Deuteronomy 25:19?

   . . . .

transformation

8. In Esther 2 kindhearted Mordecai went unrewarded. In chapter
   3 we see evilhearted Haman receive advancement from the king.

   Journal about a time when you felt your kind intentions
   went unrecognized while someone with ulterior motives
   got ahead. How did you feel?

   . . . .

   . . . .

   . . . .

   . . . .

explanation

5
AGAG'S RULE
Agag was an Amalekite king. The Amalekites became bitter enemies of Israel after their exodus from Egypt. They remained enemies of the Israelites up to the time we meet Haman. Exodus 17:16 tells us, "The Lord has sworn: the Lord will have war with Amalek from generation to generation."

7
FEARLESS
Haman's ancestors didn't fear God. They despised His people and used devious tactics against them. Because Israel's King Saul disobeyed God by not killing King Agag, Saul lost his crown (see 1 Samuel 15). Centuries later Saul's descendant, Mordecai, would face Haman, a deadly descendant of Agag.

8
PERSPECTIVE
The psalmist lost balance viewing life from an earthly perspective: "My feet had almost stumbled . . . when I saw the prosperity of the wicked" (Psalm 73:2-3). He regained balance with an eternal view: "I went into the sanctuary of God; then I understood their end" (Psalm 73:17).

ENEMY
The word *enemy* occurs frequently in the Old Testament, focusing on the idolatrous nations of the ancient world. Israel's enemies were regarded as God's enemies. But in the New Testament, our enemies are primarily spiritual in nature (adapted, *Nelson's*).

10

FEAR GOD
Fear can be either a feeling of reverence and respect or an unpleasant emotion caused by danger (adapted, *Nelson's*). A healthy fear is reverence or respect directed toward God or people. The Bible teaches that the fear of the Lord is the beginning of knowledge and wisdom (see Proverbs 1:7; 16:16).

9. During Old Testament times the Amalekites and Israelites were enemies for several generations. In the New Testament Jesus taught us how to love our enemies: "I say to you, love your enemies, bless those who curse you, do good to those who hate you, and pray for those who spitefully use you and persecute you" (Matthew 5:44).

Name someone who treats you like an enemy, then journal through the following steps.

Step One: "Bless those who curse you." Journal a blessing for your enemy.

. . . .

. . . .

Step Two: "Do good to those who hate you." Journal about a way you will do something good for your enemy.

. . . .

. . . .

Step Three: "Pray for those who . . . persecute you." Journal a prayer for your enemy.

. . . .

. . . .

10. Two kings, Agag and Saul, who did not fear God, reaped the consequence of strife that would last for generations. Fill in the following chart to discover the rewards for fearing God.

SCRIPTURE	REWARDS FOR FEARING GOD
Ps. 25:14	. . . .
Ps. 34:7	. . . .
Ps. 145:19	. . . .
Ps. 147:11	. . . .

A group of boys were playing war games. They set the rules of combat: "When you shoot your rifle, say, 'Bang, bang.' To stab with your bayonet, say, 'Stab, stab.' When throwing your hand grenades, say, 'Lob, lob.'"

One of the young soldiers saw his enemy and said, "Bang, bang," but nothing happened. He ran forward and said, "Stab, stab," but nothing happened. Finally, he fell back and said, "Lob, lob," but still nothing happened. He yelled at the enemy soldier and said, "Hey, you're not playing fair. I said 'Bang, bang,' and 'Stab, stab,' and 'Lob, lob,' and you didn't die."

The other boy replied, "Rumble, rumble. I'm a tank."

Nobody likes a cheater, someone who doesn't play fair. It's not right to change the rules mid-game, and yet it seems that those who do are the ones who get ahead. It's hard to believe the adage saying, "Cheaters never prosper."

It was disappointing to see nice guy Mordecai go unrewarded for doing what was right. It is even more disappointing to watch bad guy Haman get ahead for promoting what is wrong. But in games, as in life, "The game isn't over till it's over." Our lesson last week left us waiting for Mordecai to get his just reward. This week we observe one chapter in the life of Haman where he appears to get ahead through manipulative means. But the book isn't finished. In the chapters to come God makes sure that this cheater doesn't prosper.

contemplation
God sat in silence while the sins of the world were placed upon his Son. Was it right? No. Was it fair? No. Was it love? Yes. In a world of injustice, God once and for all tipped the scales in the favor of hope.
Max Lucado

DAY 2 RESISTING EVIL PEOPLE

preparation

The world and the evil in it scare me sometimes. But I know I need to stand tall on Your behalf. Please give me courage, Lord. Amen.

COURAGE

Be strong and courageous! Do not be afraid of them! The Lord your God will go ahead of you. He will neither fail you nor forsake you. Deuteronomy 31:6, NLT

Viktor Frankl wrote about his experience when the Nazis imprisoned him during World War II for the crime of being born a Jew. Although he survived, his wife, children, and parents were exterminated. The Gestapo agents forced him to strip, and he was left standing naked before them. While they removed his wedding ring, Viktor thought, *You can take away my wife, you can take away my children, you can strip me of my clothes and my freedom, but there is one thing no person can ever take away from me—and that is my freedom to choose how I will react to what happens to me!*

History is full of brave survivors who teach us that life is 10 percent what happens and 90 percent how we respond. Daniel happened to live under a Babylonian dictator who would throw all people who refused to pray to him into a den of lions. Daniel responded in civil disobedience, openly praying to his God. Mordecai happened to live under King Ahasuerus who issued a decree forcing all people in his kingdom to pay homage to Haman, an enemy of the Jews. Taking a stand for God and His people, Mordecai refused to bow to the king's decree.

Sometimes wickedness crashes in on us with such brutality that we're tempted to buckle under its tremendous pressure. But we have a choice. Either we'll bend our knees and surrender our wills or stand tall and defend our faith.

exploration

Haman, the villain of the plot, came on the scene, having gained a high position in Ahasuerus's court. Today we see that Haman's position took on religious overtones.

Review Esther 3; then focus on verses 2-4.

And all the king's servants who were within the king's gate bowed and paid homage to Haman, for so the king had commanded concerning him. But Mordecai would not bow or pay homage. Esther 3:2

1. Explain what the king commanded concerning Haman and how the people responded to this command.

. . . .

. . . .

2. How did Mordecai show that, in his eyes, Haman was unworthy to receive honor?

. . . .

Then the king's servants who were within the king's gate said to Mordecai, "Why do you transgress the king's command?" Now it happened, when they spoke to him daily and he would not listen to them, that they told it to Haman, to see whether Mordecai's words would stand; for Mordecai had told them that he was a Jew. Esther 3:3-4

3. What was Mordecai doing by refusing to honor Haman?

. . . .

4. How often did the servants challenge him concerning his behavior? How did he respond?

. . . .

. . . .

5. What reason do you think Mordecai gave for his refusal to pay homage to Haman?

. . . .

6. To whom did the king's servants go concerning Mordecai's actions?

. . . .

explanation

2
UNWORTHY
Mordecai wasn't holding a personal grudge. But for righteousness' sake he practiced civil disobedience. He refused to honor someone with whom God was at war. "O Lord, shouldn't I hate those who hate you? . . . Yes, I hate them with complete hatred, for your enemies are my enemies" (Psalm 139:21-22, NLT).

4
DAILY GRIND
Mordecai was hounded daily to conform to the world around him. His peers pressured him to do what they did. "Do not be conformed to this world, but be transformed by the renewing of your mind, that you may prove what is that . . . perfect will of God" (Romans 12:2).

REFUSAL
Mordecai's refusal to bow reflected his Jewish upbringing not to honor anyone above God. "Never worship or bow down to them, for I, the Lord your God, am a jealous God who will not share your affection" (Deuteronomy 5:9, NLT). Mordecai, a Jewish conscientious objector, refused to idolize a dishonorable man.

SET APART
Sanctification is the process through which believers are separated *from* the world and set apart *for* God's purposes. This setting apart results in holiness in the life of God's people. "You can be sure of this: The Lord has set apart the godly for himself" (Psalm 4:3, NLT).

BEING DIFFERENT
Being different isn't bad, it's just *different*. Believers who are different from others receive rewards. "My servant Caleb is different from the others. He has remained loyal to me, and I will bring him into the land. . . . His descendants will receive their full share of that land" (Numbers 14:24, NLT).

7. What vital piece of information did Haman receive concerning Mordecai?

. . . .

transformation

8. Mordecai practiced civil disobedience. He set himself apart from the world around him not for personal reasons but for pious principles. Fill in the chart to discover other men and women in the Bible who practiced civil disobedience and why.

SCRIPTURE	PEOPLE AND THEIR MOTIVES
Exod. 1:15-17	
Dan. 3:10-12, 16-18	
Acts 5:27-29	

9. The servants in the king's gate did not want Mordecai to be different from them, so they hounded him daily to do what they did. Check off any influences that pressure you to copy the world's actions.

— Fashion magazines   — Hollywood's habits

— Campus curriculums   — Friend's expectations

— Keeping up with the Joneses   — Family traditions

— Political agendas   — Other_____

Journal a prayer to God for help to overcome the peer pressure you are most vulnerable to. Ask Him to help you to be different from the world.

. . . .

. . . .

. . . .

. . . .

. . . .

10. Mordecai was a good example of how to resist peer pressure by refusing to listen to persuasive arguments.

Journal about someone who has been successful in resisting peer pressure.

. . . .

. . . .

. . . .

. . . .

10
RESISTANCE
Resisting peer pressure includes *running from evil* and *running to God*. "Submit to God. Resist the devil and he will flee from you. Draw near to God and He will draw near to you" (James 4:7-8). Don't just shout at the dark-ness; remember to light a candle!

Christians living in the United States may think that civil disobedience is a thing of the past. But it's not! Did you know that there are a number of recent zoning cases that have affected the right to worship in private homes? In Colorado Springs, minister Richard Blanche has been repeatedly cited for holding religious meetings in his home in violation of a city zoning ordinance. In Fairhaven, Massachusetts, local zoning officials ruled that Bible studies were home occupations and therefore prohibited under the town's property-use ordinances. In Los Angeles, officials ruled that home-occupancy regulations forbade Orthodox Jews from holding prayer meetings in their homes.

In the instances of civil disobedience cited in the Bible, the dissenting Jews and Christians remained respectful while upholding biblical principles. The Hebrew midwives steadfastly refused to kill Jewish babies. Shadrach, Meshach, and Abednego refused to bow down to an idol. The early Christians respectfully chose to obey God rather than human authorities. And Mordecai patiently stood his ground while others bowed their knees to Haman. These godly people did not incite riots or practice civil rebellion. Instead, they took a firm position regarding what—or Who—they were *for* rather than who or what they were *against*. The principle emerges that civil disobedience is valid only when it is based on biblical convictions.

contemplation
Rather let my head stoop to the block than these knees bow to any, save to the God of heaven.
William Shakespeare

141

DAY 3 ROLLING THE DICE

preparation

Lord, there are enemies who want to set traps for me simply because I am one of Your children. Please rescue me from their harmful plans. I trust You to shield and protect me. Amen.

PROTECTION

He will rescue you from every trap and protect you from the fatal plague. He will shield you with his wings. He will shelter you with his feathers. His faithful promises are your armor and protection. Psalm 91:3-4, NLT

Haman decided to play a deadly game in which the fate of Mordecai and his people would be decided by a simple roll of the dice. He was willing to flirt with death as long as it wasn't his own. Casting lots or rolling the deadly dice is eerily similar to another life threatening game: Russian roulette.

Russian roulette is a high-stakes "game" for those willing to gamble their lives with the spin of a gun chamber. Russian roulette was started by the KGB to extract information from those they interrogated. A single bullet was placed into one of the six chambers of a revolver. The KGB agents would then demand information from their prisoners. If the captive refused to cooperate, the cylinder was spun, the hammer was cocked, and the gun was placed on the victim's temple. Then the prisoner was forced to pull the trigger. If the chamber was empty, the prisoner lived long enough to be questioned further. If the hammer struck the bullet-filled chamber, the prisoner would perish. Countless victims died at the hands of KGB agents who played Russian roulette with the lives of others.

Once Mordecai revealed his Jewish background, he became Haman's mortal enemy and was pulled into a high-stakes game with his life on the line. His refusal to pay homage to Haman was like a bullet in the loaded gun of prejudice, which Haman willingly aimed at Mordecai and his people.

exploration

Haman had achieved a powerful position in King Ahasuerus's kingdom. Now we see that he was willing to use his power to promote death and destruction.

Review Esther 3; then focus on verses 5-7.

When Haman saw that Mordecai did not bow or pay him homage, Haman was filled with wrath. Esther 3:5

1. Describe the emotion that consumed Haman and its source.

. . . .

But he disdained to lay hands on Mordecai alone, for they had told him of the people of Mordecai. Instead, Haman sought to destroy all the Jews who were throughout the whole kingdom of Ahasuerus—the people of Mordecai. Esther 3:6

2. Why was taking revenge on Mordecai not sufficient for Haman?

. . . .

3. What was the extent of Haman's plan for the Jews?

. . . .

In the first month, which is the month of Nisan, in the twelfth year of King Ahasuerus, they cast Pur (that is, the lot) before Haman to determine the day and the month, until it fell on the twelfth month, which is the month of Adar. Esther 3:7

4. How did Haman determine a favorable time to initiate his plan?

. . . .

5. What date did he arrive at? . . . .

. . . .

6. How much time would there be between the casting of the lot and the initiation of Haman's plan?

. . . .

7. How do you think this time frame might help the Jews?

. . . .

explanation

1

WRATHFUL
Wrath means violent anger or rage with an eye toward retribution for an offense. It represents a settled habit of the mind with the intention of revenge. "[My enemies] bring down trouble upon me, and in wrath they hate me" (Psalm 55:3).

4

CASTING LOTS
Casting lots was a way of making decisions in Bible times, similar to drawing straws. Casting lots occurs seventy times in the Old Testament and seven in the New Testament. Most occur in the early period when God apparently approved of this means for determining a course of action (adapted, *Nelson's*).

7

GOD'S TIMING
God's providential hand was working to protect the Jews even in the timing of events. Through the casting of Pur, God gave the Jews time to prepare and Esther and Mordecai time to act. The casting of Pur became the source of the name for the Feast of Purim.

transformation

8 PEACEMAKERS
Jesus said peacemakers
are called God's chil-
dren. Paul teaches
how to make peace:
(1) "Never pay back evil
for evil to anyone";
(2) "Do things in such a
way that everyone can
see you are honorable";
(3) "Do your part to live
in peace with everyone"
(Romans 12:17-18, NLT).

9 ROLLING DICE?
There are no games
of chance for those
devoted to God's will.
He wants His children to
discover His will. In His
providence He orches-
trates circumstances to
get us where He wants
us to go. "We may
throw the dice, but the
Lord determines how
they fall" (Proverbs
16:33, NLT).

10 PERFECT TIMING
God is never late; He's
always right on time.
But our timing isn't
always His timing. We
may think He's late
when we're feeling
desperate. But that is
God's perfect time to
rescue us! "When we
were utterly helpless,
Christ came at just the
right time and died for
us sinners" (Romans 5:6,
NLT).

8. Wrath filled Haman and motivated him to take revenge on Mordecai and his people, the Jews. Watch the evening news or read your local newspaper. Describe a situation where people today are venting their wrath and taking revenge on one another.

. . . .

. . . .

Journal a prayer asking God to bring a peaceful resolution to this situation, using this verse: "Turn away from evil and do good. Work hard at living in peace with others" (Psalm 34:14, NLT).

. . . .

. . . .

. . . .

. . . .

9. Haman cast the Pur to determine when he would take revenge on the Jews. Fill in the following chart to discover other reasons for casting lots.

SCRIPTURE	WHY LOTS WERE CAST
Lev. 16:8-10	. . . .
Josh. 18:8-10	. . . .
Jon. 1:6-7	. . . .
Matt. 27:35	. . . .
Acts 1:24-26	. . . .

10. Rolling the dice gave Mordecai and the Jews time for God to intervene on their behalf.

Journal about a time when God worked with perfect timing to protect or provide for you.

. . . .

. . . .

. . . .

. . . .

. . . .

. . . .

. . . .

"Man overboard!" came the cry from an Atlantic steamer. A man heard this desperate cry as he lay in his bunk during a raging storm. He was battling a severe case of seasickness and couldn't join the rescue operation.

"May God help that poor fellow," he prayed, "but there's nothing I can do." Then he thought, *I can at least put my lantern in my small window,* and with an effort he did so. The man was finally rescued. In recounting the story the next day he said, "I was going down in the darkness for the last time when someone put a light in a porthole. It shone on my hand, and a sailor in the lifeboat grabbed it and pulled me in."

Timing is everything. So far in the book of Esther, no one has mentioned God's name or asked for His help. You see, until you realize you're drowning, you don't think you need to be saved. Haman's hatred is about to crash in on the Jews with waves of prejudice and persecution. His goal is to sweep them away in a tidal wave of vengeance. Like men going under for the last time, they will need to be rescued. And when they call out to God at just the right time, His light will shine through, and they will be lifted up.

contemplation
God has said he will exalt you in due time, but remember, he is referring to his time and not yours!
A. W. Tozer

DAY 4 REWARDING HATE CRIMES

preparation

Thank You, Lord, that
although evil people
aren't always punished,
in the end they will
receive their just
deserts. I praise You
that I will receive
Your just rewards for
righteous deeds. I want
to live to please You.
Amen.

JUST REWARDS
"There truly is a reward
for those who live for
God; surely there is a
God who judges justly
here on earth." Psalm
58:11, NLT

"Palestinian Youths Train for Warfare" declared a current headline in the *International Herald Tribune*. Each year thousands of Palestinian teenagers are sent to summer camps where they learn the arts of kidnapping, ambushing, and using assault weapons. They stage mock kidnappings of Israeli leaders that end with bodyguards being brutally murdered. They practice attacks on replicas of Israeli military posts, and they have opportunities to master the stripping and reassembling of Kalashnikov rifles. Typical summer camps end with "Parents' Day" festivities where ribbons are awarded to the best campers.

Unfortunately rewarding others for committing hate crimes is nothing new. Ku Klux Klan members reward their members' crimes of hate with white robes and elevated ranks and titles within the organization. Gangs on urban streets reward new inductees' acts of vandalism and violence with acceptance into "the family."

Haman wanted to reward hate crimes in the Persian Empire with monetary compensation. He even offered to fill the king's treasury so the king would approve of his plans of violence against the Jews. Some groups or people may reward evil actions with visible compensation, but God will repay violent actions with eternal judgment. "The Lord shall repay the evildoer according to his wickedness" (2 Samuel 3:39).

exploration

Today we see the methods Haman used to convince Ahasuerus to comply with his murderous plot. However, Haman was hiding his true motives from the king.

Review Esther 3; then focus on verses 8-11.

Then Haman said to King Ahasuerus, "There is a certain people scattered and dispersed among the people in all the provinces of your kingdom; their laws are different from all other people's, and they do not keep the king's laws. Therefore it is not fitting for the king to let them remain." Esther 3:8

1. Describe where the Jews were living within the kingdom of Persia.

. . . .

 2. What two wrongs did Haman accuse the Jews of committing, and what was his conclusion?

. . . .

"If it pleases the king, let a decree be written that they be destroyed, and I will pay ten thousand talents of silver into the hands of those who do the work, to bring it into the king's treasuries." Esther 3:9

3. What did Haman ask for, and how did he manipulate the king to get his way?

. . . .

So the king took his signet ring from his hand and gave it to Haman, the son of Hammedatha the Agagite, the enemy of the Jews. And the king said to Haman, "The money and the people are given to you, to do with them as seems good to you." Esther 3:10-11

4. How did Ahasuerus show he approved the plan concerning the Jews?

. . . .

5. What phrase reveals that Haman was committing hate crimes?

. . . .

6. How would the destruction of the Jews enrich Haman?

. . . .

explanation

2
MISUNDERSTOOD
Persian Jewish immigrants were law-abiding citizens who kept the king's laws and their Mosaic laws. Haman implied that Jews were disobedient citizens with their own legal system. Contrary to Haman's portrayal, historians suggest that these Jews were obedient citizens who made positive contributions to society.

3
MANIPULATING
Haman knew that money talks. A bribe would be appealing to a greedy king whose costly war had depleted the royal treasury. Ten thousand talents of silver weighed about 750,000 pounds, worth millions in U.S. dollars. Haman was an incredibly wealthy man who used his money to manipulate.

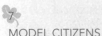

7

MODEL CITIZENS
Jews obeying God's laws were good citizens in foreign lands. Christians are citizens of heaven; we're foreigners here on earth. Jesus tells us how to be model citizens: "Do for others what you would like them to do for you. This is a summary of all that is taught in the law" (Matthew 7:12, NLT).

8

BRIBERY
A *bribe* is "money or favor given or promised in order to influence the judgment or conduct of a person in a position of trust; something that serves to induce or influence" (*Webster's*). "You shall take no bribe, for a bribe blinds the discerning and perverts the words of the righteous" (Exodus 23:8).

9

HATE
The Hebrew word for *hate* carries the idea of ugliness and deformity; therefore, to regard with feelings contrary to love; to loathe (adapted, *Unger's*). Jesus tells Christians, "Everyone will hate you because of your allegiance to me. But those who endure to the end will be saved" (Mark 13:13, NLT).

7. Read Jeremiah 29:4-7 to discover five things God expected of Jewish captives in foreign lands. Elaborate on the list of behaviors they should exhibit.

a. Homes: . . . .

. . . .

b. Land: . . . .

. . . .

c. Marriage: . . . .

. . . .

d. Children: . . . .

. . . .

e. City: . . . .

. . . .

8. Haman offered the king lots of silver in order to manipulate him and get his way.

> Journal about a time when you may have manipulated others with money or when you may have been influenced by a bribe of some kind.

. . . .

. . . .

. . . .

9. Haman promoted his plot of prejudice and bribed others to join him in committing hate crimes against God's people. Describe a time when you were a victim of someone's prejudice or hateful malice.

. . . .

. . . .

Believers often experience prejudice because of their faith. Journal a prayer of thanksgiving to God for the blessing of being like Jesus through rewriting the following verse. Personalize it by putting your name in each time the word *you* is used. "Blessed are you when men hate you, and when they exclude you, and revile you, and cast out your name as evil, for the Son of Man's sake. Rejoice in that day and leap for joy! For indeed your reward is great in heaven" (Luke 6:22-23).

. . . .

. . . .

. . . .

. . . .

A recent newspaper article discussed how Germany is trying to quash a rise in hate crimes. The paper stated that a series of violent attacks against Jews has sparked a national debate on what Germany can do to control the embers of hatred that are flaring up. In western Germany, cemeteries have been desecrated with swastikas and other Nazi symbols. Web site regulators approved a site named www.heil.hitler much to the consternation of political officials. In Düsseldorf a bomb injured ten immigrants, six of whom were Jewish. Echoes of Hitler's rhetoric can be heard on the lips of contemporary Germans: "We have 4 million unemployed people. I don't know that we need them [immigrants] here." Some of Germany's solutions for ending hate crimes include creating and enforcing tougher laws, outlawing those who encourage and finance right-wing extremism, and cracking down on employees who participate in racial attacks.

Today we combat hate crimes with legislation and law enforcement. In Ahasuerus's kingdom hate crimes were encouraged by propaganda from Haman, who manipulated the facts to suit his purposes. He even stooped to bribe the king and those who would commit these crimes against the Jews by promising financial gain. Hate began in the heart of one man and spread throughout a nation. Will love from the heart of one woman stop the madness?

contemplation

Wherever you see persecution, there is more than a probability that truth is on the persecuted side.
Hugh Latimer

DAY 5 RECORDING LETHAL LEGISLATION

preparation

Holy God, there is none like You in heaven or on earth. Your words are eternal, living, and powerful; none will ever remain unfulfilled. I willingly submit my life to Your laws above human laws. Amen.

GOD'S LAW
For assuredly, I say to you, till heaven and earth pass away, one jot or one tittle will by no means pass from the law till all is fulfilled.
Matthew 5:18

"So let it be written, so let it be done," were the words proclaimed by Pharaoh Ramses, portrayed by Yul Brynner in Cecil B. DeMille's classic movie *The Ten Commandments.* Picture his sleek, muscular physique as he stood with his heels dug in, hands on his hips, head cocked, arrogantly surveying the city built with the sweat and blood of Hebrew slaves. His whims and wishes became law and were executed without question.

Biblical scholars believe that Pharaoh Ramses was the ruler in Egypt during the time of Moses. The Egyptians believed he was the incarnation of the god Horus. It was his "divine responsibility" to rule the land. He owned everything, and the power of life and death was on his lips. He ruthlessly recorded lethal legislation, telling the Hebrew midwives, "When you do the duties of a midwife for the Hebrew women, . . . if it is a son, then you shall kill him" (Exodus 1:16).

Fast-forward a few centuries into the Persian Empire, and you will see that rulers haven't changed much. Picture King Ahasuerus, whose name means "mighty man." A powerful and sometimes cruel potentate, Ahasuerus gave his signet ring to Haman, putting his stamp of approval on the plot to kill all of the Jews in all of the Persian provinces. When he did, he was saying, "So let it be written; so let it be done!"

exploration

The king foolishly agreed to Haman's diabolical scheme. Today we see that Haman wasted no time in initiating his plan.
Review Esther 3; then focus on verses 12-15.

Then the king's scribes were called on the thirteenth day of the first month, and a decree was written according to all that Haman commanded—to the king's satraps, to the governors who were over each province, to the officials of all people, to every province according to its script, and to every people in their language. In the name of King Ahasuerus it was written, and sealed with the king's signet ring. Esther 3:12

1. To what extent did Haman spread his evil decree?

. . . .

2. How would the people know this was the king's law?

. . . .

And the letters were sent by couriers into all the king's provinces, to destroy, to kill, and to annihilate all the Jews, both young and old, little children and women, in one day, on the thirteenth day of the twelfth month, which is the month of Adar, and to plunder their possessions. A copy of the document was to be issued as law in every province, being published for all people, that they should be ready for that day. Esther 3:13-14

3. Describe the fate decreed for the Jews and who was targeted.

. . . .

4. What incentive did Haman offer the Persians to turn against their neighbors?

. . . .

The couriers went out, hastened by the king's command; and the decree was proclaimed in Shushan the citadel. So the king and Haman sat down to drink, but the city of Shushan was perplexed. Esther 3:15

5. How did Haman distract the king?

. . . .

2
SIGNET
An official used a signet or seal just like a personal signature giving validity to a document. It was also an emblem of royal authority. "Without a seal no document is considered authentic. In a similar manner coffers, doors of houses, and tombs were sealed" (*Unger's*).

4
PLUNDER
Plunder may mean "booty or spoil of war." It includes anything and everything a soldier or army captures from an enemy and carries off (adapted, *Vine's*). "You may keep for yourselves all the women, children, livestock, and other plunder. You may enjoy the spoils of your enemies" (Deuteronomy 20:14, NIT)

6

PERPLEXED
Haman played on Ahasuerus's weakness for alcohol to take his mind off the horrendous incident he had agreed to. The people did not have the luxury of numbing their minds to the decree's implications—they struggled with uncertainty and questions. "If he would do this to the Jews, might he do this to us?"

7

ROYAL SEAL
God has placed His royal stamp of approval on His children. This stamp guarantees that you belong to Him. "He who establishes us with you in Christ . . . is God, who also has sealed us and given us the Spirit in our hearts as a guarantee" (2 Corinthians 1:21-22).

8

OUR ENEMY
Becoming God's friend makes you Satan's enemy. Before salvation he seduced you with pleasure to keep you out of God's camp. As Christians, Satan's goal is to attack our thoughts, making us POWs and people missing in action. "Watch out for attacks from the Devil, your great enemy" (1 Peter 5:8, NLT).

6. How did the people respond?

. . . .

transformation

7. King Ahasuerus used his signet ring to seal a document and make it legal. Fill in the following chart to discover other uses of a ruler's ring.

SCRIPTURE	USE OF SIGNET RING
Gen. 41:42	. . . .
Num. 31:50	. . . .
Dan. 6:17	. . . .
Hag. 2:23	. . . .

Journal about a ring or other gift you have been given that seals or symbolizes love and acceptance from someone dear to you (examples: engagement, graduation, sixteenth birthday, family heirloom).

. . . .

. . . .

. . . .

8. Haman, acting as enemy of the Jews, began an unholy war in which those who joined his army could plunder vanquished Jews. Jesus calls Christians to a holy war against forces of wickedness. Read 2 Corinthians 10:3-5 and answer the following questions:

   a. Explain how Christians do *not* wage war and how our weapons are different.

   . . . .

   b. What plunder can Christians take captive?

   . . . .

9. Today we learned that war plunder included not only things but also people. Similarly, our enemy the devil has taken people's hearts and minds captive. As believers we are called to help people escape the devil's snare.

> Journal a prayer based on this Scripture passage for someone you know who has been taken captive by the devil's snare. "Teach those who oppose the truth. Perhaps God will change those people's hearts, and they will believe the truth. Then they will come to their senses and escape from the Devil's trap" (2 Timothy 2:25-26, NLT).

. . . .

. . . .

. . . .

. . . .

Haman is one in a long line of leaders who have attempted to destroy God's chosen people, the Jews. But religious persecution is not limited to the Jews. Christians have suffered under regimes attempting to destroy them as well. In the Roman Empire from the time of Nero to Diocletian there were ten persecutions of the church. Emperor Diocletian set up a stone pillar honoring himself on which these words were inscribed: "For Having Exterminated the Name Christian from the Earth." He might be rather embarrassed if he could see that monument today! Another Roman leader built a coffin to mark his intention to "bury the Galilean" once and for all by killing His followers. However, he soon learned that no onslaught could destroy the corporate body of Christ, and he eventually became a follower of Christ.

More Christians have been martyred in the twentieth century than in all of the previous nineteen centuries. Sudan, China, Ethiopia, Kuwait, and Egypt are a few of the many countries in which atrocities have been documented. Yet the church flourishes despite the plans of wicked people, fulfilling the words of Jesus: "I will build my church, and all the powers of hell will not conquer it" (Matthew 16:18, NLT).

OUR HERO
Jesus is the greatest of heroes because He rose from the grave! When He rose, He plundered the devil by releasing captives from death and hell. "When He ascended on high, He led captivity captive" (Ephesians 4:8).

contemplation
God has set a Savior against sin, a heaven against a hell, light against darkness, good against evil, and the breadth and length and depth and height of grace that is in himself for my good, against all the power and strength and subtlety of every enemy.
John Bunyan

Such a Time as This

"Such a time as this" experiences happen when you are in the right place at the right time with a righteous cause. They begin the moment the cogs in God's cosmic clock tumble into place, setting in motion a series of events that sweep you into action.

As I was typing this introduction, my phone rang. A beautiful young mother named Michelle Grey said, "I've been too shy to call for weeks. But my husband said, 'Who knows how your story might encourage others?'" Here is her "such a time" story.

One time Michelle had prayed, "Lord, use me to help women avoid abortions." Soon after, she became pregnant and made a pre-natal appointment to coincide with the tenth week of her pregnancy. Tragically, at seven weeks she miscarried. Paula, the obstetrical nurse and a fellow believer, canceled Michelle's appointment but providentially neglected to erase her name. The morning of Michelle's unneeded appointment, a desperate woman called to discuss having an abortion. Paula said there was nothing available. Then she spotted Michelle's name and gave her the opening. When the woman arrived, Paula shared with her about the sanctity of life and referred her to a life-affirming clinic. The woman kept the baby. Through the loss of Michelle's pregnancy a baby's life was spared.

Queen Esther had her "such a time as this" experience when Mordecai challenged her to use her life to save others. When we make ourselves available, God does amazing things. This week consider "whether you have come to the kingdom for such a time as this" (Esther 4:14).

DAY **1** A TIME TO MOURN

exploration

preparation

Lord, I grieve over the things that grieve You. As I look at the world around me and see so many reasons to mourn, I can rejoice knowing that one day You will set things right. Amen.

GOOD NEWS

He has sent me to tell those who mourn that the time of the Lord's favor has come, and with it, the day of God's anger against their enemies. Isaiah 61:2, NLT

Over the past few weeks we have seen how God raised Esther and Mordecai to places of prominence according to His good plan for their lives. Esther had been queen for four years, and all had been well. But when Haman's evil decree was set in motion, the plot took an unexpected twist in this ancient drama, and it became a time to mourn.

Read Esther 4; then focus on verses 1-4.

> **When Mordecai learned all that had happened, he tore his clothes and put on sackcloth and ashes, and went out into the midst of the city. He cried out with a loud and bitter cry. He went as far as the front of the king's gate, for no one might enter the king's gate clothed with sackcloth.** Esther 4:1-2

1. Describe how Mordecai's actions and apparel revealed his grief about Haman's decree.

   . . . .

2. Where did Mordecai choose to grieve? . . . .

   . . . .

3. Explain why he might feel personally responsible for the edict against the Jews.

   . . . .

4. How were the inhabitants of the palace sheltered from the realities and sadness of the outside world?

. . . .

. . . .

> *And in every province where the king's command and decree arrived, there was great mourning among the Jews, with fasting, weeping, and wailing; and many lay in sackcloth and ashes. So Esther's maids and eunuchs came and told her, and the queen was deeply distressed. Then she sent garments to clothe Mordecai and take his sackcloth away from him, but he would not accept them.*
> Esther 4:3-4

5. How did the Jews' reaction mirror Mordecai's response to the king's decree?

. . . .

6. Describe how Esther learned of Mordecai's grief and how she responded emotionally.

. . . .

. . . .

7. What action did Esther take to comfort Mordecai? . . . .

. . . .

8. How did Mordecai respond to Esther's gift? Why do you think he responded this way?

. . . .

. . . .

transformation

9. Mordecai grieved that his people were under a death sentence. Fill in the chart to learn some scriptural ways to mourn.

---

explanation

4
CLOISTERED
Some mistakenly believe that what you don't know can't hurt you and choose to remain detached from others' grief. Christians should not be cloistered away from the world of pain. Instead they are to "go into all the world and preach the Good News to everyone, everywhere" (Mark 16:15, NLT).

7
COVER-UP
Esther's response to Mordecai's distress was to cover it up with new clothes. We do the same thing, "dressing up" our problems and sins. But believers should recognize and mourn evil rather than cover it up. "Let there be tears for the wrong things you have done" (James 4:9, NLT).

9
MOURNING
Mourning is "the experience or expression of grief, as at a time of death or national disaster. In biblical times, the customs of most cultures encouraged a vivid expression of grief. The people of that time would be puzzled by our more sedate forms of mourning" (*Nelson's*).

Gen. 23:2	. . . .
1 Kings 13:29-31	. . . .
Isa. 32:11-13	. . . .
John 11:33-35	. . . .
James 4:8-9	. . . .

BOTTLED UP

Don't keep your mournful tears bottled up inside of you. Instead pour them out to God, and He will catch every drop in a special bottle. "You keep track of all my sorrows. You have collected all my tears in your bottle. You have recorded each one in your book" (Psalm 56:8, NLT).

SHARING

Sharing another's sorrow shows that we care. Paul said, "Weep with those who weep" (Romans 12:15). Jesus shared the sorrow of Mary and Martha at the death of their brother Lazarus. "Jesus wept. The people who were standing nearby said, 'See how much he loved him'" (John 11:35-36, NLT).

10. Do you display your grief vocally and visibly like Mordecai, or are you a mourner who holds grief inside? Place a check beside the items in the following list that have caused you to grieve:

— Rising abortion rate
— Loved one's death
— Proliferation of pornography
— Natural disasters
— Unsaved loved ones
— Tragic news events
— Immoral legislation
— Other_____

Review the preceding checklist, and journal about one of the situations that grieves you the most. How do you express your grief? Why do you think you are touched so deeply?

. . . .

. . . .

. . . .

. . . .

. . . .

11. Esther was cloistered away from tragedy and its painful effects, and she tried to have others cover their grief with new clothes.

Journal about some ways you have distanced yourself from another's tragedy or have tried to cover that person's grief with trite platitudes.

· ·

· ·

· ·

· ·

When I was younger, I made the same mistake Esther did when she attempted to cover up grief instead of comforting those who are grieving. As a self-centered teenager I intensely avoided showing emotions. One night I chose to party with my friends rather than attend Sunday dinner with my family. As I walked into the house later, my mother called saying, "Grandpa died tonight while taking a nap on his favorite couch." To maintain composure, I declined to drive to Grandma's house to comfort and be comforted. I avoided expressing my grief for weeks by attending more parties. But covering up my sorrow with superficial laughter didn't make me feel better; it just bottled up the sorrow that would one day overflow. Solomon said, "Sorrow is better than laughter; for by a sad countenance the heart is made better" (Ecclesiastes 7:3).

Joyce Rigsby, in her book *How to Feel Another's Pain*, suggests ways to comfort those who mourn:

1. Treat the bereaved person as a unique individual by not presuming to know how he or she feels.
2. Avoid trite expressions of condolence.
3. Understand that it is important for mourners to talk about their feelings if they wish.
4. Don't be uncomfortable with silence.
5. Use touch appropriately to communicate concern.
6. Refrain from giving a Bible study when the hurting person asks why.
7. Be willing to reveal your own feelings by weeping.

contemplation

Those who can sit in silence with their fellowman, not knowing what to say but knowing that they should be there, can bring new life in a dying heart. Those who are not afraid to hold a hand in gratitude, to shed tears in grief, and to let a sigh of distress arise straight from the heart can break through paralyzing boundaries and witness the birth of a new fellowship, the fellowship of the broken.
Henri J. M. Nouwen

DAY 2 RUNNING OUT OF TIME

preparation

Father, help me to live in the awareness that time is running out. Give me the urgency to tell others that the day of salvation is at hand. Amen.

DAY OF SALVATION
The night is almost gone; the day of salvation will soon be here. So don't live in darkness. . . . Clothe yourselves with the armor of right living, as those who live in the light. Romans 13:12, NLT

In June 1999 Michele Wetteland, wife of pitcher John Wetteland, burst into tears and prayer while reading a *Fort Worth Star Telegram* article: "Family Shattered: Mother of 3-Day-Old Twins Faces Loss of Husband, Son." Also a mother of twins, Michele sympathized with a woman experiencing birth and death simultaneously. She steadfastly prayed for the bereaved mother.

Months later the grieving mother, Kathy Mogayzel, left her house for the first time since the tragic accident when a friend enticed her with tickets to see the Baltimore Orioles play the Texas Rangers. Since the Orioles were her deceased husband's favorite team, Kathy agreed to attend. That's when Michele and Kathy had a "such a time as this" moment. While buying hot dogs, the women happened to strike up a conversation. Michele realized that *this* was the same woman she had grieved for and empathized with, and she invited Kathy to watch the game in her private sky box. Michele introduced Kathy to her husband's hero, Cal Ripken Jr., who signed her jersey. As the two women parted, Michele told Kathy, "When you think of this night, remember that there's hope in Christ, who will bring joy to your life again."

Later Kathy wrote, "I do believe that God put me in the right place at the right time and then opened a little window in the clouds." Mordecai knew Esther was in the right place at the right time too. He encouraged her to leave her comfort zone, grieve for her people, and get busy praying. They were running out of time.

exploration

British politician Edmund Burke observed, "All that is required for evil to triumph is for good men to do nothing." Mordecai, a good man, did what he could to fight evil; he publicly protested and warned the queen of the danger facing their people.

Review Esther 4; then focus on verses 5-9.

> *Then Esther called Hathach, one of the king's eunuchs whom he had appointed to attend her, and she gave him a command concerning Mordecai, to learn what and why this was.* Esther 4:5

1. How did Esther and Mordecai communicate with one another?

. . . .

2. What was Hathach told to learn from Mordecai? . . . .

. . . .

> *So Hathach went out to Mordecai in the city square that was in front of the king's gate. And Mordecai told him all that had happened to him, and the sum of money that Haman had promised to pay into the king's treasuries to destroy the Jews. He also gave him a copy of the written decree for their destruction, which was given at Shushan, that he might show it to Esther and explain it to her, and that he might command her to go in to the king to make supplication to him and plead before him for her people.* Esther 4:6-8

3. What specific details did Mordecai give to Hathach?

. . . .

4. What evidence did he produce that his story was accurate?

. . . .

5. What did Mordecai want Hathach to do with this piece of evidence?

. . . .

6. How did Mordecai urge Esther to respond to the facts?

. . . .

---

explanation

2

FACT-FINDING
Previously, since others may have distorted Mordecai's grief as a public spectacle, Esther had sent him clothes. Before acting again, Esther planned a fact-finding mission. She wouldn't rely on hear-say, just the facts. "What a shame, what folly, to give advice before listening to the facts!" (Proverbs 18:13, NLT).

4

KINGLY DECREES
A kingly decree is an "official order, command, or edict issued by a king or other person of authority. The decrees of kings were often delivered to distant towns or cities by messengers and publicly announced at . . . public places" (*Nelson's*). "I, Darius, have issued this decree. Let it be obeyed with all diligence" (Ezra 6:12, NLT).

MESSENGER
Hathach, whose name means "good," was a reliable messenger who represented the facts accurately. His agenda was to be a conduit for communication. He played a vital role in God's plan to save the Jews. "An unreliable messenger stumbles into trouble, but a reliable messenger brings healing" (Proverbs 13:17, NLT).

RUMORS
Rumors contain a grain of truth but are, in fact, distortions of the truth. "The rumor spread among the . . . believers that [John] wouldn't die. But that isn't what Jesus said at all. He only said, 'If I want him to remain alive until I return, what is that to you?'" (John 21:23, NLT).

GOD'S DECREES
Kings are not the only ones who make decrees. God made a decree that one day His Son will rule and reign, "I will declare the decree: The Lord has said to Me, 'You are My Son, today I have begotten You. . . . I will give You the nations for Your inheritance" (Psalm 2:7-8).

So Hathach returned and told Esther the words of Mordecai. Esther 4:9

7. In what way did Hathach prove to be a faithful servant?

. . . .

. . . .

transformation

8. Esther wanted to base her decisions on the facts, not on hearsay or rumors.

 Journal about a rumor you've heard recently. Whom did it affect and how? Did you propagate it or squelch it?

. . . .

. . . .

. . . .

. . . .

. . . .

9. Mordecai gave Esther's messenger a copy of the king's decree. Fill in the following chart to discover some other decrees found in Scripture.

SCRIPTURE	DECREE
Ezra 5:13	
Ps. 2:7-8	
Jer. 5:22	
Dan. 3:10-11	
Luke 2:1	

10. Esther sent a faithful messenger to collect and convey factual information. Think about a situation in which you've served as a messenger or liaison between two people. (Examples: argument between friends, dispute between family members, negotiations at work)

> Journal about your role as a messenger. Were you a faithful or faulty messenger? What was the outcome of your involvement?

. . . .

. . . .

. . . .

. . . .

Abraham Lincoln's coffin was unearthed and opened twice. The first time was in 1887, twenty-two years after his assassination. It wasn't to see if he had died of a bullet fired from John Wilkes Booth's derringer or to bury him in a more presidential grave. The reason? To dispel a rumor that Lincoln's body wasn't in his coffin. A group of witnesses verified that the rumor was false. Then the casket was resealed and buried again.

In spite of protests from Lincoln's son Robert, fourteen years later the president's body was exhumed again. This time more witnesses were present. What was the reason for disturbing his grave a second time? The rumor had resurfaced! People didn't believe that Lincoln was dead and they wanted proof. The rumors were laid to rest along with the Civil War president when his corpse was permanently interred at Springfield.

Have you been taken for a ride by unsubstantiated rumors? Has there been an Elvis sighting at your local Burger King? Do you know someone who was abducted by aliens? Has some well-meaning Christian fed you the line that Madalyn Murray O'Hair is attempting to ban Christian radio and television, even though she's dead and buried in Texas? Like Esther, perhaps it's time you checked out the facts before you jump on the bandwagon. She found eyewitnesses and gathered concrete evidence before she sprung into action. Scripture says, "The facts of the case must be established by the testimony of two or three witnesses" (Deuteronomy 19:15, NLT).

10

MESSAGE
What good is a messenger without a message? God has an important message for the world, and we are His ambassadors. "This is the message he has given us to announce to you: God is light and there is no darkness in him at all" (1 John 1:5, NLT).

contemplation
Be careful what you say. Be careful how you say it. Be careful that you send the right message, and that you send it to the right person, and that you do so with the right motive.
Charles Swindoll

preparation

Heavenly Father, my only hope is in You. I need access to Your presence to find help in time of need. Thank You that in the name of Your Son, Jesus, I have open access to Your throne of grace. Amen.

ENTRANCE
Yes, I am the gate. Those who come in through me will be saved. Wherever they go, they will find green pastures. John 10:9, NLT

Gaining access to powerful people is next to impossible for ordinary folks. How would you try to gain a sitting with Queen Elizabeth? If you marched up to Buckingham Palace, knocked on the gilded gates, and said, "Long time no see," it wouldn't be funny, and you probably wouldn't get in. Dorothy of Kansas desperately needed to see the Great and Powerful Oz. So the timid girl marched up to Emerald City and knocked on its massive doors at the risk of incurring the wizard's wrath. When the gatekeeper peered out, Dorothy reverently requested, "If you please, sir, we want to see the wizard right away. All four of us."

He gruffly replied, "Orders are nobody can see the Great Oz, not nobody, not nohow."

They made headway when the Scarecrow said, "But she's Dorothy."

Incredulously the guard replied, "You're Dorothy? The witch's Dorothy? Well, that makes a difference. Wait here. I'll announce you at once."

For Dorothy, access was granted because of her reputation as the girl who killed the wicked witch of the East when her house landed in Oz.

Esther was a meek girl who needed help too. The only person powerful enough to help her was the king of Persia. But "not nobody, not nohow" got invited into his throne room unless they had a personal invitation. It had been a long time since Esther had seen the king. Would she be willing to risk his displeasure and her life by marching into the throne room uninvited?

exploration

Mordecai warned Esther of the evil to come and encouraged her to take action. Today we see that she was unsure how to respond in light of her present circumstances.

Review Esther 4; then focus on verses 10-12.

> *Then Esther spoke to Hathach, and gave him a command for Mordecai: "All the king's servants and the people of the king's provinces know that any man or woman who goes into the inner court to the king, who has not been called, he has but one law: put all to death, except the one to whom the king holds out the golden scepter, that he may live. Yet I myself have not been called to go in to the king these thirty days." So they told Mordecai Esther's words.* Esther 4:10-12

1. Describe the law concerning anyone who went into the king's inner court.

. . . .

2. Who was familiar with this law?

. . . .

3. What was the penalty for anyone who broke this law?

. . . .

4. Why do you think Esther wanted Mordecai to be aware of this law?

. . . .

5. What sign would the king give to show she was welcome in the throne room?

. . . .

6. Explain why Esther thought she might be unwelcome.

. . . .

7. What phrase reveals that the servants did not withhold any information from Mordecai?

. . . .

explanation

1

INVITATION ONLY
Entrance into the court of King Ahasuerus was by invitation only; all others were excluded. God has an invitation list for His throne room in heaven. "Anyone whose name was not found recorded in the Book of Life was thrown into the lake of fire" (Revelation 20:15, NLT).

3

DEATH PENALTY
Going to see the king was a matter of life or death. Even his wife could not enter without permission. Ahasuerus was given to fits of rage. He had banished one queen. If Esther's presence did not please him, there was a real possibility he might kill her.

5

SCEPTER
A *scepter* was "the official staff of a ruler, symbolizing his authority and power. Originally the scepter was the shepherd's staff, since the first kings were nomadic princes. In some instances the scepter was a strong rod" (*Nelson's*). "O God . . . a scepter of righteousness is the scepter of Your kingdom" (Psalm 45:6).

THRONE

A throne is a symbol of royal government and may refer to the king's role as a judge. "Since God is the true King, it is natural that throne should apply to His royal authority, especially His authority as Judge" (*Nelson's*). "The Lord says: 'Heaven is my throne'" (Isaiah 66:1, NLT).

GOD-SIZED

God-sized prayers are the kind that soar high above all human possibilities. Prayers are not wishful thinking but faithful believing. God is bigger than your biggest prayer. He "is able to do exceedingly abundantly above all that we ask or think, according to the power that works in us" (Ephesians 3:20).

SELF-SACRIFICE

Love motivated God to make the greatest sacrifice—His only Son. Jesus willingly sacrificed His life to save us from sin and death. The Bible teaches us to follow His self-sacrificing example: "Greater love has no one than this, than to lay down one's life for his friends" (John 15:13).

8. Ahasuerus's throne room was inaccessible to the majority of people in Persia. In the book of Isaiah we see that God gave Isaiah the prophet special access to His throne room. Read Isaiah 6:1-5, and answer the following questions:

   a. Describe the One who sat on the throne.

   . . . .

   b. Describe those who attended the Lord. What did they proclaim?

   . . . .

   c. How did Isaiah respond to his experience?

   . . . .

9. The blood of Jesus offers believers unlimited access to God's throne in heaven. Think of a prayer request so great that only God could fulfill it. Take the time now to access His throne with your "God-sized" request.

   Journal your request by rewriting the following verses into a personal prayer: "Dear brothers and sisters, we can boldly enter heaven's Most Holy Place because of the blood of Jesus. Let us go right into the presence of God, with true hearts fully trusting him. . . . Without wavering, let us hold tightly to the hope we say we have, for God can be trusted to keep his promise" (Hebrews 10:19, 22-23, NLT).

   . . . .

   . . . .

   . . . .

   . . . .

10. Esther realized that to serve her people, she might have to sacrifice her life. Jesus said, "If you try to keep your life for yourself, you will lose it. But if you give up your life for me, you will find true life" (Matthew 16:25, NLT). Place a check

on the following lines that represent ways you have sacrificed your life for Christ.

— Left unhealthy friendships   — Moved to new location
— Changed occupation   — Gave up financial security
— Altered lifestyle   — Other_____

Journal about one of the unique ways Christ has asked you to lay down your life to begin a new one with Him.

. . . .

. . . .

. . . .

. . . .

A soldier in the Union army had lost his brother and father in the Civil War. He decided to ask President Lincoln for an exemption from military service so he could help his mother on the farm. When he arrived in Washington, D.C., he went to the White House and asked to see the president. He was told, "You can't see the president! Don't you know there's a war on?"

Discouraged, he sat on a bench near the White House, cradling his head in his hands. A little boy ran up and asked, "What's wrong?" The soldier explained that he was the only one left to help his mother and had come to ask for the president's help, but he'd been turned away. The boy took the soldier by the hand and led him to the White House, through the back door, and straight to the president's office. He opened the door and walked in with his new friend.

Although President Lincoln was busy, he looked up and asked, "What can I do for you, Tad?"

Tad said, "Daddy, this soldier needs to talk to you." The soldier immediately pled his case, and Lincoln sympathetically exempted him from service.

It helps to know people in high places: the soldier gained an instant audience with the president through his son Tad. Believers obtain access to the heavenly Father through His Son, Jesus. And Esther will rely on her relationship with God to gain access to the king of Persia.

contemplation
Christ is not one of many ways to approach God, nor is he the best of several ways; he is the only way.
A. W. Tozer

DAY 4

NO TIME LIKE THE PRESENT

preparation

God, sometimes I feel powerless to stand up in a world of powerful people who oppose Your truth. Thank You that it's not by might, nor by power, but by Your Spirit that I can accomplish Your will. Amen.

PROMISE

God deliberately chose things the world considers foolish in order to shame those who think they are wise. And he chose those who are powerless to shame those who are powerful.
1 Corinthians 1:27, NLT

Gay lobbyists promoting a radical agenda flooded into New Mexico during the 1990s to bring their pro-homosexual platform into schools, businesses, and churches via a bill known as SB-91. This legislation would amend New Mexico's constitution, giving gays preferential treatment normally reserved for legitimate minorities. I had never been involved in politics, but Bill Clinton's position on gays in the military forced me to my knees. I prayed, *What can I do to defend America's biblical heritage?*

God answered my prayer. A politician named Greg Zanetti encouraged me to oppose SB-91. I said, "No, I wouldn't know where to begin."

Then Tom Terry, a disc jockey, told me the people who had lobbied against the bill were out of action and asked, "Why don't *you* take their place?"

Next, Ted Luera, a physicist, inquired whether I was opposing SB-91. "No," I said, "but you're the third person who's asked." Ted reminded me of Esther's example and said, "Who knows whether you've been called for such a time as this?"

Thus began my initiation into the political maelstrom. I organized coalitions, rallies, phone trees, letters from businesspeople, and opposition speakers to testify before the legislators. Amazingly, I obtained an appointment with the governor, giving him petitions containing thousands of signatures. I even got to pray with him. In the end, SB-91 was defeated against all odds.

Like me, Esther had never been involved politically, but bad legislation forced her to take action. We both learned that when it comes to defending the faith, there's no time like the present.

exploration

Mordecai had captured a glimpse of God's plan for Esther, so he gave her some good reasons to take action.

Review Esther 4; then focus on verses 13-14.

> **And Mordecai told them to answer Esther: "Do not think in your heart that you will escape in the king's palace any more than all the other Jews."** Esther 4:13

1. Why might Esther think she would escape the king's decree?

. . . .

2. How did Mordecai remind Esther that she was not exempt from the king's decree?

. . . .

> **"For if you remain completely silent at this time, relief and deliverance will arise for the Jews from another place, but you and your father's house will perish. Yet who knows whether you have come to the kingdom for such a time as this?"** Esther 4:14

3. What was Mordecai afraid Esther would do? . . . .

. . . .

4. Explain what would happen even if she kept quiet.

. . . .

5. Though the Jews would be delivered, explain what Esther's silence would cost her and her family.

. . . .

6. What pertinent question did Mordecai ask Esther to help her realize that her position in the palace was not a mere coincidence?

. . . .

. . . .

explanation

1

NO ESCAPE
All of humanity is under a death sentence. There is no escaping the clutches of the grim reaper. The statistics on death are sobering: one out of every one person will die. "It is appointed for men to die once, but after this the judgment" (Hebrews 9:27).

3

SILENCE
Silence isn't always golden. To close our mouths when the truth should be told is like trying to contain a volcano. "As I stood there in silence . . . the turmoil within me grew to the bursting point. My thoughts grew hot within me and began to burn, igniting a fire of words" (Psalm 39:2-3, NLT).

5

UNSTOPPABLE
Mordecai knew God was unstoppable in keeping His covenant to preserve the Jews and make them a great nation (see Genesis 12:1-3). God would accomplish His purpose with or without Esther's help. Theologian Warren Wiersbe says, "When God isn't permitted to rule, He overrules!"

ETERNAL LIFE

When you're planning a rescue operation to those dying in sin, make sure you offer them the only lifeline that will last—Jesus Christ! "This is the way to have eternal life—to know you, the only true God, and Jesus Christ, the one you sent to earth" (John 17:3, NLT).

8

NEGLECT GOOD

When you neglect to perform good deeds, in God's eyes you've sinned. "Remember, it is sin to know what you ought to do and then not do it" (James 4:17, NLT). Good deeds not only benefit the people you help; they help you become a better person.

transformation

7. Mordecai enlisted Esther's help to rescue the Jews from impending death. James taught, "He who turns a sinner from the error of his way will save a soul from death and cover a multitude of sins" (James 5:20). Write down the names of some people who are under the spiritual death sentence that sin brings.

. . . .

. . . .

Journal a prayer asking God to use you to reach out to the people on your list with the good news of God's grace and forgiveness.

. . . .

. . . .

8. Esther did a good deed by helping her people in trouble. Christian women should perform good deeds too.

Journal your answers to Paul's questions in 1 Timothy 5:10 (NLT) with examples of deeds you've done.

"Has she brought up her children well?"

. . . .

"Has she been kind to strangers?"

. . . .

"Has she served other Christians humbly?"

. . . .

"Has she helped those who are in trouble?"

. . . .

"Has she always been ready to do good?"

. . . .

9. Mordecai had confidence in an unstoppable God. You can be confident that nothing can stop God from loving you. Examine Romans 8:38-39, then underline the forces that are powerless to stop God's love. "I am convinced that nothing can ever separate us from his love. Death can't, and life can't. The angels can't, and the demons can't. Our fears for today, our worries about tomorrow, and even the powers of hell can't keep God's love away. Whether we are high above the sky or in the deepest ocean, nothing in all creation will ever be able to separate us from the love of God that is revealed in Christ Jesus our Lord" (Romans 8:38-39, NLT).

10. God not only had a "such a time as this" moment for Esther's life, but He has a plan for your life as well (see Jeremiah 29:11-13).

> Journal a prayer asking God to use you in your world, "for such a time as this."
>
> . . . .
>
> . . . .
>
> . . . .

He or she who hesitates is lost. If Esther hesitated too long, she might lose out on her providential moment. Mordecai's message was urgent, and procrastination could mean the death of Esther, her family, and the nation of Israel. It was vital that Esther learn there is no time like the present. Another historic figure learned this lesson the hard way.

During the war for America's independence, Colonel Rahl, commander of the British troops at Trenton, New Jersey, was engaged in a game of cards. A messenger interrupted to deliver an urgent message revealing that General George Washington was crossing the Delaware River. More concerned with having fun than with doing his duty, Rahl foolishly put the letter into his pocket to read after the game was finished. By the time he did, it was too late. Washington and his men were close at hand; the British troops could not be organized in time to face their enemy's onslaught. Colonel Rahl's procrastination cost him his reputation, the lives of many of his men, and the liberty of the remainder of his regiment. It has been well said, "Tomorrow is the excuse of the lazy and the refuge of the incompetent."

TIMELY

The best "such a time as this" experience is at salvation. If you haven't experienced that moment, perhaps *now* is the time. "Behold, now is the accepted time; behold, now is the day of salvation" (2 Corinthians 6:2). Once you've been saved, many more timely moments are sure to follow.

contemplation

To sin by silence when they should protest makes cowards out of men.
Abraham Lincoln

DAY 5 TIMELY PRAYER

preparation

Father, thank You that Your call to fast comes with a promise of great reward. I want to put Your kingdom first. Help me to treasure Your words and will more than my necessary food. Amen.

FASTING

When you fast, comb your hair and wash your face. Then no one will suspect you are fasting, except your Father, who knows what you do in secret. And your Father, who knows all secrets, will reward you.
Matthew 6:17-18, NLT

I hadn't eaten solid food for three days, and it wasn't because I was sick. I was obeying God's command to fast and pray. Someone told me Jesus had said, "*When* you fast" not "*If* you fast," so I figured it was time to fast. My plan was to consume juices and broth, replacing my eating time with praying time.

One evening during my fast, I went for a walk on the beach to pray. I was carrying on a silent conversation with God while meditating on Matthew 6:33, "Seek first the kingdom of God and His righteousness, and all these things shall be added to you." I sat down on the sand to thank God for the beautiful sunset when I heard His quiet voice say, "You should pray for that guy in the water." So I did.

Then God said, "Why don't you tell Him about Me?"

I quickly responded, "If that's You speaking to me, then have him come over here and I'll witness to him."

Amazingly, he got out of the water, walked over, and struck up a conversation. I spent hours sharing my faith. I introduced him to other Christians, took him to church, and gave him a Bible. Fasting not only made me sensitive to God's voice and available for His service but also showed someone else the way to heaven.

When Esther wanted to hear God's voice and make herself available to His will, she decided to fast and pray and encouraged others to join her.

exploration

The persecution of Esther's people and God's call on her life transformed her from a fearful woman to a faithful woman. At this point, Esther took command of the situation and surrendered herself physically and spiritually to perform her duty for God and her people.

Review Esther 4; then focus on verses 15-17.

> *Then Esther told them to reply to Mordecai: "Go, gather all the Jews who are present in Shushan, and fast for me; neither eat nor drink for three days, night or day. My maids and I will fast likewise. And so I will go to the king, which is against the law; and if I perish, I perish!"* Esther 4:15-16

1. What did Esther ask Mordecai to have the Jews in Shushan do for her?

   . . . .

2. How long were they to take this action? . . . .

   . . . .

3. What did Esther say she would do? . . . .

   . . . .

4. Who would she enlist to support her? . . . .

   . . . .

5. Describe the illegal action she promised to take on behalf of the Jews.

   . . . .

6. What did Esther say to reveal she was committed to helping her people?

   . . . .

> *So Mordecai went his way and did according to all that Esther commanded him.* Esther 4:17

7. How did Mordecai respond to her queenly commands?

   . . . .

explanation

1

STOP EATING
To *fast* means to voluntarily go without food or drink. Old Testament fasting included humbling or afflicting the soul, surrendering the will through personal sacrifice. "Is it a fast that I have chosen, a day for a man to afflict his soul? Is it to bow down his head like a bulrush?" (Isaiah 58:5).

4

START PRAYING
Esther's fast was likely accompanied by prayer. The New Testament often unites fasting and prayer: When you stop eating, you should start praying. "Paul and Barnabas . . . prayed for them with fasting, turning them over to the care of the Lord" (Acts 14:23, NLT). Esther prayed before petitioning the king.

6

RISKY BUSINESS
Whether through Haman's lethal legislation or the king's deadly reprisal, Esther risked her life. She decided she'd rather die sooner *for* her people, than later *with* her people. Perhaps her life could save others. "So we also ought to give up our lives for our Christian brothers and sisters" (1 John 3:16, NLT).

STOP FASTING
There is a time to fast and a time for fasting to end. "This is what the Lord Almighty says: The traditional fasts and times of mourning you have kept . . . are now ended. They will become festivals of joy and celebration for the people of Judah" (Zechariah 8:19, NLT).

9

KEEP PRAYING
While there is a time to stop fasting, there is never a time to stop praying. Jesus didn't give up on prayer; He prayed the same prayer three times in Gethsemane, "Your will be done." Paul taught, "Keep on praying. No matter what happens, always be thankful" (1 Thessalonians 5:17-18, NLT).

10

NOT ASHAMED
Paul risked much to preach the gospel. He willingly suffered "in tribulations, in needs, in distresses, in stripes, in imprisonments, in tumults, in labors, in sleeplessness, in fastings" (2 Corinthians 6:4-5). He did it because he was "not ashamed of this Good News about Christ" (Romans 1:16, NLT).

transformation

8. Esther proclaimed a three-day fast for herself, the Jews, and her personal servants. Fill in the following chart to determine what accompanied fasting in Scripture:

SCRIPTURE	ACCOMPANIED FAST
Ezra 8:21	
Ezra 9:5	
Neh. 1:4	
Dan. 9:3-4	

9. Esther didn't just fast, she also prayed. Perhaps it's time for you to fast and pray too.

> Journal a prayer asking God to show you how and when to fast. Start each sentence with a word that corresponds to each letter in the word *P-R-A-Y*. (Example: Please . . . , Remember . . . , Answer . . . , You. . . .)

P. . . . .

. . . .

R. . . . .

. . . .

A. . . . .

. . . .

Y. . . . .

. . . .

10. It was risky business for Esther to intervene on behalf of her people. You may need to take risks when standing up for the Lord in the circumstances you face.

Journal about a situation in which you felt intimidated to make a stand for Christ. How did you respond? What were the results?

. . . .

. . . .

. . . .

. . . .

. . . .

. . . .

. . . .

. . . .

Are you contemplating a fast? Understanding what fasting will and will not do is vital. Fasting can't twist God's arm, but it can turn His ear. Fasting doesn't change God's mind, but it does change your heart. Fasting isn't a heavenly diet, but it is a holy discipline. Fasting isn't to impress others; it is to implore God. Examine your motivation to fast. If you're doing it for the wrong reasons, you're just losing weight. If you've got the right attitude, then you're gaining His promises.

I (Penny) attempted a fast a few years ago and failed. My friends and I made a commitment to fast twenty-four hours for the National Day of Prayer. It went great through breakfast and lunch. But by midafternoon, the fast triggered a raging migraine. I ended up in the emergency room with uncontrollable dry heaves. I concluded that fasting from food wasn't for me.

But I've discovered that there are different ways to fast. Daniel and his friends didn't give up vegetables; they did give up the king's delicacies (see Daniel 1). A delicacy is defined as an indulgence or a luxury. One of my greatest luxuries is reading—I have an insatiable appetite for it. There are seasons when I fast from reading other books to read the Bible. Lenya fasts from television to focus on her family. Another friend fasts from expensive perfume and gives to the poor. If you've fasted and failed, don't give up! Try a different form of fasting.

contemplation
Jesus has many who love his heavenly kingdom, but few who bear his cross. Many want consolation, but few desire adversity. Many are eager to share Jesus' table, but few will join him in fasting.
Thomas à Kempis

Let the Games Begin

Why do people play games? To win, of course! Vince Lombardi said, "Winning isn't everything, it's the only thing." To be a winner you must be a master of strategy. Chess is *the* game of strategy where you learn to outwit, outmaneuver, and outlast your opponent. If you can learn to conquer the chessboard, you can use your strategic skills to conquer the battlefield or the boardroom.

In chess, players take turns moving one piece at a time in an effort to attack their opponent's position and defend their own. The goal is to hunt down and immobilize your opponent's king, placing him in checkmate. The chess pieces are miniature representations of a medieval army. Each player possesses two rooks (the castle), two knights (the cavalry), two bishops (the church), a queen and king (the monarchy), and eight pawns (the lowly foot soldiers). Historians believe chess originated in India and eventually spread to Persia. From Persia the game of chess reached the rest of the world.

If games imitate life, then life in Persia was beginning to resemble a clever chess match. The key players in this deadly contest were plotting strategic maneuvers, attempting to stay several moves ahead of their opponents. The queen (Esther) and the bishop (Haman) were posturing themselves in order to win the king's favor. Mordecai (a knight) was strategically positioned to block Haman's advance. Now it's Esther's move. Let the game begin!

DAY 1
Approaching the King

DAY 2
The Queen Makes Her Move

DAY 3
The Knight's Advantage

DAY 4
The Bishop's Promotion

DAY 5
Bishop Takes Knight?

DAY 1 APPROACHING THE KING

APPROACHING
THE KING

exploration

Esther revealed that she was willing to risk her life to save her people when she decided to go unbidden to the king to expose Haman's evil plot. Before intervening, she wisely sought God's favor through prayer and fasting and encouraged others to do the same. This time of preparation gave Esther confidence to make her move and approach the king.

Review Esther 5; then focus on verses 1-3.

> *Now it happened on the third day that Esther put on her royal robes and stood in the inner court of the king's palace, across from the king's house, while the king sat on his royal throne in the royal house, facing the entrance of the house.* Esther 5:1

1. How did Esther prepare herself to enter the palace?

. . . .

2. Where did Esther go to attract the king's attention?

. . . .

3. Describe where the king was sitting. . . . .

. . . .

> *So it was, when the king saw Queen Esther standing in the court, that she found favor in his sight, and the king held out to Esther the golden scepter that was in his*

preparation

Lord, You are the King of kings. We can strategize and plot, but You are immovable and remain forever victorious. When battle lines are drawn, I choose to be on Your side. Amen.

IMMOVABLE KING
The kings of the earth prepare for battle; the rulers plot together against the Lord. . . . But the one who rules in heaven laughs. The Lord scoffs at them.
Psalm 2:2-4, NLT

explanation

STEP OF FAITH
Esther took an unwavering step of faith by walking into the throne room. She placed her confidence in the faithful God rather than the unpredictable king. "Now the just shall live by faith; but if anyone draws back, My soul has no pleasure in him" (Hebrews 10:38).

hand. Then Esther went near and touched the top of the scepter. Esther 5:2

4. How did the king respond to seeing the queen? . . . .

. . . .

5. What indication did he give that Esther was welcome in the inner court?

. . . .

6. Explain how Esther showed her acceptance of the king's favor.

. . . .

And the king said to her, "What do you wish, Queen Esther? What is your request? It shall be given to you— up to half the kingdom!" Esther 5:3

7. What did the king say to show he was interested in her petition?

. . . .

8. To what extent was he willing to grant her request?

. . . .

transformation

9. Esther was invited to pass through the royal courtyard, enter the throne room, and approach the king who was seated on his throne. As a believer, you will one day be invited to approach God's heavenly throne. Read Revelation 4:1-6, then answer the following questions to catch a glimpse of God's throne room.

a. Describe the One who sat on the throne (v. 3).

. . . .

b. Describe who and what surrounded the throne (v. 4).

. . . .

GOLDEN SCEPTER
The golden scepter signified the king's favor, power, and protection. When the king extended the scepter, he extended his favor and removed the barrier of power that kept him out of reach. When Esther touched the tip of the scepter, she received his protection.

INVITATION
"What do you wish?" God's children can also be bold to make requests of God because they have an open invitation. "Keep on asking, and you will be given what you ask for. . . . For everyone who asks, receives. Everyone who seeks, finds. And the door is opened to everyone who knocks" (Matthew 7:7-8, NLT).

WHITE ROBES
As the bride of Christ, believers will be beautifully adorned in robes of white to meet their Husband and King, Jesus Christ. "The time has come for the wedding feast of the Lamb, and his bride has prepared herself. She is permitted to wear the finest white linen" (Revelation 19:7-8, NLT).

FAITH

FAITH

Faith is "a belief in or confident attitude toward God, involving commitment to His will for one's life. According to Hebrews 11, faith was already present in the experience of many people in the Old Testament as a key element of their spiritual lives" (*Nelson's*).

11

TESTED FAITH

Trouble in Persia tested Esther's and Mordecai's faith, causing it to flourish. Trials in your life test whether your faith will flourish or falter. "Whenever trouble comes your way, let it be an opportunity for joy. For when your faith is tested, your endurance has a chance to grow" (James 1:2-3, NLT).

c. Describe the sounds and sights that filled the throne room (v. 5).

. . . .

d. Describe what was before and around the throne (v. 6).

. . . .

10. After Esther fasted and prayed she had the faith to do what she needed to do. Hebrews 11, known as the great hall of faith, repeats the phrase "by faith." Skim Hebrews 11, then check off the qualities you would like to have by faith.

— By faith Abel made a pleasant offering to God.
— By faith Enoch pleased God.
— By faith Noah feared God.
— By faith Abraham obeyed God.
— By faith Sarah received God's promise.
— By faith Moses chose suffering rather than pleasures of sin.
— By faith the walls of Jericho fell down.

Journal about a recent situation when you lacked faith and explain why. Which saint's example in Hebrews 11 can you imitate to increase your faith? (Examples: please God, fear God, obey God, etc.)

. . . .

. . . .

. . . .

. . . .

. . . .

11. Like Esther and the Old Testament saints, Christians must resolutely exercise their faith to do what God asks and to receive His promises.

Journal a prayer asking God to strengthen your faith by rewriting the following verse: "It is impossible to please God without faith. Anyone who wants to come to him must believe that there is a God and that he rewards those who sincerely seek him" (Hebrews 11:6, NLT).

. . . .

. . . .

. . . .

. . . .

Stepping out in faith as Esther did isn't easy, but when you do, God does amazing things. In 1981 I was unsure whether God wanted me to step out in faith, marry Skip, and move to New Mexico. One night I decided to fast from sleep until I knew God's will for my life. Praying Jacob's prayer, "I will not let you go unless you bless me" (Genesis 32:26, NIV), I wrestled with God for a promise to hold on to. He brought Isaiah 49 to mind. I quickly turned there and was astounded by God's answers to my questions as I personalized this passage (Isaiah 49:11-12, NIV). I wrote the date 5/15/81 in my Bible and scribbled in green marker my understanding of God's promises.

I underlined "desert heat" and "mountains" from verses 10 and 11 and wrote, "New Mexico" in the margin. Beside "from the west" (v. 12) I wrote "from California." I circled "like a bride" (v. 18) and wrote "Yes, a bride!" I believed the passage predicted what God would do through our union. "The children born . . . will yet say . . . , 'This place is too small for us; give us more space to live in'" (v. 20). I had faith God would give us many spiritual children. I wrote in the margin, "God will multiply in New Mexico."

I took the leap of faith, and everything God promised has come true. I was a bride who moved to New Mexico from California. Because of rapid growth, our church has moved five times and expanded our current facility three times. Calvary of Albuquerque is now home to fourteen thousand spiritual children.

contemplation
If all things are possible with God, then all things are possible to him who believes in him.
Corrie ten Boom

DAY 2 THE QUEEN MAKES HER MOVE

preparation

Lord, this world can be a scary place full of people with ulterior motives, seeking to take advantage of others. Give me the wisdom to avoid their traps and humbly oppose their agendas. Amen.

WISDOM
Behold, I send you out as sheep in the midst of wolves. Therefore be wise as serpents and harmless as doves.
Matthew 10:16

For centuries chess was a slow, strategic game. However, things really perked up at the end of the 1400s with the invention of two long-range pieces: the bishop and the queen. The game became more fast paced and tactical when these attacking pieces were introduced. While bishops have the freedom to move diagonally an unlimited number of squares, queens can move diagonally, backward or forward, left or right an unlimited number of squares. Both pieces are extremely deadly because of their mobility, but the queen reigns supreme as the most powerful piece on the chessboard.

Queen Esther got into the game by getting into the throne room. Ahasuerus broadened her power base when he offered her anything "up to half the kingdom." With her newfound mobility she played the game with tactical finesse. To accomplish her purpose she showed how shrewd, clever, and resourceful a queen can be.

Haman was promoted from "pawn" to "bishop" when everyone in the kingdom was forced to bow as he passed by. He believed that he had all the right moves with unlimited power. Little did he know that there was someone more powerful and adroit who could take him out of action. Both the king and Haman were unaware that the queen was ready to make her move. She invited them both to a banquet, strategically placing them in positions that would be to her advantage.

exploration

Esther boldly entered the throne room, trusting God to protect her. Today we see that she patiently awaited God's perfect timing to reveal Haman's destructive plan to the king.

Review Esther 5; then focus on verses 4-8.

So Esther answered, "If it pleases the king, let the king and Haman come today to the banquet that I have prepared for him." Then the king said, "Bring Haman quickly, that he may do as Esther has said." So the king and Haman went to the banquet that Esther had prepared. Esther 5:4-5

1. What reasonable request did Esther make? . . . .

. . . .

2. Describe the king's response to Esther's invitation.

. . . .

3. How do you know the king was eager to please Esther?

. . . .

At the banquet of wine the king said to Esther, "What is your petition? It shall be granted you. What is your request, up to half the kingdom? It shall be done!" Then Esther answered and said, "My petition and request is this: If I have found favor in the sight of the king, and if it pleases the king to grant my petition and fulfill my request, then let the king and Haman come to the banquet which I will prepare for them, and tomorrow I will do as the king has said." Esther 5:6-8

4. What did the king again want to know? . . . .

. . . .

5. What assurance did the king give that he would grant her request?

. . . .

6. Rather than immediately exposing Haman's plot, what did Esther do?

. . . .

. . . .

1

BANQUET
Rather than demanding the king's protection, Esther sought the king's company. She invited him to a banquet and suggested he bring Haman, her enemy. Perhaps she remembered God's promise, "You prepare a table before me in the presence of my enemies" (Psalm 23:5).

5

ASK ANYTHING
The king assured Esther whatever she asked would be done. Jesus assures us, "Yes, ask anything in my name, and I will do it!" (John 14:14, NLT). Esther's limitations were "up to half the kingdom." Our limitations are to "ask him for anything in line with his will" (1 John 5:14, NLT).

PATIENCE

Esther understood that patience is a virtue, so she did not hurry her request to the king. Patiently she refrained from making her petition. Esther was sensitive to God's timing and showed she would "be patient in trouble, and always be prayerful" (Romans 12:12, NLT).

8.

QUICKLY

Quickly means "rapidly, speedily, or intently" and is marked by readiness or promptness. Over ten times in the New Testament, Jesus urged his followers to act quickly. Jesus wants us to be in a constant state of preparedness. He said, "Look, I am coming quickly" (Revelation 3:11, NLT).

9.

ASSURANCE

Jesus said, "I tell you the truth"—now that's assurance. To have assurance means to know that you know the truth, free from doubt and uncertainty. Biblically, assurance is believers' full confidence that their sins are forgiven and that they will enjoy eternal life because of Christ's finished work on the cross.

7. When would she reveal what she wanted from the king?

. . . .

transformation

8. The king quickly gave Haman the invitation to Esther's banquet. He was ready and willing to share the news. Similarly, the angel at Christ's tomb told the women to "go quickly and tell his disciples he has been raised from the dead" (Matthew 28:7, NLT). Check the box that indicates how quick *you* usually are to tell others about the good news of salvation in Jesus.

— Right away
— Sooner or later
— Later than sooner
— Never

Journal a prayer asking God to help you pick up the pace when sharing the gospel with others.

. . . .

. . . .

. . . .

. . . .

9. The king offered words of assurance to Esther when he offered to fulfill her request within reason. Jesus gives us assurance too. Fill in the chart to discover some of the assurances He has given.

SCRIPTURE	ASSUREDLY—"I TELL YOU THE TRUTH"
Matt. 5:18 . . . .
Matt. 17:20 . . . .
Mark 3:28-29 . . . .
Mark 10:29-30 . . . .

10. Esther and Haman each had a strategy for getting what they wanted. Esther exercised patient planning while Haman engaged in power plays. Proverbs 16:32 extols patience over power.

Journal a prayer asking God to help you learn how to exercise patience in the difficult circumstances you face by rewriting the following verse. "It is better to be patient than powerful; it is better to have self-control than to conquer a city" (Proverbs 16:32, NLT).

. . . .

. . . .

. . . .

. . . .

10
ACT PATIENTLY
Patience does not sit idly by as time marches on; it is active, not passive. Patient people pursue godly activities while they wait. Pray while you wait, watch while you wait, or work while you wait. "But you, O man of God, flee these things and pursue . . . patience" (1 Timothy 6:11).

Guess who's coming to dinner? Have you thought of including your enemy on your guest list? Solomon did: "If your enemies are hungry, give them food to eat. If they are thirsty, give them water to drink. You will heap burning coals on their heads, and the Lord will reward you" (Proverbs 25:21-22, NLT). My husband, Skip, took Solomon's advice when he invited Damien out for coffee.

Damien, who dabbled in the occult, had been calling the church for weeks, scaring the receptionists with threats to burn down the building, assassinate Skip, and harm Nathan and me. The women trembled at the sound of his low, growling voice, "This is Damien. I'm gonna burn the church."

One day Damien phoned, and Skip grabbed the receiver, saying, "I think you're a coward calling and scaring my staff. Are you brave enough to meet me for coffee so we can talk?"

And he was. Damien wasn't a threat; he was a runaway teenager suffering with AIDS. Skip led him to the Lord, had him apologize to the secretaries, and paid his bus fare home.

Esther invited her enemy Haman to dinner not once but twice. Perhaps she wanted to see whether she could turn an enemy into a friend. Paul said, "If it is possible, as much as depends on you, live peaceably with all men" (Romans 12:18). But as we'll see, there are some with whom it is impossible to live peaceably.

contemplation
Patience and gentleness is power.
Leigh Hunt

185

DAY 3 THE KNIGHT'S ADVANTAGE

preparation

Father, there are times in the heat of a battle when I want to run and hide. Help me to stand my ground in the power of Your might. Keep me steady with Your truth and righteousness. Amen.

STANDING SURE
Stand your ground, putting on the sturdy belt of truth and the body armor of God's righteousness.
Ephesians 6:14, NLT

In the game of chess, bishops and knights are almost evenly matched, wielding nearly the same amount of power. However, knights possess two strategic advantages. First, they are the only pieces that aren't stopped by opponents in their path because of their ability to hop over obstacles. Second, when knights maintain position in the center of the board, they strictly limit the mobility of all the other pieces that run a greater risk of being captured. Because of this middle-ground advantage, chess players warn against positioning knights on the rim (edge) or in the corners of the chessboard. Two cute sayings sum up this game-winning philosophy: "A knight on the rim is dim," and "A knight in the corner makes you a mourner."

Mordecai, in Persia's life or death contest, adopted both of the strategic advantages possessed by knights in a chess game. First, Mordecai found a way to jump over Haman's egotistical demands by refusing to bow down to him. And up to this point Haman couldn't stop Mordecai's civil disobedience. Second, Mordecai stood his ground right in the middle of the king's gate, effectively blocking Haman's way and limiting his progress. As a result, Haman's countenance grew dim as Mordecai avoided the rim. Unable to force Mordecai into the corner, Haman became a mourner.

exploration

Esther put her game plan into action by inviting Haman and the king to two banquets. Today we see how Haman responded to an encounter with Mordecai after leaving the first banquet.

Review Esther 5; then focus on verses 9-10.

So Haman went out that day joyful and with a glad heart; but when Haman saw Mordecai in the king's gate, and that he did not stand or tremble before him, he was filled with indignation against Mordecai.
Esther 5:9

1. How was Haman feeling as he went his way after the banquet?

. . . .

. . . .

2. Remembering yesterday's lesson, what would account for Haman's feelings?

. . . .

3. Where did Haman encounter Mordecai? . . . .

. . . .

4. How did Mordecai again defy Haman? . . . .

. . . .

5. Explain how seeing Mordecai affected Haman's joy.

. . . .

. . . .

Nevertheless Haman restrained himself and went home, and he sent and called for his friends and his wife Zeresh. Esther 5:10

6. Rather than attacking Mordecai, what did Haman do?

. . . .

. . . .

7. Whom did Haman gather around him? . . . .

. . . .

explanation

2

UPS
Haman had every reason to be happy: the king's promotion, the people's respect, and the queen's invitations. He should enjoy the "up" while it lasts. "Enjoy prosperity while you can. But when hard times strike, realize that both come from God. . . . Nothing is certain in this life" (Ecclesiastes 7:14, NLT).

5

DOWNS
Haman's bitterness toward Mordecai became like an anchor—every time he tried to get up, it dragged him down. Warning! "Jealousy and selfishness are not God's kind of wisdom. Such things are earthly, unspiritual, and motivated by the Devil" (James 3:15, NLT).

7

ALL AROUND
When Haman became upset, he attempted to settle himself back down by surrounding himself with people who could comfort him. When you are down, it's a good idea to find friends who will lift you up. "Bear one another's burdens, and so fulfill the law of Christ" (Galatians 6:2).

UPS AND DOWNS

Emotions can soar one minute then sink the next. What goes up eventually comes back down. Happiness based on circumstances is like a roller-coaster ride. Joy in the Lord, not circumstances, remains constant. "Let all who take refuge in you rejoice; let them sing joyful praises forever" (Psalm 5:11, NLT).

9

BITTER

The root word for *bitter* means "to cut or to prick." Literally, *bitter* means pointed, sharp, and pungent to taste or smell (adapted, *Vine's*). In the New Testament, a "root of bitterness" is a wicked person or a sin that leads to denial of the faith (see Hebrews 12:15; adapted, *Nelson's*).

transformation

8. Circumstances in Haman's life made him sink or soar. What gets you up? What brings you down? Place an arrow pointing up ↑ or down ↓ next to the items in the following list to show which direction they take you.

— Your children   — Your job

— Your marriage   — Your health

— World news   — The weather

— The stock market   — The government

Journal about a day that was full of ups and downs. What caused the changes? What could you have done to find stable ground?

. . . .

. . . .

. . . .

9. The reason Haman's feelings were brought low so readily was because of his bitter heart. With this in mind, place the attributes listed in the following passage in the appropriate columns. "Let all bitterness, wrath, anger, clamor, and evil speaking be put away from you, with all malice. And be kind to one another, tenderhearted, forgiving one another, just as God in Christ forgave you. Therefore be imitators of God as dear children. And walk in love" (Ephesians 4:31–5:2).

Bitter Behavior   **Better Behavior**

. . . .

. . . .

. . . .

. . . .

. . . .

. . . .

10. When Haman was attempting to restrain his indignation, he surrounded himself with friends and family. Whom do you turn to when you are upset?

. . . .

Journal a prayer asking God to surround you with His presence when you are feeling emotionally vulnerable. Rewrite the following passage as part of your prayer: "I will cry to you for help, for my heart is overwhelmed. Lead me to the towering rock of safety, for you are my safe refuge, a fortress where my enemies cannot reach me" (Psalm 61:2-3, NLT).

. . . .

. . . .

RESTRAIN ANGER
Time will tell if Haman has completely restrained his anger or if he's letting it simmer. His friends will either defuse the situation or stir up the pot. "Be . . . slow to get angry. Your anger can never make things right in God's sight" (James 1:19-20, NLT).

Haman had a major anger problem. Instead of resolving conflict, he went postal. From airport rage to school shootings, it's obvious that people today don't know how to deal with their anger either. Psychologist Richard Driscoll offers this anger test: (1) Do you feel mistreated by others? (2) Do you take minor inconveniences personally? (3) Do you complain often? (4) Do you exaggerate the actions of others? (5) Do you frequently yell at other drivers? If you answered yes more than you answered no, your anger quotient is too high. Here are some suggestions to bring it down.

Change or accept: When you feel anger welling up, take a change it or accept-it approach. If you can do something constructive to change the situation, do it. If nothing can be done, learn to accept it.

Don't take it personally: If you've thought, *That shouldn't have happened to me* or *I don't deserve that,* you're taking things too personally. Smart people adopt a water-on-the-back-of-a-duck approach when dealing with life's unfairnesses.

Stop dwelling on the past: If you remember a minor infraction long after it happened, it's time to let go. Life has moved on and so should you. Think of the problem as having been caused by the situation, not the person.

Adjust your routine: Avoid upsetting situations. If long lines upset you, don't shop on crowded weekends. Avoiding frustrating situations helps defuse anger.

contemplation
Don't get angry at the person who acts in ways that displease you. Give him the smile he lacks. Spread the sunshine of your Lord's limitless love.
Joni Eareckson Tada

preparation

God, I am reminded that Your ways are not our ways. We boast and bargain to receive a promotion. You ask us to humble ourselves and serve others. Help us to exalt You, and then we will be exalted! Amen.

PROMOTION
Therefore humble yourselves under the mighty hand of God, that He may exalt you in due time, casting all your care upon Him, for He cares for you.
1 Peter 5:6-7

If you march a pawn all the way across a chessboard to your opponent's side, you get a huge reward. A pawn that advances from one end of the board to the other is "promoted" and can be changed into any piece of your choosing except a king. Most of the time players promote their pawns to queens since that is the most powerful piece. But every once in a while it's best to select another piece when promoting a pawn.

Haman has been on the march since early in the book of Esther. He has plowed through enemy territory, reaching his opponents' side. As a result the king has promoted him and required all the people in Persia to pay him homage—in effect, to worship him. "Bishop" Haman even raised the finances necessary to support a holy war to annihilate his enemy, "Knight" Mordecai, and all the Jews who refused to deny their God and bow to worship a mere man. God explicitly warns His people against worshiping either man or beast, heavenly constellations or gods: "You shall have no other gods before Me. You shall not make for yourself a carved image, or any likeness of anything that is in heaven above, or that is in the earth beneath, or that is in the water under the earth; you shall not bow down to them nor serve them" (Exodus 20:3-5). Haman was not content with the king's promotion but felt the need to promote himself.

exploration

Haman was a man of many emotional ups and downs. He was up in the presence of the king and queen and down in the presence of Mordecai. Today we will see how he acted in the presence of his friends and family.

Review Esther 5; then focus on verses 11-12.

Then Haman told them of his great riches, the multitude of his children, everything in which the king had promoted him, and how he had advanced him above the officials and servants of the king. Esther 5:11

1. What things did Haman boast about concerning his personal life?

. . . .

. . . .

2. What did he boast about concerning his professional life?

. . . .

3. Why do you think Haman felt the need to boast after running into Mordecai?

. . . .

. . . .

Moreover Haman said, "Besides, Queen Esther invited no one but me to come in with the king to the banquet that she prepared; and tomorrow I am again invited by her, along with the king." Esther 5:12

4. Explain what Haman boasted about concerning the first banquet.

. . . .

5. What future event did he boast about? . . . .

. . . .

6. What phrase did he use to put himself on the same level as the king?

. . . .

. . . .

explanation

I'M RICH!
Boasting in riches is foolish because they are fleeting. Trusting in God is wise because He is eternal. "Command those who are rich in this present age not to be haughty, nor to trust in uncertain riches but in the living God, who gives us richly all things to enjoy" (1 Timothy 6:17).

4
I'M IMPORTANT!
Haman bragged about his riches, children, and position and concluded that he was a VIP (very important person). But really he was a VAP (very arrogant person). The Bible would call him a VEP (very evil person). "You boast in your arrogance. All such boasting is evil" (James 4:16).

I'M EXALTED!
Haman's boasting had reached epic proportions—he was as good as a king! Apparently his pride knew no end. Boasting means to speak with excessive pride and usually implies exaggeration and glorifying oneself. The biblical definition is picturesque: to "lift up the neck" (adapted, *Vine's*).

IGNORE THEM

When people boast, they reveal what they love most. Girls may love their pearls, while boys might love their toys. The reason people boast is to get others to notice them. Paul urged a tough-love approach to people who boast—ignore them! "From such people turn away!" (2 Timothy 3:5).

BOAST IN GOD

Not all boasting is bad. Boasting in God is very good—for you and those around you. "My soul shall make its boast in the Lord; the humble shall hear of it and be glad. Oh, magnify the Lord with me, and let us exalt His name together" (Psalm 34:2-3).

transformation

7. Paul warned about men in the last days who would behave much like Haman did. Read 2 Timothy 3:1-5, and answer the following questions:

   a. Which characteristics in this list remind you of Haman?

   . . . .

   b. Which characteristics have you ever displayed?

   . . . .

   c. According to Paul, how should believers respond to those who exhibit these traits?

   . . . .

   > Journal a prayer of repentance asking God to forgive you for displaying any of the character traits listed in this passage.

   . . . .

   . . . .

   . . . .

8. Haman sinfully boasted about his accomplishments, his family, and his riches. Jeremiah 9:23-24 reveals what we should and should not boast in. Place the phrases from the following passage in the appropriate columns. "Let not the wise man gloat in his wisdom, or the mighty man in his might, or the rich man in his riches. Let them boast in this alone: that they truly know me and understand that I am the Lord who is just and righteous, whose love is unfailing, and that I delight in these things" (NLT).

Sinful Boasting	Holy Boasting
. . . .	. . . .
. . . .	. . . .
. . . .	. . . .
. . . .	. . . .

9. Haman exalted himself. Take the time now to exalt the Lord.

Journal a list of great things God has done for you. Then share your list with someone else in order to boast about God's goodness.

. . . .

. . . .

. . . .

. . . .

A wealthy Texas rancher invited his pastor to dinner. After a lavish meal served on the finest china, they moved to the balcony to enjoy the view and drink coffee.

Pointing to the oil wells bobbing in the distance the Texan boasted, "Twenty-five years ago I didn't own a thing. Today those gushers are all mine." Pointing in the opposite direction at his vast fields of grain, he said, "All those acres are mine." Turning to his numerous herds of cattle, he bragged, "They're all mine." Then directing the pastor's attention to a beautiful forest, he exclaimed, "That's mine too."

Puffed up with pride, he waited for his pastor's admiration. Instead, the man of God placed one hand on the man's shoulder, pointed in the air with the other, and inquired, "How much do you have in that direction?"

The deflated rancher hung his head and muttered, "I never thought of that." An eternal perspective brought that Texan down a notch or two.

Haman and the Texas rancher were full of pride, strutting their stuff to impress others. Haman pointed to his children, to his large bank account, and to his connection with important people. He even made a point of comparing himself to the king. But Scripture reminds us, "Pride goes before destruction, and haughtiness before a fall" (Proverbs 16:18, NLT). Haman, beware! When you build yourself up too high, the only way to go is down.

9
EXALT GOD
Boasters need a perspective check. Instead of pridefully looking down on others, they should humbly look up to God. Seeing the greatness of God makes us mindful of the smallness of humanity. "Be exalted, O God, above the highest heavens! May your glory shine over all the earth" (Psalm 57:5, NLT).

contemplation

If there's anything small, shallow, arrogant, or ugly about a person, giving him a little authority will bring it out.
Unknown

DAY 5 BISHOP TAKES KNIGHT?

preparation

Lord, in the game of life it is difficult to know what moves to make. Thank You for seeing the whole game plan and showing me the right path. I want to listen to Your instructions so I can emerge victorious. Amen.

RIGHT PATH

Lead me in the right path, O Lord, or my enemies will conquer me. Tell me clearly what to do, and show me which way to turn. Psalm 5:8, NLT

A piece may *capture* any opposing chess piece that stops its progress. A player makes a capture by moving a piece to a space occupied by an enemy piece. The player removes the captured piece from the board and replaces it with the capturing piece on the space. A piece in danger of being captured is considered *under attack* and risks being taken from the game.

Each piece in chess captures in its own prescribed manner. For instance, the pawn captures differently than the way it moves. The pawn, like the foot soldier in war, marches forward one square at a time but can only capture diagonally, as if fighting to the side with a short sword. Knights capture by jumping directly on top of an enemy piece. Since the bishop cannot jump over other pieces that block its progress as a knight can, it must capture those pieces that impede him.

"Knight" Mordecai has persistently blocked "Bishop" Haman's progress and jumped over his demands. Since Haman can't jump over Mordecai, who is in his way, he is convinced his only option is to take the enemy out. Because Mordecai has dominated the center of this game, he has effectively forced Haman into a corner. For Haman to advance, he must *capture* his enemy. Now Mordecai is *under attack* and in danger of being taken out!

exploration

Haman convened his friends and family to listen to his many accomplishments. Today we see him turn his boasting party into a war party.

Review Esther 5; then focus on verses 13-14.

"Yet all this avails me nothing, so long as I see Mordecai the Jew sitting at the king's gate." Esther 5:13

1. Why was Haman filled with self-pity despite the honors he had received?

. . . .

. . . .

2. Explain the "problem" that preoccupied Haman.

. . . .

Then his wife Zeresh and all his friends said to him, "Let a gallows be made, fifty cubits high, and in the morning suggest to the king that Mordecai be hanged on it; then go merrily with the king to the banquet." And the thing pleased Haman; so he had the gallows made. Esther 5:14

3. Describe the plan Haman's wife and friends hatched concerning Mordecai.

. . . .

. . . .

4. What were the dimensions of this deadly contraption?

. . . .

. . . .

5. How would Haman feel after Mordecai was put to death?

. . . .

6. What would Haman do after Mordecai's death?

. . . .

7. How did Haman respond to this deadly plot?

. . . .

---

explanation

1

OFF BALANCE
Haman's system of accounting was off balance. He had a huge list of assets and only one deficit: Mordecai. But in Haman's mind, his hatred toward Mordecai weighed more than his happiness from his accomplishments. When you assess your circumstances wrongly, it will rob you of your joy.

4

OVERKILL
A cubit was typically measured from the elbow to the fingertip, about 18-20 inches. In modern measurements Haman's gallows would stand 75 feet high. When Haman made an execution device for Mordecai, he made sure that everyone would see it. It was like killing a fly with a sledgehammer—overkill.

5

BACKWARD
Haman's friends had a skewed perspective, thinking Haman could murder Mordecai, then go merrily along. But murder is not merry! "Destruction is certain for those who say that evil is good and good is evil; that dark is light and light is dark" (Isaiah 5:20, NLT).

COMPARISONS
Comparing means finding differences and likenesses to establish relative value. God's values and the world's values aren't always the same. "God chose . . . things counted as nothing at all, and used them to bring to nothing what the world considers important" (1 Corinthians 1:28, NLT)

NO COMPARISON
We should never compare God to anyone or anything else. He is beyond compare! "For who in all of heaven can compare with the Lord? What mightiest angel is anything like the Lord? . . . Where is there anyone as mighty as you, Lord?" (Psalm 89:6-8, NLT).

CONTAGIOUS
Bad attitudes can be as contagious as a pesky virus. When people sneeze, they cover their mouth to stop spreading germs. It's good to cover your mouth before spreading any decaying sayings. "Don't be fooled by those who say such things, for 'bad company corrupts good character'" (1 Corinthians 15:33, NLT).

transformation

8. When Haman wrongly compared all his assets to the one deficit of knowing Mordecai would not bow down to him, he was left feeling bankrupt. Do you allow the few deficits you experience to outweigh your assets? In the columns provided, list your assets and deficits. Consider all areas of your life.

Many Assets   **Few Deficits**

. . . .

. . . .

. . . .

. . . .

. . . .

. . . .

. . . .

9. When Paul rightly compared all his personal accomplishments with the greatest asset of knowing Christ, he saw them for what they really were—nothing. Look at the list of your assets and realize they, too, are nothing compared to Christ.

> Journal Philippians 3:7-8 into a personal prayer acknowledging Christ's worth: "What things were gain to me, these I have counted loss for Christ. Yet indeed I also count all things loss for the excellence of the knowledge of Christ Jesus my Lord, for whom I have suffered the loss of all things, and count them as rubbish, that I may gain Christ."

. . . .

. . . .

. . . .

10. Haman's bitterness infected his friends and family so that they were willing to plot evil against Mordecai too.

Journal about a time when someone's sinful attitude infected yours or when your bad attitude influenced someone else for evil.

. . . .

. . . .

. . . .

. . . .

Winners in chess are the ones who have the best strategy, tactically moving each piece without losing sight of the master plan. Winners act like the coach of a sports team, utilizing the strengths and full potential of each player. Every piece working together effectively achieves victory. One piece alone probably wouldn't be able to attack the opponent's king with much success, but the combined strength of several pieces makes a powerful attacking force.

So far it appears that Haman and Mordecai have fought this battle *mano a mano.* However, while Haman has focused his attack on Mordecai, another battle has been started on a different front. Esther has strategically gathered her forces to flank Haman and blindside him.

A well-played chess game has three stages. In the *opening,* the players bring out their forces in preparation for combat. The *middle game* begins as the players maneuver for position and carry out attacks and counterattacks. The final stage is the *endgame* when, with fewer pieces left on the board, it is safer for the kings to come out and join the final battle.

In Esther 3 and 4 we witnessed the opening of this contest of wills when Haman and Mordecai made their opening moves. In chapter 5 we've seen the middle game played as "Bishop" Haman, "Knight" Mordecai, and Queen Esther have strategically maneuvered for position. In chapter 6 we'll see the endgame begin when King Ahasuerus enters the fray! Who will outwit, outmaneuver, and outlast in this life-and-death game?

contemplation

God alone knows all the facts, sets all the goals, and determines morality. Nowhere in Scripture are his principles to be replaced in favor of human calculation. He allows us to play the game; he does not allow us to make the rules.
Erwin W. Lutzer

Pecking Order

In the animal kingdom an order of dominance is established by a "might makes right" mentality. With cattle it is called the "horning order." Among sheep it is spoken of as the "butting order." In a pen full of chickens it is referred to as the "pecking order." Each species utilizes their strongest asset, whether a horn or a beak, to bully one another in an attempt to possess the best grazing or the most desirable breeding partner.

Pecking is a prevalent problem among game bird flocks and can lead to cannibalism if not dealt with severely. The problem usually begins by innocent pecking or pulling feathers as they establish the social order and can escalate until it is out of control. Generally an arrogant, cunning, and domineering bird will bully any bunch of birds, maintaining its position of prestige by driving other birds or chicks away from the best grazing. This continuous conflict and jealousy within the flock can be quite detrimental. The birds cannot lie down, rest in contentment, or lay eggs. The flock becomes edgy, tense, discontented, and restless. They lose weight and become irritable. Some even get pecked to death.

Haman has become a domineering bully in Persia. He has thrown around his weight and pushed his way to the top of the pecking order. But he will get his feathers ruffled when Mordecai struts his stuff at the king's command.

DAY 1
Night Owl

DAY 2
Early Bird

DAY 3
Proud As a Peacock

DAY 4
Eating Crow

DAY 5
Dead Duck

DAY **1** NIGHT OWL

preparation

Father, it's hard to sit on the sidelines as others soar to new heights. Help me to wait on You for new strength. Give me wings to fly above my circumstances. Amen.

FLYING HIGH
*Those who wait on the Lord will find new strength. They will fly high on wings like eagles. They will run and not grow weary. They will walk and not faint.
Isaiah 40:31, NLT*

explanation

INSOMNIA
There's something the rich and famous have that you don't want— insomnia. Throughout Scripture, kings and noblemen frequently had their sleep inter- rupted. "People who work hard sleep well, . . . but the rich are always worrying and seldom get a good night's sleep" (Ecclesi- astes 5:12, NLT).

exploration

Things looked bad for the Jews. Their mortal enemy Haman had attained great prominence in the land, second only to the king. The edict had been dispersed calling for their destruction. But God providentially placed Esther on the throne, gave her favor with Ahasuerus, and remembered Mordecai's service to the king. God was at work behind the scenes in Persia and would fulfill His promise to protect His chosen people from their enemies. Today we'll see how the God "who watches over Israel never tires and never sleeps" (Psalm 121:4, NLT). He was busy at work in the king's palace throughout the night.

Read Esther 6; then focus on verses 1-3.

> *That night the king could not sleep. So one was commanded to bring the book of the records of the chronicles; and they were read before the king.*
> Esther 6:1

1. What condition disturbed the king the night after Esther's first banquet?

. . . .

2. How did the king deal with his restlessness? . . . .

. . . .

3. What was done with these records? . . . .

. . . .

And it was found written that Mordecai had told of Bigthana and Teresh, two of the king's eunuchs, the doorkeepers who had sought to lay hands on King Ahasuerus. Esther 6:2

4. What treasonous story was read to the king? . . . .

. . . .

5. Explain why Mordecai was the hero of this story.

. . . .

. . . .

Then the king said, "What honor or dignity has been bestowed on Mordecai for this?" And the king's servants who attended him said, "Nothing has been done for him." Esther 6:3

6. What question did the king ask concerning Mordecai?

. . . .

7. How did his servants respond? . . . .

. . . .

transformation

8. God used insomnia in this king's life to accomplish His will. Fill in the chart to discover why the sleep of other biblical figures was disrupted.

SCRIPTURE	WHY DISRUPTED SLEEP
Dan. 2:1-3	
Dan. 6:16-19	
Matt. 1:20-24	
Matt. 27:17-19	

DIVINE READING
Ahasuerus maintained an elaborate log of his twelve-year reign, detailing his daily events and especially recording the deeds of those who had served him well. Providentially, the librarian chose the text containing Mordecai's good deed. God can direct the books people read as well as the sleep patterns of kings.

7
OVERSIGHT
Persian rulers used rewards to maintain loyalty among their subjects. The king realized that failing to honor the man who had saved his life was a serious oversight. In retrospect, we see that God providentially delayed Mordecai's reward to come at the perfect time when his people needed rescuing.

8
TIME TO SLEEP
When King Ahasuerus couldn't sleep, he read a boring book. When you can't sleep, try reading the Good Book. "I will lie down in peace and sleep, for you alone, O Lord, will keep me safe" (Psalm 4:8, NLT). It will teach you to count your blessings instead of sheep.

RIGHT TIMING
It's not just *what* you say that matters but *when* and *how* you say it. Blurting out information prematurely is not always beneficial. Saying the right thing at the right time is better. "A word fitly spoken is like apples of gold in settings of silver" (Proverbs 25:11).

10

TIMELY REWARD
In God's kingdom no service, however small, goes unnoticed. If you feel unrecognized or uncompensated in some part of your life, take heart—God sees and remembers and will reward you in due season. "He is a rewarder of those who diligently seek Him" (Hebrews 11:6).

Journal about a time when your sleep was disrupted. What were you thinking about? What did you do?

. . . .

. . . .

. . . .

. . . .

9. Mordecai knew how to keep privileged information concealed, such as the lineage of Esther. He also knew when to reveal a secret matter, especially if it pertained to life and death. In the appropriate columns, list the things you should secretly conceal or openly reveal.

Conceal	**Reveal**
(Example: Your husband's bad habits)	(Example: Teenage neighbor seen smoking)
. . . .	. . . .
. . . .	. . . .
. . . .	. . . .
. . . .	. . . .
. . . .	. . . .

10. Ahasuerus had forgotten and failed to reward Mordecai's service. God's rewards are sure to come to His saints.

Journal Isaiah 40:10 into a prayer of hope for your sure and coming rewards: "Yes, the Sovereign Lord is coming in all his glorious power. He will rule with awesome strength. See, he brings his reward with him as he comes" (NLT).

. . . .

. . . .

. . . .

Let's face it, ruling the world has got to be stressful. I'm sure King Ahasuerus had worries of his own: the affairs of state or the queen's mysterious request. Perhaps he was tormented by the "could haves" and "should haves" of his life. He could have controlled his temper with Vashti, and he should have rewarded Mordecai.

Insomnia has plagued my family for many generations. In the wee hours of the night, a glowing light from my grandma's bedroom meant she was up playing solitaire. My mother inherited the nasty gene, and on many a sleepless night she can be found with a Diet Pepsi in one hand and the TV remote control in the other. As you may have guessed, I also suffer from insomnia.

I've concluded that my disrupted sleep patterns don't come from some genetic predisposition but a personal propensity to worry. (And I'm pretty sure that's why my ancestors couldn't sleep either.) I worry about Skip's health, Nathan's future, and all the "could haves" and "should haves" in my life. Playing cards, watching TV, and reading books has not helped. In desperation I told one of the staff pastors at our church that I couldn't sleep. Amazingly, he said that he couldn't either. Just knowing we weren't the only ones gave us comfort. We decided that if we couldn't sleep, we would start to pray. Shifting the focus off of self and onto others helped me to fall asleep. I discovered, "He gives His beloved sleep" (Psalm 127:2), when we trust Him with the details of our lives.

contemplation
A weary Christian lay awake one night trying to hold the world together by his worrying. Then he heard the Lord gently say to him, "Now you go to sleep, . . . I'll sit up."
Ruth Bell Graham

preparation

Lord, sometimes I look for riches in my bank account, honor from my friends, and long life from the gym. Those are the wrong places to look. Teach me to be humble and to wait for Your rewards. Amen.

HONOR
True humility and fear of the Lord lead to riches, honor, and long life. Proverbs 22:4, NLT

There are two things my dad loves: the birds that visit his feeder and the fish that live in his pond. Every morning he puts fresh birdseed out, then retires to the sunroom to record which birds from his bird-watcher's book have come to visit. And each evening he strolls out to his rock waterfall to feed the fish who swim happily in his koi pond.

Trouble in paradise began when a rare sandhill crane was migrating through New Mexico and spotted my dad's pond. He quickly realized that he had discovered a buffet just there for the taking. This bird had uncanny timing, knowing that the early bird gets the worm, or in this case the koi. On the first morning my dad caught him gulping down mass quantities of fish. Dad came running with arms flailing, shouting, "Get away from my fish!" The next morning the first koi to go was my dad's favorite fish named Chubby. Dad watched the crane fly away with Chubby hanging out of his beak. He tried to guard the pond and his precious fish, but the crane got up too early. Before long, he no longer had a koi pond, he just had a pond. So the crane moved on.

Haman was the early bird moving in for the kill. He believed that Mordecai was a big fish, just there for the taking. Little did he know that trouble was brewing in paradise.

exploration

A sleepless night reminded the king that he had not rewarded Mordecai for saving his life. Before Ahasuerus decided how to respond, he sought counsel from the early bird, Haman.

Review Esther 6; then focus on verses 4-6.

So the king said, "Who is in the court?" Now Haman had just entered the outer court of the king's palace to suggest that the king hang Mordecai on the gallows that he had prepared for him. The king's servants said to him, "Haman is there, standing in the court." And the king said, "Let him come in." Esther 6:4-5

1. What was the first question the king asked? . . . .

. . . .

2. Why had Haman come early to the palace? . . . .

. . . .

3. What did the king do upon hearing of Haman's presence in the court?

. . . .

4. How might this action have bolstered Haman's sense of confidence?

. . . .

So Haman came in, and the king asked him, "What shall be done for the man whom the king delights to honor?" Now Haman thought in his heart, "Whom would the king delight to honor more than me?" Esther 6:6

5. What theoretical question did the king ask Haman?

. . . .

. . . .

6. Who was the king really thinking of honoring? . . . .

. . . .

7. Describe what Haman was thinking. . . . .

. . . .

explanation

2
EARLY RISER
Haman couldn't sleep until he set in motion the bitter scheme that was running through his mind. "Evil people cannot sleep until they have done their evil deed for the day. They cannot rest unless they have caused someone to stumble" (Proverbs 4:16, NLT).

5
HONOR
To *honor* means several things. It is respect paid to superiors, such as God, parents, or kings, and includes submission and service. It also refers to the esteem due to another based on virtue, wisdom, or reputation. Finally, it is the reward or position given to faithful subjects (adapted, *Unger's*).

7
ASSUMPTIONS
Haman made the mistake of assuming he was the one who should be honored. Assumptions often lead to misunderstandings and disappointment. Jesus' parents "assumed he was with friends among the other travelers. . . . When they couldn't find him, they went back to Jerusalem to search for him there" (Luke 2:44-45, NLT).

transformation

8

RISE AND SHINE
God is always up, tireless in His desire to meet with you daily, encouraging you to do good. "I earnestly exhorted your fathers in the day I brought them up out of the land of Egypt, until this day, rising early and exhorting, saying, 'Obey My voice'" (Jeremiah 11:7).

9

GOD HONORS
When we honor God, He returns the compliment and honors us as well. But when we dishonor Him, we become a disappointment to Him. "Now the Lord declares: . . . 'Those who honor me I will honor, but those who despise me will be disdained'" (1 Samuel 2:30, NIV).

8. Haman rose early to fulfill an evil deed. The Bible encourages believers to rise early to do *good* deeds. Fill in the following chart for some ideas of what to do when you rise early.

SCRIPTURE	RISING EARLY
Gen. 31:55	
1 Sam. 1:19	
Ps. 63:1	
Mark 1:35	
John 8:2	

Journal about your internal time clock. Do you stay up late or rise early? When do you spend time with the Lord?

. . . .

. . . .

. . . .

. . . .

9. The king considered what he might do to honor a man in whom he delighted.

Journal about someone who has brought you joy and delight recently. Write about some of the ways you might show him or her honor.

. . . .

. . . .

. . . .

. . . .

10. Mordecai had done a good deed that brought delight to the king's heart. The Bible gives the Christian many ways to delight her King. Place a check beside the deeds you've done that delight God.

— "The Lord's delight is in those who honor him, those who put their hope in his unfailing love" (Ps. 147:11, NLT).
— "He delights in honesty" (Prov. 11:1, NLT).
— "He delights in those who have integrity" (Prov. 11:20, NLT).
— "Those who deal truthfully are His delight" (Prov. 12:22).
— "The prayer of the upright is His delight" (Prov. 15:8).

Skip and I weren't looking for special honors; we just wanted time to heal during a time of grief. On the day I lost a pregnancy, Skip lost his father. I was rushed to the hospital, while Skip rushed to the airport. We met in California for the funeral two days later. The next day we were scheduled to attend a Billy Graham Crusade in Atlanta but didn't know if we should go. The privacy of being in a hotel room to grieve together, the opportunity to sit as a couple during a service (which never happens for pastors' families), and the chance to be ministered to by peers convinced us that we should attend the crusade.

We walked into the stadium and took two seats high in the bleachers opposite the stage. We had just settled in when Franklin Graham's assistant found us and invited us to sit on the platform with the honored guests. We felt so privileged and said, "Someday we'll tell our grandchildren we sat on the same stage as Billy Graham."

Jesus said, "When you are invited, take the lowest place, so that when your host comes, he will say to you, 'Friend, move up to a better place.' Then you will be honored in the presence of all your fellow guests. . . . He who humbles himself will be exalted" (Luke 14:10-11, NIV). This is the kind of advice Haman refused to hear. He couldn't imagine anyone besides himself being honored.

DELIGHT
In Hebrew, *delight* means "to incline oneself to, to bend toward." Today it means to be pleased with; something giving great joy or satisfaction. A Christian's greatest delight should be in the Lord, not in people or things. "Delight yourself in the Almighty and look up to God" (Job 22:26, NLT).

contemplation
It is a worthier thing to deserve honor than to possess it.
Charles R. Swindoll

DAY 3 PROUD AS A PEACOCK

preparation

Lord, help me not to be a show-off, putting on fancy duds to impress fickle people. Instead, help me to put on a beautiful attitude to please You. Amen.

BEAUTY
Don't be concerned about the outward beauty that depends on fancy hairstyles, expensive jewelry, or beautiful clothes. You should be known for the beauty that comes from within.
1 Peter 3:3-4, NLT

The peacock unfurled his feathers like a fine Chinese fan and proudly strutted. It was as if the peacock were saying: "Look, aren't I the most beautiful creature you've ever beheld?" The envious animals knew exactly what he was thinking, wishing they could be as beautiful as he.

One fateful day a fox came prowling with a glint in his eye. He was up to no good, you see. The only reason he was in the forest was to gobble up another animal! All the other animals scattered, but there in a clearing stood the peacock in all his glory—the sunlight giving a brilliant luster to his adorning colors. "Good day, Peacock. How beautiful you are. What amazing colors," remarked the fox. The peacock started to glow.

"I don't suppose . . . ," said the fox. "Oh no, I couldn't."

"What, what . . . ?" inquired the puffed-up peacock.

"You're so exquisite, could you come closer so I can see how beautiful you are?"

The peacock was pleased with himself, so he drew nearer. "That's fine," said the fox with a grimace and pounced on the prideful peacock. All that remained were a few feathers and the stories the animals told of the vain peacock.

Haman believed he was the most honorable creature in Persia. He felt that the king should put him in magnificent attire to strut around to the envy of all. Vain and foolish Haman didn't know that pride comes before a fall.

exploration

This week we have seen the "night owl" Ahasuerus ask the "early bird" Haman for advice on how to honor a special man, Mordecai. Now Haman, proud as a peacock, gladly offers his advice.

Review Esther 6; then focus on verses 7-9.

And Haman answered the king, "For the man whom the king delights to honor, let a royal robe be brought which the king has worn, and a horse on which the king has ridden, which has a royal crest placed on its head."
Esther 6:7-8

1. How was the man the king wished to reward referred to?

. . . .

2. Describe Haman's suggestion for the honoree's apparel.

. . . .

3. How was the man the king delighted in to be transported?

. . . .

4. What was the significance of the adornment on the horse?

. . . .

"Then let this robe and horse be delivered to the hand of one of the king's most noble princes, that he may array the man whom the king delights to honor. Then parade him on horseback through the city square, and proclaim before him: 'Thus shall it be done to the man whom the king delights to honor!'" Esther 6:9

5. How was the honoree to receive this kingly array, and where would he be led?

. . . .

6. What would be proclaimed? . . . .

. . . .

7. Why was Haman so excited about his suggestion?

. . . .

. . . .

explanation

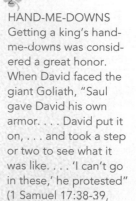

2
HAND-ME-DOWNS
Getting a king's hand-me-downs was considered a great honor. When David faced the giant Goliath, "Saul gave David his own armor. . . . David put it on, . . . and took a step or two to see what it was like. . . . 'I can't go in these,' he protested" (1 Samuel 17:38-39, NLT).

3
HORSEBACK
Donkeys were the typical mode of transportation for commoners in ancient times, while horses were reserved for the rich and noble. Haman's desire to ride the king's horse could have been interpreted as a bid for the king's throne. He hoped people would consider him to be the heir apparent.

5
ON PARADE
A parade is a pompous show; a public procession to exhibit ostentatiously. Haman's suggestion reveals how important prestige was to him. He could have asked for power or riches but preferred to dress as a king and receive public acclaim. He was a proud peacock on parade.

HANDOUTS

Christians are asked to share their clothes. "Do not withhold your tunic either. Give to everyone who asks of you" (Luke 6:29-30). Clothing someone in need, in essence, clothes the Lord. Jesus said, "Whatever you did for one of the least of these . . . , you did for me" (Matthew 25:40, NIV).

HORSEPOWER

Ancient men relied on horses to bring victory. Modern folk rely on tanks and missiles. What do you rely on? "Don't count on your warhorse to give you victory— . . . it cannot save you. But the Lord watches over those . . . who rely on his unfailing love" (Psalm 33:17-18, NLT).

8. Haman asked for hand-me-downs from King Ahasuerus to display his power. Read Genesis 41:41-44 to discover how Pharaoh delighted to honor Joseph.

   a. Describe the hand-me-downs in which Joseph was adorned.

   . . . .

   b. Describe the mode of transportation he was offered.

   . . . .

   c. How were the people to respond? . . . .

   . . . .

   Journal about how you could bless someone with one of your hand-me-downs. Would you give the person your castoffs or your crown jewels? How might your gifts meet a need? How would they make the person feel?

   . . . .

   . . . .

   . . . .

   . . . .

   . . . .

9. We have discovered that horses were a sign of power and nobility, largely reserved for war. Fill in the following chart to learn about other biblical people who rode horses.

SCRIPTURE	THOSE WHO RIDE HORSES
1 Kings 20:20-21	
2 Chron. 1:16-17	
Rev. 6:2	
Rev. 19:11, 13-14	

10. Haman loved a parade, especially if it was in his honor.

> Journal 1 Corinthians 13:4-5 into a prayer, asking God to keep you from showy displays of pride. "Love does not parade itself, is not puffed up; does not behave rudely, does not seek its own."

. . . .

. . . .

. . . .

. . . .

10
PRIDE
Pride is inordinate self-esteem and haughtiness. It carries the idea of being puffed up in an attempt to be noticed. People who act proudly assume they are superior to others. "They wear pride like a jeweled necklace, and their clothing is woven of cruelty" (Psalm 73:6, NLT).

I love a parade, and my good friend Lisa Davis knew it. When I turned thirty, she planned the ultimate surprise party. As our car pulled into her driveway, I heard chanting, singing, and loud kazoos humming. I looked up to see a parade of my closest friends and family dressed in colorful costumes marching down the street with streamers flying and banners waving. It was the best birthday ever and made me feel like a queen.

I'm not the only one who loves a parade; most Americans do too. That's why so many cities host them. New York City's biggest parade is held on St. Patrick's Day, painting the town green with Irish pride. On New Year's Eve, Miami hosts the King Orange Jamboree Parade, boasting about their biggest crop. San Francisco's annual Golden Dragon Parade most honorably celebrates the Chinese New Year, complete with elaborate fireworks. New Orleans has the most ostentatious of all parades, hosting the Mardi Gras parade, which elevates hedonism to new heights.

Haman was fond of a good parade himself. He wanted King Ahasuerus to sponsor the first annual "Haman's Day Parade," complete with elaborate costumes and a decorated horse. The people would never have participated in a parade honoring Haman of their own free will. So, with the king's permission, the crowds would be forced to march and chant, "Heil Haman, the king's right-hand man!" He was determined that he would be treated like a king.

contemplation
A proud man is always looking down on things and people; and, of course, as long as you're looking down, you can't see something that's above you.
C. S. Lewis

DAY 4 · EATING CROW

preparation

God, because You are my heavenly Father, You provide good things for my life. Thank You that if I ask for bread, You will not give me a stone. The good things You provide satisfy my soul. Amen.

GOOD THINGS
[The Lord] satisfies your mouth with good things, so that your youth is renewed like the eagle's. Psalm 103:5

Eating crow is similar to eating humble pie. The phrase means to abase oneself or to do something extremely disagreeable. Like most pithy sayings, "eating crow" has an interesting origin. The phrase evolved from an incident during a cease-fire in the War of 1812. Food was scarce, so soldiers were forced to hunt. On one expedition, a misguided New Englander crossed the river in search of game. Coming up empty, he shot and killed a crow for target practice.

A British officer heard the shot and rushed to find the Yank reloading his gun. Since the officer was unarmed, he complimented the soldier on his marksmanship and asked to see his impressive weapon. The naive soldier handed it over, and the officer pointed it at him, berating him for trespassing. Then, to humiliate him, he ordered the soldier to take a bite of crow. After the Yank swallowed his pride along with the crow, the officer returned his weapon and ordered him to leave. As the Englishman departed, the Yank thought, *I'll force that arrogant Brit to eat the rest of the crow.* Though the officer begged, the soldier was unrelenting. Faced with death, he ate crow.

Haman had vainly tried to get Mordecai to eat humble pie. He planned for the ultimate humiliation to come, not at the end of a gun, but at the end of a rope. As the tables were turned, Haman was forced to eat crow.

exploration

Haman believed *he* was to be honored and drafted the highest accolade imaginable—a parade fit for a king. But things are not always what they seem, as Haman soon found out.

Review Esther 6; then focus on verses 10-12.

Then the king said to Haman, "Hurry, take the robe and the horse, as you have suggested, and do so for Mordecai the Jew who sits within the king's gate! Leave nothing undone of all that you have spoken." Esther 6:10

1. What was Haman ordered to do for Mordecai? . . . .

. . . .

2. What word makes you think that the king's command was urgent?

. . . .

3. How thorough was Haman to be in carrying out his own suggestions?

. . . .

So Haman took the robe and the horse, arrayed Mordecai and led him on horseback through the city square, and proclaimed before him, "Thus shall it be done to the man whom the king delights to honor!" Esther 6:11

4. How did Haman prepare Mordecai for his parade?

. . . .

5. What did he shout for all to hear? . . . .

. . . .

Afterward Mordecai went back to the king's gate. But Haman hurried to his house, mourning and with his head covered. Esther 6:12

6. What did Mordecai do after the pageant? . . . .

. . . .

7. What did Haman do after the pageant? . . . .

. . . .

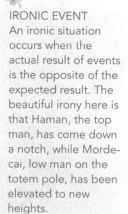

explanation

1
IRONIC EVENT
An ironic situation occurs when the actual result of events is the opposite of the expected result. The beautiful irony here is that Haman, the top man, has come down a notch, while Mordecai, low man on the totem pole, has been elevated to new heights.

5
CHANGED TUNE
Haman had been harping on Mordecai for years. He encouraged others to play a funeral dirge on behalf of the Jews. Haman loved to sing his own praises, but he was forced to change his tune. Haman's lips had to offer Mordecai a blessing instead of a curse.

6
AFTERMATH
After Mordecai was honored, he didn't gloat or manipulate others. He returned to his regular place, serving the king. "Officials lord it over the people beneath them. But among you it should be quite different. Whoever wants to be a leader . . . must be your servant" (Matthew 20:25-26, NLT).

transformation

8

TABLES TURNED
God can turn the tables in our lives, changing bad things into better things. For Joseph, being sold into slavery ultimately provided the opportunity for him to become prime minister and save his people. "You meant evil against me; but God meant it for good" (Genesis 50:20).

9

OFFER BLESSING
Christians can turn the other cheek, offering a blessing instead of a curse because God will ultimately right all wrongs. Abraham was told not to worry about the way others treated him, for God said, "I will bless those who bless you and curse those who curse you" (Genesis 12:3, NLT).

8. Today we saw the beautiful irony of Mordecai and Haman switching places. Having tried to force Mordecai to bow to him, Haman now was forced to exalt Mordecai. Jesus also experienced exquisite irony. Read Philippians 2:5-11, and answer the following questions:

   a. Although equal to God, what did Jesus choose to do (vv. 6-7)?

   . . . .

   b. Describe the extent of His humility (v. 8).

   . . . .

   c. What ironic event came as a result of His humility (v. 9)?

   . . . .

   d. What is the response required of those placed beneath Him (vv. 10-11)?

   . . . .

9. Haman was forced to "eat crow" when he had to bless Mordecai, whom he had previously cursed. Describe a situation in which you've said unkind things about another person.

   . . . .

   . . . .

   Journal a prayer asking God to bless that person by rewriting the following verse: "Love your enemies, bless those who curse you, do good to those who hate you, and pray for those who spitefully use you and persecute you" (Matthew 5:44).

   . . . .

   . . . .

   . . . .

   . . . .

10. Mordecai got back to business when he was honored. Haman covered his head in shame.

Journal about a time when you were honored. Did you respond with humility or pride?

. . . .

. . . .

. . . .

. . . .

Journal about a situation when someone you view as "unworthy" was honored. How did you respond?

. . . .

. . . .

. . . .

. . . .

SYMPATHETIC
If we are to "rejoice with those who rejoice, and weep with those who weep," then it stands to reason that we should celebrate with those who get a promotion and commiserate with those who lose their jobs. We are to "be of the same mind toward one another" (Romans 12:15-16).

An old crow became extremely territorial when he claimed a piece of land on the outskirts of London. This crotchety old bird soon became a veteran of many battles. Day after day he valiantly flew out to defend his property, even though he was wounded and had lost a considerable amount of blood. Observers were amazed to watch the punch-drunk crow return to "his" house to attack his own reflection in a window. Ironically, his only enemy was the one in the pane.

Haman had become extremely territorial concerning his position in the Persian Empire. He had staked his claim and was prepared to defend his turf come what may. He mistakenly believed that Mordecai was his enemy, but in truth, his greatest enemies were his ambition, his pride, and ultimately himself. Observers will be amazed to see him build a trap big enough to capture his oversized ego.

contemplation
If you're successful, don't crow. If you fail, don't croak.
Samuel Chadwick

DAY 5 DEAD DUCK

preparation

When my enemies rise against me, I will run to You, Lord, to find protection. I will call on You with all my heart, knowing that salvation is from the Lord. Amen.

PROTECTION

My God is my rock, in whom I find protection. He is my shield, the strength of my salvation, and my stronghold. I will call on the Lord, who is worthy of praise, for he saves me from my enemies. Psalm 18:2-3, NLT

Three men went duck hunting one day. Two of them were inundated with stories from the third man about his great duck-hunting abilities. After a few hours the first two men bagged a couple of ducks each, but the braggart hadn't taken a shot. They questioned him on this, so he agreed to show his shooting abilities at the next opportunity.

A few moments later one lone duck came flying by. As promised, the braggart stood up and squeezed off one shot. But the duck kept flying!

"Gentlemen, you have just witnessed a miracle," said the braggart, pointing at the retreating duck, "for there flies a dead duck."

It seems that there were some assorted "ducks" in the kingdom of Persia. Haman believed he had placed the Jews in the position of sitting ducks. The legislation he had manipulated the king into signing would force the Jews to sit there and take it, while their former friends and neighbors annihilated them and stole their property.

However, the tables had turned. God performed a miracle in Persia, providentially elevating Mordecai the Jew to the utter humiliation of Haman the Agagite. Haman, the one who had set the trap for Mordecai and considered him as good as dead, was in reality a dead duck himself, flying along quite oblivious to his situation. "May my enemies' plans for evil be turned against them. Do as you promised and put an end to them" (Psalm 54:5, NLT).

exploration

Haman's troubles were rapidly building. The same day that Haman sought the death of his enemy would end with a deadly prediction for his own life.

Review Esther 6; then focus on verses 13-14.

When Haman told his wife Zeresh and all his friends everything that had happened to him, his wise men and his wife Zeresh said to him, "If Mordecai, before whom you have begun to fall, is of Jewish descent, you will not prevail against him but will surely fall before him."
Esther 6:13

1. To whom did Haman turn when he was humiliated?

. . . .

2. What did he relate to them?

. . . .

3. Remembering the king's counselors from Esther 1:13-21 (Lesson 5, Day 4), what additional insight do you gain into the role Haman's wise men played in his life?

. . . .

4. What did Zeresh and the wise men come to understand about Mordecai's heritage?

. . . .

5. Explain what they predicted concerning Haman's fate.

. . . .

While they were still talking with him, the king's eunuchs came, and hastened to bring Haman to the banquet which Esther had prepared. Esther 6:14

6. What phrases make you believe that there is an urgency concerning Haman's fate?

. . . .

7. Remembering last week's lesson, contrast Haman's state of mind as he prepared to go to Esther's second banquet with how he might be feeling now.

. . . .

explanation

2

VICTIMS
Haman didn't blame himself for his troubles; he thought he was a victim of circumstances, focusing on what "had happened *to* him." Adam blamed his wife for their problems; Eve blamed the serpent (see Genesis 3:12-13). Human nature doesn't accept responsibility for its actions, while a godly nature will.

5

VICTORS
Haman's pagan advisers unknowingly stated a central biblical truth: Neither Haman nor anyone can destroy God's people. "No weapon formed against you shall prosper, and every tongue which rises against you in judgment You shall condemn. This is the heritage of the servants of the Lord" (Isaiah 54:17).

transformation

CONSEQUENCES
People would rather feel like victims than believe they are experiencing the consequences of their actions. Many times people aren't victims; they're just reaping what they've sown. "Don't be misled. Remember that you can't ignore God and get away with it. You will always reap what you sow!" (Galatians 6:7, NLT).

9
HURRY UP!
Haste implies urgency, while *hurry* carries a stronger implication of agitation and bustle. Christians should make haste to complete the tasks God has given them because Jesus is coming quickly! "The great day of the Lord is near; it is near and hastens quickly" (Zephaniah 1:14).

8. Human beings come from a long line of people who see themselves as victims, from Adam and Eve to Haman. The victim mentality continues to this day. We live in a generation of people who have taken victimization to new heights, blaming everything and everyone else for our problems. Check off any of the following blame games you've played.

— "My mom raised me that way."
— "The devil made me do it."
— "It's that time of the month."
— "He just pushes my buttons."
— "She deserved what she got."
— "Uncle Sam owes me."

> Journal about which of the blame games you play the most, then write a prayer asking God to help you take responsibility for your actions instead of blaming others.

. . . .

. . . .

. . . .

. . . .

9. Haman was urged to hurry about the king's task and was hastened to the queen's banquet. Fill in the following chart to discover other people who were in a hurry.

SCRIPTURE	IN A HURRY
Gen. 19:15, 22	
Gen. 41:14	
Exod. 5:13-14	
Matt. 28:7-8	
John 13:26-27	

10. Haman's advisers realized that he could not triumph over Mordecai, one of God's chosen people. As one of His children, you can receive strength and power to triumph over your enemies too.

Journal a prayer thanking God for ultimate victory by rewriting the following verse: "Now thanks be to God who always leads us in triumph in Christ, and through us diffuses the fragrance of His knowledge in every place" (2 Corinthians 2:14).

. . . .

. . . .

. . . .

. . . .

There is an ancient story of a sentry standing day after day at his post for no apparent reason. One day a passerby asked him why he was standing there. "I don't know," the sentry replied. "I'm just following orders." The passerby then went to the captain of the guard and asked him the same question. "I don't know," the captain replied. "We're just following orders."

This prompted the captain of the guard to pose the question to a higher authority. "Why do we post a sentry at that particular spot?" he asked the king. Not knowing, the king summoned his wise men and asked them the question. They discovered that one hundred years before, Catherine the Great, empress of Russia, had planted a rosebush and ordered a sentry placed there to protect it. The rosebush had been dead for eighty years, but the sentry still stood guard.

There is an even more ancient story, written before time began, of God's establishing great promises to stand guard over His people. "Those who trust in the Lord are as secure as Mount Zion; they will not be defeated but will endure forever. Just as the mountains surround and protect Jerusalem, so the Lord surrounds and protects his people, both now and forever" (Psalm 125:1-2, NLT).

An empress's word kept a plot of ground protected for decades. God's Word kept Mordecai and his people protected for centuries, and it will continue to protect you and faithful generations to follow.

CHOSEN PEOPLE
The Jews were God's chosen people in the Old Testament. In the New Testament, Christians are also "a chosen people, . . . God's holy nation, his very own possession. This is so you can show others the goodness of God" (1 Peter 2:9, NLT).

contemplation
A providence that provides for sparrows will certainly protect the saints.
Unknown

What a Difference a Day Makes

The monotony of the daily grind can lull you into a state of lethargy, causing you to think that life is a succession of days without meaning. Yesterday nothing much happened, today nothing much is happening, and tomorrow nothing much will happen. *Until . . .* the doctor says, "It's cancer"; your boss says, "We're downsizing"; or your husband says, "We're through." That's when you realize what a drastic difference one day can make.

For instance, where were you on the day JFK was shot? I (Penny) was at my grandmother's house eating a grilled-cheese sandwich and entertaining my little brother. The television caught Mima's attention. Walter Cronkite took off his glasses and gravely reported, "President Kennedy is dead. He was shot to death by an assassin in the streets of Dallas. He was forty-five." She phoned Granddaddy, "Close the store and come home, someone's killed the president!" For countless Americans, at that moment time stood still. It seemed the shot that assassinated John F. Kennedy mortally wounded our nation's innocence and left us feeling frightened about the future. On November 22, 1963, it is said, everything changed.

Esther 7 and 8 chronicle the amazing difference one day made on June 25, 474 B.C. On that fateful day in history Esther moved from silence to supplication; Haman fell from glory to the gallows; Mordecai shifted from doom to deliverance; and the Jews moved from fear to feasting. In Persia it was the day that changed everything.

DAY 1
*From Silence
to Supplication*

DAY 2
*From Glory
to the Gallows*

DAY 3
*From Doomed
to Delivered*

DAY 4
*From Persecuted
to Protected*

DAY 5
*From Fear
to Feasting*

1 FROM SILENCE TO SUPPLICATION

preparation

Lord, help me to rejoice each and every day, whether things are happy or sad. I offer this day to You, knowing that You can save and bring success. Amen.

REJOICE
This is the day the Lord has made. We will rejoice and be glad in it. Please, Lord, please save us. Please, Lord, please give us success.
Psalm 118:24-25, NLT

explanation

1
WINING AND DINING
Esther showed incredible diplomatic skills by ensuring that the king would be amenable to her request. She first filled his stomach before filling his ears. A satisfying meal would put the king in a more likely mood to say yes.

exploration

By cross-checking ancient Hebrew lunar dates given in the book of Esther with Persian records, scholars have arrived at relatively accurate dates for some of the events we are studying. Esther became queen sometime between December 479 and January 478 B.C. Four years later in April 474 B.C., Haman cast Pur for his deadly decree, setting the future date to destroy the Jews. A short time later, Esther invited the king and Haman to her second banquet on June 25, 474 B.C., the day that set in motion the providential events leading to the Jews' deliverance.

Last week we saw Mordecai honored and Haman humiliated. Things were definitely changing in favor of the Jews. This week we will see how God sovereignly defused the dangerous situation, eliminated Haman, and transformed Esther and Mordecai into powerful advocates for their people.

Read Esther 7; then focus on verses 1-4.

> *So the king and Haman went to dine with Queen Esther. And on the second day, at the banquet of wine, the king again said to Esther, "What is your petition, Queen Esther? It shall be granted you. And what is your request, up to half the kingdom? It shall be done!"*
> Esther 7:1-2

1. What event did Haman and the king attend?. . . . .

. . . .

2. How do you know that Esther's plan to interest the king worked?

. . . .

3. How many times in the past had he made the same promise?

. . . .

> *Then Queen Esther answered and said, "If I have found favor in your sight, O king, and if it pleases the king, let my life be given me at my petition, and my people at my request."* Esther 7:3

SOCIAL GRACES
Esther used good psychology and social graces to address King Ahasuerus. "If I have found favor" reveals she wasn't telling the king what to do but making a request. "If it pleases the king" reveals Esther wasn't trying to please herself but wanted to please the king instead.

4. What two phrases let you know that Esther was placing herself at the mercy of the king?

. . . .

5. For what two things did Esther ask? . . . .

. . . .

. . . .

CITING SOURCES
Esther quoted Haman's lethal decree by repeating the words, "to destroy, to kill, and to annihilate" (Esther 3:13). She was acting as a clever attorney using the very words of her opponent to make her case against him. She did not rely on hearsay when presenting her evidence.

6. Esther had kept her heritage hidden (Esther 2:20). How did she now identify with her persecuted race?

. . . .

> *"For we have been sold, my people and I, to be destroyed, to be killed, and to be annihilated. Had we been sold as male and female slaves, I would have held my tongue, although the enemy could never compensate for the king's loss."* Esther 7:4

7. What explanation did Esther give for making this request?

. . . .

8. Describe how Esther would have reacted had her people been condemned to slavery rather than death.

. . . .

BANQUET
The word *banquet* in Hebrew literally means "drinking." Banquets were common in Bible times and were characterized by hospitality. Besides being a part of the religious observance of great festivals, banquets or feasts were given for birthdays, the weaning of a son, marriages, reunions of friends, or burials (adapted, *Unger's*).

11

ETIQUETTE
Displaying good manners isn't just cultural, it's scriptural. "Show your fear of God by standing up in the presence of elderly people and showing respect for the aged. I am the Lord" (Leviticus 19:32, NLT). By showing your respect for others, you show your respect for God.

9. What phrases reveal that this holocaust was financially motivated? Why would it not be beneficial to the king?

. . . .

transformation

10. Esther used a banquet to set the mood and soften the king's heart.

> Journal about a banquet (a special evening) you have participated in. Describe the mood and the setting. How did it make you and others feel?

. . . .

. . . .

. . . .

. . . .

11. Esther relied on good etiquette and social graces in order to find favor with the king. What social graces do you exhibit in your daily life?

— Say "Please" and "Thank You"
— Wait to eat until everyone is served
— Rise when an older person enters
— Write thank-you notes
— Pray before meals
— Offer your chair
— Don't interrupt
— RSVP

12. Esther finally came out in the open about her Jewish heritage. Sometimes Christians keep their faith secret from those around them. List some ways you or other Christians you know have hidden their spiritual heritage.

. . . .

. . . .

13. Esther wasn't a gossip; she got her facts right when making her case against Haman, quoting him exactly.

> Journal about a time when you set the record straight in a situation by revealing the facts instead of being a party to gossip.

. . . .

. . . .

. . . .

. . . .

13
ENDING GOSSIP
To stop a gossiper, let the truth be told. "Any story sounds true until someone sets the record straight" (Proverbs 18:17, NLT). When someone gossips, ask these questions: (1) "Is this beneficial?" (2) "May I quote you?" (3) "Mind if I verify the facts?" (4) "Why are you telling me this?"

The rift in their family had gone on long enough. My friend Paul told me how his two sisters had let petty grievances separate them from their stepmother for nearly two decades. But on the evening of their nephew's wedding banquet things were destined to change. The family was on their best behavior adorned in formal wear and fake smiles. Mom should have been lighthearted, but instead she was weighed down with grief. The girls she'd raised as her own wouldn't even say hello.

That's when Paul, using tact and timing, approached his sisters and said, "This ends now! You're going to tell Mom you're sorry and that you love her." In unison they replied, "We can't, too much time has passed." He reminded them that their mother loved them and would forgive them. "There's no time like the present," he said.

Next, Paul went to his mother and said, "Your daughters want to reconcile with you; it's time to make up." But she replied, "I can't, they've hurt me for too many years." He assured her that they were ready to put the past behind them.

So while dinner was being served, before the bride and groom cut the cake, Paul brought his mother and sisters together, allowing them to break down the barrier that had stood between them for so long. With tear-filled eyes they warmly embraced one another saying, "I'm sorry, I love you."

Haman had been bullying Mordecai for a long time, but on the evening of the queen's banquet, things were destined to change. Through Esther's intervention, the conflict would finally be resolved, but not the way Haman expected.

contemplation
Who can tell what a day may bring forth? Cause us, therefore, gracious God, to live every day as if it were to be our last. . . . Cause us to live at present as we shall wish we had done when we come to die.
Thomas à Kempis

FROM GLORY TO THE GALLOWS

preparation

Lord, keep me ever mindful of my humanity, that I am but dust. I want to be known for possessing a heart of meekness and humility. Amen.

MODEST

Lord, my heart is not proud; my eyes are not haughty. I don't concern myself with matters too great or awesome for me. Psalm 131:1, NLT

Nicknamed *le petit Caporal* (the little Corporal), Napoléon Bonaparte stood only five feet two inches tall. Although he was an inspirational leader, Napoléon could also be cynical and demanding. He skillfully formed key political alliances and in 1799 seized control of the French government in a coup d'etat on 18–19 *Brumaire* (November 9–10). Ultimately, he crowned himself emperor of France on December 2, 1802, at the Cathedral of Notre Dame.

Napoléon's ambition led him to overextend his power and brought about his downfall. He was demoralized in Russia, defeated at the Battle of the Nations, and devastated at the Battle of Waterloo. Napoléon twice abdicated the throne and was twice exiled—once to the tiny island of Elba and finally to the barren British island of St. Helena. Napoléon Bonaparte, once ruler of nations, spent the end of his life as emperor of a deserted island.

Haman, too, was a political opportunist with great ambitions. He had manipulated circumstances to become prime minister of Persia, and if he could have, he would have crowned himself king. He overextended his power by declaring war on the entire Jewish race. He was demoralized by Mordecai's exaltation and devastated by the knowledge of Esther's heritage. We discover that, like the great Napoléon, Haman meets his Waterloo and falls from glory.

exploration

Esther broke her silence and pleaded for the king to save her people from death. Now we learn how the king reacted to Esther's request and the impact it had on Haman.

Review Esther 7; then focus on verses 5-10.

So King Ahasuerus answered and said to Queen Esther, "Who is he, and where is he, who would dare presume in his heart to do such a thing?" And Esther said, "The adversary and enemy is this wicked Haman!" So Haman was terrified before the king and queen. Esther 7:5-6

1. What three things did the king want to know about Esther's enemy?

. . . .

2. How did Haman respond to Esther's revelation that he was the enemy?

. . . .

Then the king arose in his wrath from the banquet of wine and went into the palace garden; but Haman stood before Queen Esther, pleading for his life, for he saw that evil was determined against him by the king. Esther 7:7

3. What was the king's reaction to this revelation?

. . . .

4. To whom did Haman turn for mercy, and why?

. . . .

When the king returned from the palace garden to the place of the banquet of wine, Haman had fallen across the couch where Esther was. Then the king said, "Will he also assault the queen while I am in the house?" As the word left the king's mouth, they covered Haman's face. Esther 7:8

5. What did the king accuse Haman of doing, and why?

. . . .

6. What was the immediate result?

. . . .

explanation

1

FOUND OUT
Ahasuerus found out the who, what, and where of Esther's adversary. The king understood that insight into the enemy ensured victory. You, too, must be aware of your enemy "so that you will be able to stand firm against all strategies and tricks of the Devil" (Ephesians 6:11, NLT).

3

TIME OUT
When aroused to wrath, the king took time out to think. Perhaps he was coming to terms with the realization that he'd signed his wife's death warrant. Maybe he was examining his folly in trusting Haman or devising a plan to eliminate Haman and save his wife.

7

OUT OF TOUCH
The king was out of touch with what was obviously going on in his kingdom. A eunuch had to inform him about the 50-cubit gallows—hard to miss—and its intended purpose. Once informed, the king let Mordecai off the hook and hung Haman with his own rope.

8

HIS ENEMY
Esther's enemy became the king's enemy. God says that if we are obedient children, our enemies will become His. "If you are careful to obey [God], following all my instructions, then I will be an enemy to your enemies, and I will oppose those who oppose you" (Exodus 23:22, NLT).

9

GET CONTROL
Tempers are meant to be controlled. When you don't, you're foolish. "Those who control their anger have great understanding; those with a hasty temper will make mistakes" (Proverbs 14:29, NLT). When your temper flares, (1) Count to ten; (2) Take a walk; (3) Catch your breath; (4) Compose yourself.

> *Now Harbonah, one of the eunuchs, said to the king, "Look! The gallows, fifty cubits high, which Haman made for Mordecai, who spoke good on the king's behalf, is standing at the house of Haman." Then the king said, "Hang him on it!" So they hanged Haman on the gallows that he had prepared for Mordecai. Then the king's wrath subsided.* Esther 7:9-10

7. Contrast the original intent of the gallows with how it was actually used.

. . . .

transformation

8. For Christians as well as King Ahasuerus, knowing our enemy is the key to victory. Fill in the following chart to become familiar with the scheming ways of your enemy, the devil.

SCRIPTURE	THE ENEMY'S SCHEMES
Luke 22:31-32	
2 Cor. 11:13-15	
1 Pet. 5:8-9	
Rev. 12:9-10	

9. Though he was righteously angry, Ahasuerus wisely took time out before responding to Haman's offense.

> Journal about how you behaved the last time you were provoked to anger. How might you have been better served to take some time out?

. . . .

. . . .

. . . .

. . . .

10. The king was out of touch with the life-threatening plot to the Jews that was so obvious to others. What destructive things are happening in your city, right in front of your eyes? (Examples: adult bookstores or gang activity)

. . . .

Journal a prayer asking God to dismantle these destructive traps by rewriting the following verse: "How quickly I would escape—far away from this wild storm of hatred. Destroy them, Lord, and confuse their speech, for I see violence and strife in the city" (Psalm 55:8-9, NLT).

. . . .

. . . .

. . . .

. . . .

GET REAL
There's a difference between "not seeing" and "refusing to see." Hard hearts see the truth but refuse to respond! "For the hearts of these people are hardened, . . . and they have closed their eyes—so their eyes cannot see, . . . and their hearts cannot understand" (Matthew 13:15, NLT).

King Ahasuerus heard Esther's evidence against Haman and sentenced him to death by hanging. It has been said that those who don't learn from history are doomed to repeat it. The Nazi leaders in the twentieth century could have learned a lesson from Haman's fall, but instead they repeated it.

At the end of World War II high-ranking German officials were put on trial for committing "crimes against humanity," especially the mass murder of Jews. The International Military Tribunal began in November 1945 in Nuremberg, Germany. Reminiscent of Haman, all those indicted pleaded not guilty. Some claimed that they were merely following orders; others argued that the court had no jurisdiction. Concentration camp survivors testified about their experiences. There was undeniable proof that crimes against humanity had been committed.

Just like Haman centuries before, eleven German officials were sentenced to death by hanging. At 1:11 A.M. on October 16, 1946, Joachim von Ribbentrop walked to the gallows. A black hood was pulled over his head. The noose was slipped around his neck. A trapdoor opened. Two minutes later, the next in line, Field Marshal Keitel, stepped up the gallows stairs. The others followed. By 2:45 A.M. it was over.

contemplation
The wrongs which we seek to condemn and punish have been so calculated, so malignant and so devastating that civilization cannot tolerate their being ignored because it cannot survive their being repeated.
Robert Jackson, U.S. Supreme Court Justice

DAY 3 FROM DOOMED
TO DELIVERED

preparation

*God, I know that I have
rightfully lived under a
death sentence because
the wages of sin is
death. But You have
filled me with songs
of deliverance because
the blood of Your Son
has set me free. Amen.*

DELIVERANCE
*You are my hiding
place; You shall
preserve me from
trouble; You shall
surround me with
songs of deliverance.
Psalm 32:7*

On February 12, 2001, Earl Washington Jr. walked out of prison
after spending nine and one-half years on death row for a murder
he didn't commit. Washington, who was largely illiterate, had
confessed to the 1982 rape and slaying of Rebecca Lynn Williams
even though no biological evidence ever tied him to the crime.

In 1985, forty-year-old Washington escaped being executed
in the electric chair by just nine days when he was granted a stay.
As a result of a 1993 DNA test, which raised doubts about his
guilt, his death sentence was commuted to life in prison. Later,
additional DNA tests discovered genetic material linking the crime
to two other men, so in 2001 the Virginia governor pardoned
Washington. "It made me happy," Washington said in an interview. "[The governor] did a good job by my book."

On June 25, 474 B.C., in Shushan, Persia, Mordecai the Jew
was set free after spending a long time under a wrongful death
sentence. Cross-examining a key witness in this case brought new
evidence to light. Haman had been like a perjurer, twisting facts,
to get the wrong man convicted while he, the real culprit, was
free to torment others. Not only was Mordecai delivered from his
pending doom, he was also elevated to a new position within the
Persian government and lavishly rewarded. Mordecai could have
said, "The king did a good job by my book!"

exploration

Haman had sown death; therefore he reaped death (see Galatians
6:7). But Esther and Mordecai had acted righteously and were
delivered from death.

Read Esther 8; then focus on verses 1-8.

On that day King Ahasuerus gave Queen Esther the house of Haman, the enemy of the Jews. And Mordecai came before the king, for Esther had told how he was related to her. So the king took off his signet ring, which he had taken from Haman, and gave it to Mordecai; and Esther appointed Mordecai over the house of Haman. Esther 8:1-2

1. What gift did the king give to Esther? . . . .

. . . .

2. What did Mordecai receive from the king? from Esther?

. . . .

Now Esther spoke again to the king, fell down at his feet, and implored him with tears to counteract the evil of Haman the Agagite, and the scheme which he had devised against the Jews. Esther 8:3

3. Describe the queen's posture and emotional state as she spoke to the king.

. . . .

And the king held out the golden scepter toward Esther. So Esther arose and stood before the king, and said, "If it pleases the king, and if I have found favor in his sight and the thing seems right to the king and I am pleasing in his eyes, let it be written to revoke the letters devised by Haman, the son of Hammedatha the Agagite, which he wrote to annihilate the Jews who are in all the king's provinces. For how can I endure to see the evil that will come to my people? Or how can I endure to see the destruction of my countrymen?" Esther 8:4-6

4. What did Esther ask the king to do concerning Haman's legislation?

. . . .

5. What personal reasons did she give for this request?

. . . .

1

GENEROSITY
When a traitor was executed in Persia his property reverted to the crown. The king could have gained a fortune by keeping Haman's property for himself, yet he chose to give the estate to Esther. Esther, through God's grace and the king's generous gift, became independently wealthy.

2

PROMOTION
Mordecai received generous gifts from Queen Esther and King Ahasuerus. The signet ring was a delegation of authority, raising Mordecai to second in command. Esther gave him oversight over Haman's vast estate. Through God's providence, there was a Jewish queen and prime minister in the greatest empire on earth.

IRREVOCABLE
The king could not revoke his old decree. Daniel 6:8 says, "A law of the Medes and Persians, . . . cannot be revoked" (NLT). However, the king *could* sign a new decree to protect the Jews that would supersede his previous law. Haman wrote a life-threatening edict. Mordecai and Esther would enact life-saving legislation.

8

NEW TESTAMENT
Jesus replaced the law, that brought death, with grace, which brings life. "He is the mediator of the new testament, . . . for the redemption of the transgressions that were under the first testament, they which are called might receive the promise of eternal inheritance" (Hebrews 9:15, KJV).

9

GIFT GIVER
Anything good in your life *is* a gift from God. "Every good and perfect gift is from above, coming down from the Father of the heavenly lights, who does not change like shifting shadows" (James 1:17, NIV). Don't take His generosity for granted; thank Him for the little things as well as the big things.

Then King Ahasuerus said to Queen Esther and Mordecai the Jew, "Indeed, I have given Esther the house of Haman, and they have hanged him on the gallows because he tried to lay his hand on the Jews. You yourselves write a decree concerning the Jews, as you please, in the king's name, and seal it with the king's signet ring; for whatever is written in the king's name and sealed with the king's signet ring no one can revoke." Esther 8:7-8

6. How did the king remind Queen Esther and Mordecai of his good will toward them?

. . . .

7. What was the king's solution, and why would it be effective?

. . . .

transformation

8. Ahasuerus countermanded an old decree with a new decree. This is a picture of what God has done for all of sinful humanity under an irrevocable death sentence: He has provided a "new decree" to spare us from certain death.

   a. According to Ezekiel 18:4, what is the "old decree" for us?

   . . . .

   b. According to Romans 6:23, what "new decree" does God offer to save us?

   . . . .

9. Jesus, our king, gives generous gifts to us.

   Journal a prayer thanking God for His generosity by rewriting the following verse: "It is a good thing to receive wealth from God and the good health to enjoy it. To enjoy your work and accept your lot in life—that is indeed a gift from God" (Ecclesiastes 5:19, NLT).

. . . .

. . . .

. . . .

. . . .

10. Mordecai and Esther both enjoyed promotion from the king. God promotes His people too. Draw a line between what you *were* to what you *are* now in Christ.

Promoted From	Promoted To
Slave to Sin	Child of light
Stranger and alien	New man
Dead in trespasses	Saint
Child of wrath	Citizen of heaven
Sinner	Alive in Christ
Morally bankrupt	Inheritance in Christ
Old Man	Free indeed

10
ELEVATED
Ahasuerus elevated Esther to queen and Mordecai to statesman, giving them authority in Persia. God has elevated us and "raised us up with Christ and seated us with him in the heavenly realms" (Ephesians 2:6, NIV). God gives us authority so that " we will reign with him" (2 Timothy 2:12, NLT).

While reviewing his troops one day, Napoléon's horse bolted out of control. A young private broke ranks, running to rein in the horse and rescue the emperor. "Thank you, *Captain*," said Napoléon. With one word he instantly promoted the soldier from private to captain. Not missing a beat, the quick-witted soldier asked, "Of what regiment, sir?" "Of my guards," replied Napoléon as he rode away, continuing his inspection.

Taking the emperor at his word, the private-turned-captain then walked into the middle of an officer's meeting. "What does he think he's doing here?" quipped a high-ranking official. "I am a captain of the guards," replied the young man, still wearing his private's uniform. "I can see by your markings that you're just a private! Who says you're a captain?" the indignant officer said. Pointing to the emperor the soldier confidently answered, "He did!" The officer saluted and said, "I beg your pardon, Captain. I was not aware of your promotion."

Like the private, Mordecai had saved his ruler's life. Just as the word of Napoléon was enough to instantly promote a private to a captain, the word of a king was all it took to immediately promote Mordecai to a place of authority in the Persian Empire. And Ahasuerus gave Mordecai the signet ring so everyone in the kingdom would be aware of his promotion. He had been doomed, but now he was delivered, and he was in a position to help rescue his people.

contemplation
Spiritual authority flows not from titles and positions but from a life that is genuine.
Wayne Jacobsen

preparation

Lord, thank You for Your unfailing love. I simply cannot comprehend the many ways You have protected me and been faithful to me. Today I look to You for new mercies. Amen.

NEW DAY
The unfailing love of the Lord never ends! By his mercies we have been kept from complete destruction. Great is his faithfulness; his mercies begin afresh each day. Lamentations 3:22-23, NLT

There were quite a few double takes in Beeville, Texas, when the Borntrager family went in their horse-drawn buggy and sold corn, quilts, and jellies on the courthouse square. The Amish family made quite a stir when they settled in the small south Texas town, a community of 18,000 people. "I thought it was strange, just like everybody else," said Danny Madrigal, a sheriff's inspector.

Perhaps because the Amish were different, some local boys began mocking them with taunts and mischievous acts. Things got out of hand when four teenage boys riddled the Borntragers' horses with bullets, killing the pregnant mare and injuring the stallion. A local citizen, Pat Finch, said, "It was just a senseless, terrible act. It stripped those poor Amish folks of their family pets, transportation, and financial assets in one fell swoop."

Finch set up a fund to make amends and replace the mare. The town has raised half of the $4,100 needed to ship a new mare from Tennessee. Beeville is very protective of this Amish family now, most citizens refusing to tell outsiders where the family resides in order to protect their privacy.

The Jews most likely turned a few heads when they "moved" into Persia as exiles with their unusual ways. Haman, the bully, began persecuting them with taunts and mischievous legislation. When the king heard about it, he became very protective of the strangers who dwelt in his land.

exploration

Haman was dead, and Mordecai and Esther had been rewarded for their faithful service to the king. However, there was still an irrevocable death sentence in effect for the persecuted Jews.

Review Esther 8; then focus on verses 9-14.

So the king's scribes were called at that time, in the third month, which is the month of Sivan, on the twenty-third day; and it was written, according to all that Mordecai commanded, to the Jews, the satraps, the governors, and the princes of the provinces from India to Ethiopia, one hundred and twenty-seven provinces in all, to every province in its own script, to every people in their own language, and to the Jews in their own script and language. And he wrote in the name of King Ahasuerus, sealed it with the king's signet ring, and sent letters by couriers on horseback, riding on royal horses bred from swift steeds. Esther 8:9-10

1. On what date were the king's scribes called to record Mordecai's commands?

. . . .

2. Who received the new decree? How do you know they understood it?

. . . .

3. How did Mordecai sign and seal the letters? . . . .

. . . .

By these letters the king permitted the Jews who were in every city to gather together and protect their lives—to destroy, kill, and annihilate all the forces of any people or province that would assault them, both little children and women, and to plunder their possessions, on one day in all the provinces of King Ahasuerus, on the thirteenth day of the twelfth month, which is the month of Adar. Esther 8:11-12

4. Explain what the king allowed the Jews to do and why this was fair.

. . . .

5. Where and on what day was the decree to become effective?

. . . .

3
NAME DROPPING
Although Mordecai was given authority to write a new decree, he did so in the name of Ahasuerus to ratify this new law. Legislation in Mordecai's name couldn't counteract the previous law Haman had written in the king's name. Only the king's decree could supersede his previous legislation.

4
SELF-DEFENSE
The Jews wouldn't attack others but would defend themselves. The new law allowed them to unite and protect their lives and possessions. They were no longer sitting ducks. The Persians understood that Ahasuerus was on the Jews' side and this would be a deterrent from acting on Haman's previous legislation.

PONY EXPRESS
The swift steeds chosen to carry this urgent message were the equivalent of today's racehorses, bred from royal mares. They were also known as chariot steeds. When the couriers were commanded to hurry, they were being encouraged to use these swift steeds to their full potential. Mordecai didn't waste time.

HIS NAME
As Christians, we are given permission to use the name of Jesus in everything we do and in everything we say. "Whatever you do in word or deed, do all in the name of the Lord Jesus, giving thanks to God the Father through Him" (Colossians 3:17).

HIS GLORY
When you ask something in Jesus' name and then receive it, make sure that God gets the glory. "You can ask for anything in my name, and I will do it, because the work of the Son brings glory to the Father" (John 14:13, NLT).

A copy of the document was to be issued as a decree in every province and published for all people, so that the Jews would be ready on that day to avenge themselves on their enemies. The couriers who rode on royal horses went out, hastened and pressed on by the king's command. And the decree was issued in Shushan the citadel. Esther 8:13-14

6. Why did the couriers hurry? . . . .

. . . .

transformation

7. Mordecai wrote new legislation in the name of the king. Jesus tells Christians to take advantage of the things He offers when we act in His name.

SCRIPTURE	IN HIS NAME
Matt. 18:20 . . . .
Mark 9:39-41 . . . .
Luke 9:48 . . . .
John 14:26. . . . .

Journal about which of these things you've done in the name of Jesus.

. . . .

. . . .

8. Mordecai used the king's name and got results. Jesus invites those who love Him to use His name, guaranteeing both results and joy!

Journal a prayer asking Jesus for something in His name by rewriting this verse: "The truth is, you can go directly to the Father and ask him, and he will grant your request because you use my name. . . . Ask, using my name, and you will receive, and you will have abundant joy" (John 16:23-24, NLT).

. . . .

9. Mordecai wrote enforceable legislation because he had received the king's permission and authority to do so. Those who use the name of Jesus also must receive His "permission" to do so by believing in Him or reap the consequences. Read Acts 19:13-16, and answer the questions about who did not have authority to act in Christ's name.

a. How did some Jews use Jesus' name, and what words did they recite (vv. 13-14)?

. . . .

b. Who commissioned these exorcists (v. 13)?

. . . .

c. How did the evil spirit respond, and what were the consequences (vv. 15-16)?

. . . .

In 1540, Martin Luther's great friend and assistant, Frederick Myconius, was dying and wrote a farewell note to Luther. When Martin Luther received the letter, he immediately sent this note: "I command thee in the name of God to live because I still have need of thee in the work of reforming the church. The Lord will never let me hear that thou art dead, but will permit thee to survive me. For this I am praying, this is my will, and may my will be done, because I seek only to glorify the name of God." Myconius regained his strength and outlived Luther by two months.

Like Mordecai's request, Luther's was granted because he asked appropriately. God will answer your prayers, too, when they line up with Scripture:

1. *In His name:* "Whatever you ask in My name, that I will do, that the Father may be glorified in the Son" (John 14:13).

2. *According to His will:* "Now this is the confidence that we have in Him, that if we ask anything according to His will, He hears us" (1 John 5:14).

3. *In faith:* "Let him ask in faith, with no doubting" (James 1:6).

4. *With a clean heart:* "But your iniquities have separated you from your God; . . . so that He will not hear" (Isaiah 59:2).

HIS HONOR
God's name will be honored even when others use it dishonorably. Though the Jewish exorcists used His name inappropriately, Jesus was still exalted. "When this became known to the Jews and Greeks living in Ephesus, they were all seized with fear, and the name of the Lord Jesus was held in high honor" (Acts 19:17, NIV).

contemplation

To pray "in Jesus' name" means to pray in his spirit, in his compassion, in his love, in his outrage, in his concern. In other words, it means to pray a prayer that Jesus himself might pray.
Kenneth L. Wilson

DAY 5 FROM FEAR TO FEASTING

preparation

When I trust You, Lord, I know that victory is soon to follow. So I will celebrate Your goodness and shout for joy when my battle is won. Amen.

CELEBRATE

Let all those rejoice who put their trust in You; let them ever shout for joy, because You defend them; let those also who love Your name be joyful in You. Psalm 5:11

On May 7, 1945, America and its allies celebrated with unbridled passion the surrender of Germany, and on September 2, Victory over Japan Day. In New York City thousands gathered in Times Square to celebrate the end of the war. The photograph that best captured the spirit of the joyous occasion was of a sailor sweeping a nurse off her feet in an exuberant embrace. In small town America jubilant citizens took to the streets honking horns, waving flags, shouting with joy, and hugging passersby.

When Prime Minister Winston Churchill announced that World War II was over, there were huge celebrations throughout England, with church bells ringing for the first time since the war began. In Newtown a children's march and a peace bonfire celebrated the end of the war, and a "Princess of Peace" was crowned.

Mary Whalley, who was a young girl living in Wales in 1945, remembers that the end of the war meant the end of food rations. "The first bananas arrived and queues formed for an allocation. I remember eating mine, but my brother gave his away. He had never seen one before, and my mother was not pleased."

As with the news of the end of World War II, good news traveled fast to the 127 provinces of the Persian Empire. The people erupted in spontaneous celebrations when they heard of Mordecai's decree allowing the Jews to protect and defend themselves. A day that began with fear of death ended with feasts of joy.

exploration

Good news was carried on swift steeds throughout the empire. The Jews were transformed from hopeless victims to hopeful victors. Today we'll see how the people celebrated throughout the land.

Review Esther 8; then focus on verses 15-17.

So Mordecai went out from the presence of the king in royal apparel of blue and white, with a great crown of gold and a garment of fine linen and purple; and the city of Shushan rejoiced and was glad. Esther 8:15

1. Describe Mordecai's updated wardrobe. . . . .

   . . . .

2. Contrast Mordecai's experience wearing new clothing at this point with the time he received new clothing from Esther back in lesson 8, day 1 (Esther 4:4).

   . . . .

3. How did the citizens of Shushan respond to Mordecai's new position?

   . . . .

The Jews had light and gladness, joy and honor. And in every province and city, wherever the king's command and decree came, the Jews had joy and gladness, a feast and a holiday. Then many of the people of the land became Jews, because fear of the Jews fell upon them. Esther 8:16-17

4. What four characteristics did these events elicit among the Jews?

   . . . .

5. Where did the joy spread? . . . .

   . . . .

6. How did all the Jews celebrate upon hearing the king's command and decree?

   . . . .

7. Describe the spiritual impact these events had on the Persian people.

   . . . .

explanation

4
BEAMING
The Jews weren't merely happy, they were lighthearted, glad, joyful, and full of honor. Lightness implies a bright and luminous spirit. Gladness expresses exceeding mirth, pleasure, or glee. Joy depicts an attitude of cheerfulness. Honor means that the Jews had regained their dignity and value as esteemed citizens.

7
CONVERTS
Gentiles throughout the empire abandoned their pagan practices and converted to Judaism. The converts couldn't be fully initiated into Judaism since the priest dwelt in Jerusalem. They were known as "God fearers." Apparently Gentiles in the kingdom now sided with the Jews and adopted their faith.

transformation

8

CASTING CROWNS
What will we do with the crowns we will receive? Cast them down. "They lay their crowns before the throne and say, 'You are worthy, O Lord our God, to receive glory and honor and power. For you created everything, and it is for your pleasure that they exist and were created'" (Revelation 4:10-11, NLT).

9

REJOICE
Salvation from their enemies brought joy and gladness to the Jews. Salvation of our souls from sin and death should bring indescribable joy. "You rejoice with joy inexpressible and full of glory, receiving the end of your faith—the salvation of your souls" (1 Peter 1:8-9).

10

CONVERSION
Conversion involves turning *away* from evil deeds and false worship and turning *toward* worshiping the Lord. Conversion marks a person's entrance into a new relationship with God, forgiveness of sins, and a new life (adapted, *Nelson's*). "You turned away from idols to serve the true and living God" (1 Thessalonians 1:9, NLT).

8. Mordecai wore a golden crown provided by the king. According to Scripture, believers will also receive crowns. Fill in the following chart to discover what kinds of crowns we will receive.

SCRIPTURE	CROWNS
1 Cor. 9:25	. . . .
2 Tim. 4:8	. . . .
James 1:12	. . . .
1 Pet. 5:4	. . . .

9. The Jews celebrated with light, gladness, joy, and honor at the great deliverance God had wrought through Esther and Mordecai.

Use the acrostic J-O-Y to journal a prayer of thanksgiving to God for the great deliverance He has brought to your life. (Example: Jesus . . . , Oh . . . , Yes . . .)

J . . . .

. . . .

O . . . .

. . . .

Y . . . .

. . . .

10. The fear of the Jews caused Gentiles in Persia to convert from their pagan practices to Judaism and the worship of the one true God.

Journal about your conversion experience. What circumstances caused you to turn from sinner to saint?

. . . .

. . . .

. . . .

. . . .

A day is a terrible thing to waste. Some people invest their time wisely, taking advantage of every minute they've been given. Others squander their time, wasting precious opportunities that may never come again. Esther and Mordecai never missed a beat, and in twenty-four short hours they changed the course of history. On June 25, 474 B.C., Haman was executed, Mordecai was promoted to prime minister, Esther was made financially secure, new legislation was enacted, couriers were dispatched to every province, the Jews began celebrating, and pagans were converted to Judaism.

As far as I can recall, I've never done anything of significance on June 25. Have you? But other men and women throughout history have made that same date one to remember:

- 1630: Governor Winthrop introduced the fork into American dining.
- 1876: Custer and the seventh Cavalry were wiped out at Little Big Horn.
- 1941: FDR issued Executive Order 8802 forbidding discrimination.
- 1962: Supreme Court ruled New York school prayer unconstitutional.
- 1972: Berenice Gera became first female umpire in professional baseball.
- 1991: Slovenia and Croatia declared independence from Yugoslavia.

Time passes quickly, and we can never get it back. Wise people use the time they've been given for something that will outlast them. What will you do with June 25, or April 10, or November 2? They're just ordinary days unless you do something extraordinary with them. Take advantage of the next twenty-four hours, and discover "what a difference a day makes!"

contemplation
Happy and strong and brave shall we be—able to endure all things, and to do all things— if we believe that every day, every hour, every moment of our life is in God's hands.
Henry van Dyke

All's Well That Ends Well

*G*reat storytellers bring memorable characters to life and dramatically teach valuable lessons. The Bible is replete with amazing true stories told by master storytellers. Ruth is a tale of redemption, shining hope in the midst of darkness. Esther tells the story of God delivering His people, the Jews.

William Shakespeare was one of the greatest storytellers of all. With keen insight he looked beyond historic events to the human condition, portraying people's successes and failures in a way everyone can personally relate to. His beautiful tales include multidimensional characters, poignant quotes, and unforgettable lessons teaching us to look at life through new eyes.

The *Merchant of Venice* is one of Shakespeare's early comedies (known as a "Christian comedy") in which good triumphs over evil. The character Shylock echoes the plight of Jews throughout history: "I am a Jew. Hath not a Jew eyes? Hath not a Jew hands, organs, dimensions, senses, affections, passions? Fed with the same food, hurt with the same weapons, subject to the same diseases, healed by the same Means, warmed and cooled by the same winter and summer, as a Christian is? If you prick us, do we not bleed? If you tickle us, do we not laugh? If you poison us, do we not die? And if you wrong us, shall we not revenge?" This week we'll see the Jews in Persia, who have been wronged, rightfully take revenge. When the good hand of God intervenes on behalf of His people, "all's well that ends well."

DAY 1
Alas, Poor Haman, We Knew Him Well

DAY 2
Two Days or Not Two Days, That Is the Question

DAY 3
Friends, Persians, Countrymen, Lend Me Your Ears

DAY 4
To Thine Own God Be True

DAY 5
Some Have Greatness Thrust upon Them

DAY 1 — ALAS, POOR HAMAN, WE KNEW HIM WELL

preparation

Lord, You guarantee a happy ending for my life in eternity, where there will be no more death or sorrow. I can't wait for the day when evil and evildoers are banished forever. Come quickly, Lord Jesus! Amen.

HAPPY ENDING
He will remove all of their sorrows, and there will be no more death or sorrow or crying or pain. For the old world and its evils are gone forever.
Revelation 21:4, NLT

exploration

Alas, poor Haman was dead, but the day to destroy the Jews, March 7, 473 B.C., was here. There remained many enemies eager to comply with Haman's decree to annihilate the Jews, including his ten sons, who knew their father well.

Read Esther 9; then focus on verses 1-10.

> *Now in the twelfth month, that is, the month of Adar, on the thirteenth day, the time came for the king's command and his decree to be executed. On the day that the enemies of the Jews had hoped to over-power them, the opposite occurred, in that the Jews themselves overpowered those who hated them.*
> Esther 9:1

1. Contrast what actually occurred on the thirteenth day of Adar with what the enemies of the Jews had hoped would happen.

. . . .

. . . .

. . . .

> *The Jews gathered together in their cities throughout all the provinces of King Ahasuerus to lay hands on those who sought their harm. And no one could withstand them, because fear of them fell upon all people.* Esther 9:2

2. Explain the Jews' strategy for opposing their enemies.

. . . .

3. Why was no one able to conquer them? . . . .

. . . .

> *And all the officials of the provinces, the satraps, the governors, and all those doing the king's work, helped the Jews, because the fear of Mordecai fell upon them. For Mordecai was great in the king's palace, and his fame spread throughout all the provinces; for this man Mordecai became increasingly prominent.* Esther 9:3-4

4. Explain who helped the Jews and why. . . . .

. . . .

> *Thus the Jews defeated all their enemies with the stroke of the sword, with slaughter and destruction, and did what they pleased with those who hated them. And in Shushan the citadel the Jews killed and destroyed five hundred men. Also Parshandatha, Dalphon, Aspatha, Poratha, Adalia, Aridatha, Parmashta, Arisai, Aridai, and Vajezatha—the ten sons of Haman the son of Hammedatha, the enemy of the Jews—they killed; but they did not lay a hand on the plunder.* Esther 9:5-10

5. How did the Jews defeat their enemies? . . . .

. . . .

6. How many did they kill in Shushan? Whose sons were among the dead?

. . . .

7. Describe how the Jews revealed that they were not using war for material gain.

. . . .

2

LIMITED REVENGE
The Jews had a controlled response toward their enemies. They exacted satisfaction for a wrong by punishing the wrongdoers. They limited their revenge to those who hated them and sought their harm, inflicting just punishment against their attackers and making sure the innocent were not injured in the process.

4

FEARED LEADER
To fear a person in an exalted position means to stand in awe of that person. It is not emotional fear but reverential respect. It recognizes the power and position of the one in charge and offers the proper respect (adapted, *Vine's*). All the king's men revered and aided Mordecai.

7

PLUNDER
Plunder is the confiscation of personal or household effects—spoil taken by the victor from an enemy in war. The Jews had the right to plunder because they had won the battle but gallantly refused to take their neighbors' possessions. They were not waging an aggressive war but defending themselves.

transformation

8. INNOCENT BLOOD
Innocent blood that is shed cries out to God. When Abel murdered Cain, God said, "Listen—your brother's blood cries out to me from the ground!" (Genesis 4:10, NLT). God takes crimes against the innocent personally. "To kill a person is to kill a living being made in God's image" (Genesis 9:6, NLT).

9. CHRIST'S BLOOD
The innocent blood of Christ shed on behalf of sinners cries out, "Forgiveness!" Since the wages of sin is death, sinners should die for the penalty of their sins. Yet, "He paid for you with the precious lifeblood of Christ, the sinless, spotless Lamb of God" (1 Peter 1:19, NLT).

8. The Jews reflected the heart of God when they limited their revenge to wrongdoers. God commanded through Moses: "Never put an innocent or honest person to death. I will not allow anyone guilty of this to go free" (Exodus 23:7, NLT).

Journal about an example you have heard or read about when wrongdoers caused the death of innocent people. How does this Scripture verse give you comfort?

. . . .

. . . .

. . . .

. . . .

9. Killing an innocent victim is something God hates. Proverbs 6:16-19, NLT, lists six other sins equally abhorrent to God. Check off any of these detestable traits you have displayed in your past. "There are six things the Lord hates—no, seven things he detests:

___ Haughty eyes,

___ A lying tongue,

___ Hands that kill the innocent,

___ A heart that plots evil,

___ Feet that race to do wrong,

___ A false witness who pours out lies,

___ A person who sows discord among brothers."

Journal a prayer to God asking Him to forgive you for doing the things He hates.

. . . .

. . . .

. . . .

. . . .

10. People feared Mordecai because *he* feared God. Fill in the following chart to discover other results of fearing God.

SCRIPTURE	FEAR OF THE LORD
2 Chron. 17:10	
2 Chron. 19:9-10	
Job 28:28	
Prov. 8:13	

10
GOD-FEARING
Many Gentiles who feared God are recorded in Scripture. These men and women became proselytes and were respected by the Jews. "A Roman army officer named Cornelius . . . feared the God of Israel, as did his entire household. He gave generously to charity and was a man who regularly prayed to God" (Acts 10:1-2, NLT).

The date Haman had selected to destroy the Jews had finally arrived. Nine months had passed since Mordecai's decree empowered the Jews to defend themselves. Providentially they had ample time to prepare as they "gathered together in their cities" for battle. No doubt "the enemies of the Jews" were a large contingency intent on fulfilling Haman's decree despite four factors: a Jewish queen, a Jewish prime minister, the king's backing, and favorable legislation.

As the two hostile camps stood face-to-face throughout the Persian Empire, several things became obvious. First, the Jews were motivated by neither hate nor greed. They showed great restraint, killing only those who were a threat and leaving the plunder behind. Second, the fear of Mordecai and the Jews caused their enemies to fall before them instead of overpowering them. Third, in this power struggle the opposite of what was expected to happen occurred, revealing an unseen power at work behind the scenes.

God's good hand is a force to be reckoned with. Those opposing seemingly weak people with nothing but God on their side are destined for defeat. David, the little shepherd boy, armed with just a sling and five smooth stones, toppled the giant Goliath, who wielded a sword, spear, and javelin (1 Samuel 17:32-51). Gideon and his three hundred men who lapped water like dogs despoiled the Midianites, whose hordes were thick as locusts and whose camels were too numerous to count (Judges 7). Deborah, a woman commanding an army without shields or spears, stopped the nine hundred chariots of the mighty Canaanite army in their tracks (Judges 4).

contemplation
If you have no power to prevail over someone, leave it to God.
Ancient Proverb

DAY 2

TWO DAYS OR NOT TWO DAYS, THAT IS THE QUESTION

preparation

When people are favor-able toward me, Lord, help me to realize that it is because Your gracious hand rests upon me. Amen.

GRACIOUS LORD
The king gave him everything he asked for, because the gracious hand of the Lord his God was on him. Ezra 7:6, NLT

In perhaps the most famous soliloquy in literature, Hamlet's words "To be or not to be" reflect the desperate state in which the Prince of Denmark finds himself. His uncle had murdered his father, the king, and married his mother to usurp the throne. Hamlet's grow-ing awareness of the betrayal by his evil uncle, Claudius, leads to a deepening sense of depression. He wrestles with the frailty of life, what lies beyond, and he questions his role in setting things right by asking himself whether he is to "suffer the slings and arrows of outrageous fortune, or to take arms against a sea of troubles, and by opposing end them?" In the end, Prince Hamlet determines to take up arms and oppose those who have betrayed his father, avenging his untimely death.

Esther, too, was dealing with the frailty of life and the desire to set things right in the kingdom. She knew that there were still many in Shushan, the capital, who opposed the Jews and would take up arms against them. She realized that the situation remained dangerous. Like a surgeon who finds more cancer than expected in the midst of surgery and determines that a more radical procedure is called for, Esther realized that the enemy was so great that given one day to defend themselves was not enough. Radical measures were needed. Esther's loyalty to her people led her to ask the king, "Two days or not two days, that is the question."

exploration

Yesterday we saw the Jews overpower those who had hoped to overpower them, as they looked behind the scenes at God's hand of protection and His empowerment for their victory. Today we find that further action was required.

Review Esther 9; then focus on verses 11-16.

On that day the number of those who were killed in Shushan the citadel was brought to the king. And the king said to Queen Esther, "The Jews have killed and destroyed five hundred men in Shushan the citadel, and the ten sons of Haman. What have they done in the rest of the king's provinces? Now what is your petition? It shall be granted to you. Or what is your further request? It shall be done." Esther 9:11-12

1. What report did the king give Queen Esther about the battle in Shushan?

. . . .

2. How did he entreat the queen? . . . .

. . . .

Then Esther said, "If it pleases the king, let it be granted to the Jews who are in Shushan to do again tomorrow according to today's decree, and let Haman's ten sons be hanged on the gallows." So the king commanded this to be done; the decree was issued in Shushan, and they hanged Haman's ten sons. Esther 9:13-14

3. What two things did Esther request of the king? Why do you think she made these requests?

. . . .

And the Jews who were in Shushan gathered together again on the fourteenth day of the month of Adar and killed three hundred men at Shushan; but they did not lay a hand on the plunder. The remainder of the Jews in the king's provinces gathered together and protected their lives, had rest from their enemies, and killed seventy-five thousand of their enemies; but they did not lay a hand on the plunder. Esther 9:15-16

4. How many men were killed on the fourteenth day of Adar in Shushan? in the provinces?

. . . .

explanation

OPEN DOOR
Ahasuerus gave Esther an open door. In the past, she had fearfully approached his throne, uninvited, with her requests. Now he freely invited her to make further requests. His past promises were conditional, "up to half the kingdom." Now he promised that whatever she asked would be granted.

PUBLIC DISPLAY
Esther's request to publicly display the bodies of Haman's sons on the gallows sent a twofold message. It told citizens that crimes against the Jews would not go unpunished, and it warned them to cease and desist from further hostilities. Those who continued this feud could meet the same fate.

ROUND TWO
Yesterday, in round one, the Jews had wounded their mortal enemies but had not completely taken them out of the game. Today, in round two, they finished the fight in a knockout round. When the day was over, they "had rest from their enemies," revealing how thorough the victory was.

5. What was the Jews' defense strategy in the provinces?

. . . .

6. What repeated phrase reveals that the Jews were not out for material gain?

. . . .

transformation

7. The king did not tire of the requests made by his queen. Instead, he openly invited her to ask more of him in the future than she had in the past. Jesus invites his bride, the church, to keep on praying too. Read Luke 18:1-8, then answer the following questions:

a. Describe the judge in this story and what changed his mind (vv. 2-5).

. . . .

b. Describe the widow in this story, and tell how she prevailed (vv. 2-5).

. . . .

c. What lesson should God's children draw from this parable (vv. 7-8)?

. . . .

8. Esther's request to hang and display the bodies of Haman's dead sons, while controversial to us, did stop the violence. Those who allow hate and anger to motivate them to senseless acts of violence ought to be punished.

Journal about your feelings on the controversy surrounding the death penalty. Where do you stand and why? How should murderers be punished?

. . . .

. . . .

. . . .

7

PERSEVERANCE
Praying is not a game; it's hard work that demands perseverance. Some give up too soon and too easily. In prayer, Christians are encouraged to keep on keeping on, "praying always with all prayer and supplication in the Spirit . . . with all perseverance and supplication for all the saints" (Ephesians 6:18).

8

JUDGMENT
Jesus goes beyond the problem of murder to the motive behind it. He said that uncontrolled anger is as deadly as murder itself: "Moses says, 'Do not murder. If you commit murder, you are subject to judgment.' But I say, if you are angry with someone, you are subject to judgment!" (Matthew 5:21-22, NLT).

9. Esther asked the king for one more day to completely eradicate the enemy. Sometimes *we* are our own worst enemies. Jesus urges us to deal radically with our sinful nature.

> Journal a prayer using the following verse, asking God to help you to completely cut away the sins that hinder you: "If your hand or foot causes you to sin, cut it off and throw it away. It is better to enter heaven crippled or lame than to be thrown into the unquenchable fire with both of your hands and feet" (Matthew 18:8, NLT).

. . . .

. . . .

. . . .

. . . .

There's no time like the present. Unfinished business today is sure to catch up with you in the future. The enemies of the Jews had been growing like weeds. The king had given Esther and her people one day to do "weed control," but it just wasn't enough to get the job done. Sin in our lives can grow like weeds and take over if we don't deal with it daily. This principle reminds me of a story my husband, Skip, tells from his childhood.

Skip's mother had told him, "A job worth doing is worth doing right." He would regret the day he ignored that advice. His parents went on an overseas trip and left Skip in charge of "weed control" in their rock garden during the two weeks they were gone. He had put off this loathsome chore until the day before they were to come home. But it was too late; so many weeds had overtaken their two-acre lot that one day would never be enough time to eliminate them all. That's when he got the bright idea: *I'll just cut 'em down with the lawn mower and nobody will be the wiser.*

However, his dad was the wiser! It became obvious in a few short days that something was rotten in the Heitzig yard. There were more weeds than rocks in the rock garden. His father led him out to the yard and said, "Skip, I can tell by the chewed mower blades that you didn't pull these weeds out by the roots; you buzzed 'em down with the mower. *Now,* do it right, and give me back your allowance!"

9.

CIRCUMCISION
Circumcision means "to cut away." Jewish males circumcised their foreskin, ratifying their covenant with God. Christians must circumcise their sinful nature. "When you came to Christ, you were 'circumcised,' but not by a physical procedure. It was a spiritual procedure—the cutting away of your sinful nature" (Colossians 2:11, NLT).

contemplation
The probability that we may fail in the struggle should not deter us from the support of a cause we believe to be just.
Abraham Lincoln

FRIENDS, PERSIANS, COUNTRYMEN, LEND ME YOUR EARS

preparation

Father, I celebrate Your promise that all sorrow and mourning will disappear. I am overcome with gladness that You are my God and I am Your child. Amen.

GLADNESS
Sorrow and mourning will disappear, and they will be overcome with joy and gladness. Isaiah 35:10, NLT

In Shakespeare's *Julius Caesar,* Mark Antony takes center stage to deliver his famous eulogy for his beloved friend Caesar, who had been assassinated by a group of conspirators. His voice rings out with passion, "Friends, Romans, countrymen, lend me your ears; I come to bury Caesar."

Antony's eloquent speech is filled with irony and innuendo, inspiring the crowd to never forget the evil deed perpetrated against Caesar, the man who had done so much good for his people. He reminds them, "The evil that men do lives after them; the good is oft interred with their bones." His rousing words mark him as a virtuous and clever statesman, able to turn the hearts of the people against the evil assassins and back to their slain ruler.

In Persia's drama, Mordecai took center stage to inspire his friends and countrymen to listen to what he had to say. He wanted to bury Haman and his conspirators along with their evil plot and put to rest the hostilities in the land. However, he knew that his people must *never* forget the good Ahasuerus had done for them and the way God had miraculously delivered them from their enemies. In the future they must always celebrate Adar, "the month which was turned from sorrow to joy for them, and from mourning to a holiday" (Esther 9:22). Mordecai's rousing words also marked him as a virtuous and clever statesman. He turned the people's hearts from war and fear to joy and feasting.

exploration

The Jews had triumphed and rooted out their enemies. Then Mordecai declared to his friends, Persians, and countrymen that it was time to celebrate.

Review Esther 9; then focus on verses 17-25.

This was on the thirteenth day of the month of Adar. And on the fourteenth day of the month they rested and made it a day of feasting and gladness. But the Jews who were at Shushan assembled together on the thirteenth day, as well as on the fourteenth; and on the fifteenth of the month they rested, and made it a day of feasting and gladness. Esther 9:17-18

1. When did the Jews at Shushan rest from battle, and how did they celebrate?

. . . .

. . . .

Therefore the Jews of the villages who dwelt in the unwalled towns celebrated the fourteenth day of the month of Adar with gladness and feasting, as a holiday, and for sending presents to one another. Esther 9:19

2. What date did the Jews outside Shushan declare a holiday? How did they celebrate?

. . . .

And Mordecai wrote these things and sent letters to all the Jews, near and far, who were in all the provinces of King Ahasuerus, to establish among them that they should celebrate yearly the fourteenth and fifteenth days of the month of Adar, as the days on which the Jews had rest from their enemies, as the month which was turned from sorrow to joy for them, and from mourning to a holiday; that they should make them days of feasting and joy, of sending presents to one another and gifts to the poor. Esther 9:20-22

3. What days did Mordecai officially declare to be annual holidays, and for what reason?

. . . .

4. How were they to commemorate this holiday?

. . . .

NEW HOLIDAY
The English word *holiday* comes from the two words *holy* and *day*. The Hebrew word for *holiday* means "quiet." It originated with the holiday Ahasuerus instituted when he took Esther as his wife, eliminating taxes in the celebration. There was also quiet on the day the Jews rested from their enemies.

MEMORIAL DAY
A day you gain rest from enemies is a day worth memorializing. The U.S. celebrates Memorial Day by honoring soldiers who have secured peace for our nation with the display of the American flag, parades, and picnics. Mordecai expanded the Jewish "Memorial Day" to a two-day celebration with feasting.

CHRISTMAS
This Jewish holiday was similar to the celebration of Christmas, with a holiday feast, tidings of joy, and gifts to one another. The Jews also included gift giving to the needy, not just those who could give something in return. This Christmas remember to practice the joy of giving to the poor.

6

REST
To rest means to be quiet or free from anxiety. In the Bible *rest* means to cease from action after hard work or from trouble after the onslaught of enemies. "The word may mean 'to set one's mind at rest,' as when a child receives the discipline of his parent" (*Vine's*).

ACTIVE REST
True rest is not so much physical ease as it is spiritual peace. God told the Israelites how they could find spiritual rest. "Look for the old, godly way, and walk in it. Travel its path, and you will find rest for your souls" (Jeremiah 6:16, NLT).

So the Jews accepted the custom which they had begun, as Mordecai had written to them, because Haman, the son of Hammedatha the Agagite, the enemy of all the Jews, had plotted against the Jews to annihilate them, and had cast Pur (that is, the lot), to consume them and destroy them; but when Esther came before the king, he commanded by letter that this wicked plot which Haman had devised against the Jews should return on his own head, and that he and his sons should be hanged on the gallows. Esther 9:23-25

5. In your own words, retell the events that led up to the institution of this holiday.

. . . .

. . . .

transformation

6. When the Jews had rest from their enemies, they celebrated with a holiday. Fill in the chart to discover what others in the Bible have done when God delivered them.

SCRIPTURE	AFTER REST FROM ENEMIES
Deut. 12:10-11 . . . .
Josh. 22:4-5. . . . .
1 Kings 5:4-5. . . . .
Isa. 14:3-7 . . . .

7. Just as the children of Israel found rest from their enemies, so Jesus wants His followers to find rest for their souls.

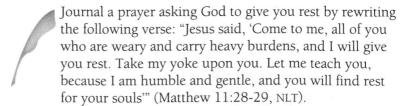

Journal a prayer asking God to give you rest by rewriting the following verse: "Jesus said, 'Come to me, all of you who are weary and carry heavy burdens, and I will give you rest. Take my yoke upon you. Let me teach you, because I am humble and gentle, and you will find rest for your souls'" (Matthew 11:28-29, NLT).

. . . .

. . . .

. . . .

8. Jews celebrated by giving gifts to the poor. Use the acrostic
G-I-F-T to journal some ways you can celebrate God's goodness
by giving to those less fortunate than yourself.

G . . . .

I . . . .

F . . . .

T . . . .

8

GIFT GIVING
A *gift* is something
voluntarily given by
one person to another
without compensation.
All gifts don't come in
pretty packages tied
up with bows. You can
give the gift of a listening ear, a helping hand,
or a pat on the back.
The gift of yourself is
the best gift you can
give.

Mordecai instituted a Jewish Memorial Day to ensure that the
people never forgot the evil planned against them and their
miraculous deliverance. It is important to bring the lessons from
the past into the present, remembering the sacrifices made and
God's deliverance. The National Vietnam Veterans Memorial in
Washington, D.C., stands as a poignant reminder of our nation's
tragic loss of life in a terrible war. Some visit The Wall to remember, some visit to forget. Some gather to find the names of fallen
soldiers etched in the shiny black granite to remember comrades
and to honor their lives.

When my (Penny's) father returned from the Korean War, he
refused to talk about it for decades, hoping to forget the horrors.
But late one night, I heard my dad moaning in his sleep. I tiptoed
into the kitchen and found him sitting at the table staring into
space. I put my hand on his shoulder and said, "Daddy, are you
okay?" He shook his head, and his war stories spilled out in a
stream of painful remembrances. He spoke of surviving for seven
days behind enemy lines, knowing that most of his platoon had
been wiped out, and of waking up in a hospital after being uncon-
scious for two months. Looking into my father's past helped me
understand the man he is today. "Remember the days of long ago;
think about the generations past. Ask your father and he will
inform you" (Deuteronomy 32:7, NLT).

contemplation
Don't forget to remem-
ber your blessings,
your triumphs, and
your victories.
William Arthur Ward

DAY 4   TO THINE OWN GOD BE TRUE

preparation

Father, I don't want to be a hypocrite, with my outward actions betraying the truth You have placed in my heart. Help me to remain true to You so that I can be true to those around me. Amen.

INNER TRUTH
Behold, You desire truth in the inward parts, and in the hidden part You will make me to know wisdom. Psalm 51:6

In *Hamlet* Polonius spoke to his son Laertes before his departure for travel abroad, giving him some earthly, fatherly advice. This instruction has been repeated throughout history by parents offering the same counsel in more modern terms.

Wisdom from Polonius	Modern Wisdom
"Give thy thoughts no tongue."	"Think before you speak."
"Nor any unproportion'd thought his act."	"Look before you leap."
"Apparel oft proclaims the man."	"Clothes make the man."
"Neither a borrower nor a lender be."	"Don't lend or borrow money."

Polonius saved his most famous advice for last: "This above all, to thine own self be true; and it must follow, as the night the day, thou canst not then be false to any man." This father believed that if you are true to yourself, you will be true to other people as well.

Mordecai, Israel's wise father figure, understood that only by being true to your God could you be true to yourself. He wanted the Jewish remnant living in Persia to rejoice in their miraculous deliverance. Rather than being ashamed of their Jewish heritage, he urged them to openly celebrate who they were by acknowledging what God had done for them. Mordecai's advice might have been a little different than that of Polonius, focusing on the heavenly rather than the earthly, "This above all, to thine own God be true." And *that* is true wisdom.

exploration

The Jews had spontaneously celebrated their deliverance from annihilation. In order to remind future generations of this great deliverance, Mordecai wrote careful instructions for all generations to follow.

Review Esther 9; then focus on verses 26-32.

> *So they called these days Purim, after the name Pur. Therefore, because of all the words of this letter, what they had seen concerning this matter, and what had happened to them, . . .* Esther 9:26

1. What was the holiday named, and why was it named this?

. . . .

> *. . . the Jews established and imposed it upon themselves and their descendants and all who would join them, that without fail they should celebrate these two days every year, according to the written instructions and according to the prescribed time, that these days should be remembered and kept throughout every generation, every family, every province, and every city, that these days of Purim should not fail to be observed among the Jews, and that the memory of them should not perish among their descendants.* Esther 9:27-28

2. For whom did the Jews establish this holiday, and why?

. . . .

3. How far into the future were they to celebrate and keep this holiday?

. . . .

4. Where should Purim be celebrated? . . . .

> *Then Queen Esther, the daughter of Abihail, with Mordecai the Jew, wrote with full authority to confirm this second letter about Purim. And Mordecai sent letters to all the Jews, to the one hundred and twenty-seven provinces of the kingdom of Ahasuerus, with words of peace and truth, to confirm these days of Purim at their appointed time, as Mordecai the Jew and Queen Esther had prescribed for them, and as they had decreed for themselves and their descendants concerning matters*

explanation

1

PURIM

Purim is plural for the Babylonian word *pur*, which meant "lot." An odd name for a holiday, it was meant to remind the Jews that Haman had cast lots to determine the day for the Jews' annihilation. He let the hands of fate determine the future, but the hand of God prevailed.

2

GENERATIONS

Retelling this story to future generations was paramount to the Jews, lest future descendants forget God's protection. Their ancestors living in the Promised Land had forgotten about God's deliverance: "They forgot what [God] had done— the wonderful miracles . . . he did for their ancestors in Egypt" (Psalm 78:11-12, NLT).

5
EVERYWHERE
Esther and Mordecai's decree was far-reaching. It not only included the 127 provinces of the Persian Empire, but also went beyond the borders of Persia to anywhere the Jews settled in the world. The feast of Purim continues to be commemorated March 7–8 in Israel today and wherever faithful Jewish communities exist.

7
FESTIVALS
Old Testament law prescribed that the Israelites observe not only daily worship but also special festivals. One Hebrew name for *festival* was derived from the word meaning "dance." When applied to religious services, this indicated that the Jewish festivals were occasions of joy and gladness (adapted, *Unger's*).

8
SECULARIZED
Our society has secularized our sacred observances, taking the "holy" out of holiday. It has taken the Resurrection out of Easter, leaving colored eggs; the One we thank out of Thanksgiving, leaving a stuffed turkey; and Christ out of Christmas, leaving Santa Claus instead.

of their fasting and lamenting. So the decree of Esther confirmed these matters of Purim, and it was written in the book. Esther 9:29-32

5. Summarize who received letters and what the letters contained.

. . . .

. . . .

6. What matters did Esther's written decree speak of?

. . . .

transformation

7. The Jews had other commemorative feasts besides Purim. Read Deuteronomy 16:1-17, then describe the feasts and how they were celebrated.

Feast of Passover/Unleavened Bread (vv. 1-8): . . . .

. . . .

Feast of Weeks/Pentecost (vv. 9-12): . . . .

. . . .

Feast of Tabernacles/Booths (vv.13-15): . . . .

. . . .

8. We also have commemorative celebrations today.

Journal about how and why you celebrate the following holidays:

Easter. . . . .

Thanksgiving . . . .

Christmas . . . .

9. All future generations were to remember Purim by retelling the story of Esther. Your children should remember the real reason

for their holidays too. "Take heed to yourself, and diligently keep yourself, lest you forget the things your eyes have seen, and lest they depart from your heart all the days of your life. And teach them to your children and your grandchildren" (Deuteronomy 4:9).

> Journal a prayer using this verse, thanking God for the real reason for the seasons you celebrate. Then commit to tell your children about them.

· ·

· ·

· ·

PASS IT ON
Children should learn about God at home. "Commit yourselves wholeheartedly to these commands. . . . Repeat them again and again to your children . . . when you are at home and when you are away on a journey, when you are lying down and when you are getting up again" (Deuteronomy 6:6-7, NLT).

The pur has evolved throughout history, taking on various forms to assist in decision making. In Haman's day it became known as casting lots, similar to drawing straws to determine a course of action. Others used rolling dice to discover the outcome of a situation. Today the lottery has been instituted to draft soldiers, fulfill quotas, or determine winners in a game of chance.

In South Korea tens of thousands anxiously await lottery results selecting candidates for a reunion with loved ones in communist North Korea. They had become separated when a heavily fortified border divided the two countries after the 1950–53 Korean War. There is no mail, phone, or any other form of communication between these divided family members.

The lottery originated with an agreement between North and South Korea in order to ease hostilities between the two countries. A computer program was designed to randomly select five hundred out of the seventy-five thousand people who had registered, all hoping to win the opportunity to see loved ones. Eighty-five-year-old Kim Sung-eun entered the lottery because she hasn't seen her eighty-eight-year-old brother in over fifty years. "My only wish is to meet my brother," she said. "If I don't get selected this time, at least I would like to know if he is still alive."

The winners of this lottery will find cause to celebrate as they are reunited with people they haven't seen in years, whereas the "winners" of Haman's lottery were doomed to death. But in the end, God gave the Jews a reason to celebrate for generations to come.

contemplation
Yet if we celebrate, let it be that he has invaded our lives with purpose.
Luci Shaw

DAY 5 SOME HAVE GREATNESS THRUST UPON THEM

preparation

God, help me to remember that although I am just Your servant, You have great plans for me. I look forward to seeing You exhibit Your greatness and power. No one is as great as You. Amen.

GREATNESS

O Sovereign Lord, I am your servant. You have only begun to show me your greatness and power. Is there any god in heaven or on earth who can perform such great deeds as yours? Deuteronomy 3:24, NLT

Twelfth Night is Shakespeare's romantic comedy in which the four main characters believe that marriage is unattainable because they love people outside their social class. The steward Malvolio, an arrogant upstart, desires to marry above his station, setting his sights on the lady he serves, the Countess Olivia. To knock him off his high horse and thus teach him a lesson, his fellow servants play a trick on him. They plant a letter in Olivia's handwriting encouraging Malvolio to ostentatiously court her.

Shakespeare commonly used humor and the most unlikely characters to make his most poignant lessons. Malvolio summed up the overriding moral of this play when he says, "Be not afraid of greatness. Some are born great, some achieve greatness, and some have greatness thrust upon them."

Malvolio, like Haman, believed he was destined for greatness but found out the hard way that "pride comes before a fall." Malvolio was imprisoned and ridiculed; Haman was humiliated and hung. The hero and heroine in *Twelfth Night,* being of noble character but not noble birth, displayed integrity and genuine compassion. In the end they had "greatness thrust upon them" as they found true love and married into nobility. Esther, our heroine, also not of noble birth but of truly noble heart, was exalted to a position of greatness when she married the king. Mordecai, our hero in this dramatic story, achieved greatness because of his loyalty to the king and love for his people.

exploration

The book that began with the power and greatness of King Ahasuerus ends focusing on the king and his vast empire. Though the book is named after Esther, she is not mentioned in the final chapter. She gracefully bows out of the picture as our attention shifts to Mordecai and the righteous impact he had on Ahasuerus's kingdom.

Read Esther 10; then focus on verses 1-3.

> **And King Ahasuerus imposed tribute on the land and on the islands of the sea.** Esther 10:1

1. Explain how the king funded his vast government.

. . . .

> **Now all the acts of his power and his might, and the account of the greatness of Mordecai, to which the king advanced him, are they not written in the book of the chronicles of the kings of Media and Persia?** Esther 10:2

2. What was recorded about the king?. . . . .

. . . .

3. Where was this recorded? . . . .

. . . .

4. How was Mordecai remembered in these chronicles?

. . . .

> **For Mordecai the Jew was second to King Ahasuerus, and was great among the Jews and well received by the multitude of his brethren, seeking the good of his people and speaking peace to all his countrymen.** Esther 10:3

5. What position did Mordecai occupy in the kingdom?

. . . .

6. What was Mordecai's reputation, and how was he received?

. . . .

7. What did Mordecai seek for his people? for his countrymen?

. . . .

explanation

1

TRIBUTE
Tribute was a compulsory fee or fine imposed on an inferior by a superior. It was a payment in acknowledgment of submission or as the price of protection. The modern equivalent is taxes. "Render therefore to all their due: taxes to whom taxes are due, . . . honor to whom honor" (Romans 13:7).

4

GREATNESS
Greatness refers to acts that distinguish a person as superior in character. A great person is one of dignity, proving to be noble and majestic. David understood that the greatness he achieved was from God. "O God, who is like You? . . . You shall increase my greatness" (Psalm 71:19-21).

7

PEACEMAKER
Although Mordecai had written a decree in the king's name allowing the Jews to defend themselves and eliminate their enemies, he was remembered as a man of peace. Sometimes the only way to achieve peace is to wage war. Jesus said, "God blesses those who work for peace" (Matthew 5:9, NLT).

transformation

TAX RELIEF
God understood the great burden taxes could be. He warned His people that if they overtaxed the poor, they would not prosper. "You trample the poor and steal what little they have through taxes and unfair rent. Therefore, you will never live in the beautiful stone houses you are building" (Amos 5:11, NLT).

GREAT GOD
All great human leaders and religious leaders pale in comparison to the God of gods. There is no one greater than He. "The Lord your God is the God of gods and Lord of lords. He is the great God, mighty and awesome" (Deuteronomy 10:17, NLT).

8. King Ahasuerus levied a tax throughout the known world. During New Testament times the Caesars also placed heavy taxes on the regions they ruled. Read Mark 12:13-17, then answer the following questions.

   a. What did the Pharisees and Herodians ask Jesus and why (vv. 13-15)?

   . . . .

   . . . .

   b. Describe the clever way Jesus responded to their inquiry (vv. 15-17).

   . . . .

   c. What lesson do you derive from this situation?

   . . . .

9. Mordecai had achieved greatness through the things that he did and said. Fill in the following chart to discover how greatness is achieved in God's kingdom.

   SCRIPTURE   ACHIEVING GREATNESS

   Matt. 5:19 . . . .

   Matt. 20:26-28 . . . .

   Luke 6:22-23. . . . .

   Luke 9:46-48. . . . .

   Journal about how you will apply these Scripture verses to begin the path to greatness.

   . . . .

   . . . .

   . . . .

   . . . .

10. Mordecai was a peacemaker in his policies; you can be a peacemaker in your prayers.

Journal a prayer of peace and blessing for God's people, the Jews, and for the place He calls His own, by rewriting the following verse: "Pray for the peace of Jerusalem: 'May they prosper who love you. Peace be within your walls, prosperity within your palaces.' For the sake of my brethren and companions, I will now say, 'Peace be within you'" (Psalm 122:6-8).

. . . .

. . . .

. . . .

. . . .

10

PRINCE OF PEACE
True peace resides not in a place but in human hearts ruled by the Prince of Peace. His peace cannot be diminished by persecution or political uprisings. "A son is given to us. . . . These will be his royal titles: Wonderful Counselor, Mighty God, Everlasting Father, Prince of Peace" (Isaiah 9:6, NLT).

Throughout this study we've gained insight into God's providence, tracing the fingerprints left by His good hand on the lives of His people. Ruth was divinely led to the right field, on the right day, and as a result experienced redemption at the hand of her kinsman-redeemer. Esther discovered that though she was destined to live in exile, she would be exalted by Ahasuerus "for such a time as this."

We have learned from Ruth and Esther that God's providence becomes more clearly recognizable in seasons of darkness than during moments of lightheartedness. For Penny, when God in His providence allowed chronic migraines to diminish her life, she discovered that God would show Himself strong despite her weakness. For Lenya, when the good hand of God allowed the loss of much-desired pregnancies, she came to understand that God's plan was to use her to birth others into God's kingdom.

We don't know what disappointing circumstances have darkened your path. But we do know that God, in His providence, has seen your plight, and His good hand will lead you to blessings beyond your imagination. When you seek God's ways, as Ruth did, you will surely glean the "handfuls of purpose" (Ruth 2:16, KJV) God has left along the way to lead you to His perfect plan. And when, like Esther, you trust Providence to work all things together for your good, you will discover that you are in the midst of your unique situation "for such a time as this" (Esther 4:14).

contemplation
Faith makes the uplook good, the outlook bright, the inlook favorable, and the future glorious.
V. Raymond Edman

Bibliography

The authors have used the following books and electronic sources in preparing the illustrations and sidebar material for this book.

Alexander, David, and Pat Alexander, eds. *Eerdmans' Handbook to the Bible*. Grand Rapids: Eerdmans, 1973.

Baldwin, Joyce G. *Esther: An Introduction and Commentary*. Downers Grove, Ill.: InterVarsity Press, 1984.

Barber, Cyril J. *Ruth: A Story of God's Grace*. Neptune, N.J.: Loizeaux Brothers, 1989.

Bible Illustrator for Windows. Parsons Technology, 1997–1998.

Cundall, Arthur E., and Leon Morris. *Judges and Ruth*. Tyndale Old Testament Commentaries. London: Tyndale, 1968.

Evans, Debra. *Six Qualities of Women of Character*. Grand Rapids: Zondervan, 1996.

Funk, Charles Earle. *A Hog on Ice*. New York: Harper & Row, 1948.

Halley, Henry Hampton. *Halley's Bible Handbook*. Grand Rapids: Zondervan, 1965.

Heitzig, Skip. *Enjoying Bible Study*. Costa Mesa, Calif.: The Word for Today, 1996.

Henry, Matthew. *Matthew Henry's Commentary on the Whole Bible: One Volume Edition, Complete and Unabridged*. Peabody, Mass.: Hendrickson, 1991.

Hewett, James S. *Illustrations Unlimited*. Wheaton, Ill.: Tyndale House, 1988.

INFOsearch™, Illustrations data and database, The Communicator's Companion™, P.O. Box 171749, Arlington, Texas 76003. Web site: <www.infosearch.com>. *Search by finding a search word in the illustration.*

Ironside, H. A. *Esther*. Rev. ed. Neptune, N.J.: Loizeaux Brothers, 2001.

Jensen, Irving L. *Jensen's Survey of the Old Testament*. Chicago: Moody Press, 1978.

Lockyer, Herbert, ed. *Nelson's Illustrated Bible Dictionary*. Nashville: Nelson, 1986. (Out of print but appears in *The PC Study Bible for Windows*.)

Merriam-Webster's Collegiate Dictionary, 10th ed.

Nelson's Quick Reference Topical Bible Index. Nashville: Nelson, 1995.

The PC Study Bible for Windows. Biblesoft, Version 3.0. Seattle: Jim Gilbertson, 1999.

Pfeiffer, Charles F., and Everett F. Harrison, eds. *The Wycliffe Bible Commentary*. Chicago: Moody Press, 1962.

Rigsby, Joyce. "How to Feel Another's Pain." *Ministry* (September 1990): 4–7.

Schultz, Samuel J. *The Old Testament Speaks*. 5th ed. San Francisco: HarperSanFrancisco, 2000.

Strong, James, ed. *Strong's Concordance of the Bible*. Nashville: Nelson, 1980.

Swindoll, Charles R. *Esther: A Woman of Strength and Dignity*. Nashville: Word, 1997.

Unger, Merrill F., and R. K. Harrison, eds. *The New Unger's Bible Dictionary*. Chicago: Moody Press, 1988. (A 1998 version appears in *The PC Study Bible for Windows*.)

Vine, W. E. *Vine's Expository Dictionary of Old and New Testament Words*. Edited by Merrill F. Unger and William White Jr. Nashville: Nelson, 1996.

Walvoord, John F., and Roy B. Zuck, eds. *The Bible Knowledge Commentary*. Wheaton, Ill.: Victor, 1985.

Wiersbe, Warren. *Be Committed: An Old Testament Study of Ruth and Esther*. Wheaton, Ill.: Victor, 1993.

With Gratitude

Lenya—I'm grateful for the incredible influence these sisters of the soul have had on my life: Suzanne Friesner, my sister by birth, you have inspired me with your poetic soul and empowering love. Linda Evans, my "Jonathan," thank you for seeing the writer in me long before anyone else did. Dianne Saber, my sister in Christ, who's stuck closer to me than any brother, especially when things got sticky. Heartfelt thanks to my other "soul sisters": Chris Borszcz, Teri Church, Lisa Davis, Angela DiPrima, Christy Schneider, and Terri Shinn for reasons too innumerable to recount.

Penny—My heart is filled with gratitude for those who have left their handprints on this book: my husband, Kerry, whose loving hands held me close in the dark times; my children—Erin, Kristian, and Ryan—whose enthusiastic hands cheered me on; my parents, Jack and Janelle Pierce, who so willingly lent helping hands; my prayer partners—Brenda, Kristi, and Pia—who unceasingly folded their hands in prayer; and my heavenly Father, whose guiding hands providentially led the way.

Thanks from both of us to the dynamic Calvary church staff, who keep us connected; to the Women at Calvary, who do most of the work while we get most of the credit; and to the Tyndale people, who are good at spotting diamonds in the rough and making them shine.

About the Authors

Lenya Heitzig was headed for a promising career in fashion merchandising when God changed her direction. After a lifetime steeped in agnosticism, Lenya was converted in 1978 and then was thrust into the explosive days of the Jesus Movement in southern California.

Her early training for ministry was forged on the anvil of servant leadership. Lenya's "job description" as a counselor for new believers included vacuuming the church sanctuary and cleaning rest rooms. After joining Youth With a Mission (YWAM) in 1980 as a single women's counselor, she once again discovered that ministry is not just telling people how to act but serving them as cook and school secretary.

These days of small beginnings were preparation for a wider scope of service. After her term with YWAM, Lenya met a determined California surfer who was undergoing his own spiritual groundwork for great things ahead. After marrying in 1981, Skip and Lenya Heitzig headed to the Rocky Mountain Southwest and settled in Albuquerque, New Mexico. Soon their home Bible study blossomed into Calvary of Albuquerque, a church exceeding 12,000 in weekly attendance.

Lenya's gift in teaching and communicating truth paved the way for a thriving women's ministry that has had a strong impact on the Southwest. Lenya has served on the executive board for a Billy and Franklin Graham Crusade and currently chairs and directs the Southwest Women's Festival, which hosts yearly conferences, sharing the podium with such speakers as Kay Arthur, Florence Littauer, and Anne Graham Lotz. Lenya is the founder of Mercy B.A.N.D. (Bearing Another's Name Daily), a nonprofit organization that remembers the victims of the September 11 terrorist attacks and encourages prayer for their loved ones.

Lenya speaks regularly to the Women at Calvary and is in demand as a conference speaker for retreats and seminars throughout the United States and Europe. In 2001 Tyndale released her first book, *Ephesians: Discovering the Path to God's Treasures.*

Skip, Lenya, and their son, Nathan, live in Albuquerque and continue this exciting pathway that God has set them on.

Penny Pierce Rose was raised in a loving Christian home and heard God call her by name while attending church camp at the age of nine. During high school and college she wandered off

God's pathway and followed the ways of the world. Soon after marriage and motherhood she became discontented with her life and grudgingly attended a Bible Study Fellowship meeting with her mother. God's Word inspired her to renew her relationship with Him. Her husband, Kerry, soon followed in the footsteps of faith, bringing salvation to their household.

Penny graduated from Texas Tech University with a degree in political science. After seven years in Bible Study Fellowship, Penny joined the leadership team of the Women at Calvary. She also serves on the board of directors of Southwest Women's Festival. Reflecting her heart to minister to women and children, she has participated as Kid's Crusade coordinator for Harvest Crusade with Greg Laurie and as secretary for the Women's Committee of New Mexico Festival '98 with Franklin Graham.

Ephesians: Discovering the Path to God's Treasures was released by Tyndale in 2001. Penny's writing has also appeared in *Why Fret That God Stuff?* and *God's Little Rule Book*. She continues to write for the Women at Calvary Bible study and is a speaker for conferences and retreats. Her fervent desire is to minister to women by teaching them to study God's Word, apply the truths to their daily lives, and embrace the Christian life as a grand adventure. Penny and Kerry live in Albuquerque with their three great kids: Erin, Kristian, and Ryan.